CAPACITY REALIZATION AND PRODUCTIVITY GROWTH IN A DEVELOPING COUNTRY

To

My mother

Capacity Realization and Productivity Growth in a Developing Country

Has economic reform had impact?

RUHUL A. SALIM
Department of Economics
Jahangirnagar University
Dhaka, Bangladesh

Ashgate

Aldershot • Brookfield USA • Singapore • Sydney

Published by
Ashgate Publishing Ltd
Gower House
Croft Road
Aldershot
Hants GU11 3HR
England

Ashgate Publishing Company
Old Post Road
Brookfield
Vermont 05036
USA

British Library Cataloguing in Publication Data
Salim, Ruhul A.
 Capacity realization and productivity growth in a
 developing country : has economic reform had impact?
 1. Industrial productivity - Bangladesh 2. Manufacturing
 industries - Bangladesh 3. Bangladesh - Economic policy
 I. Title
 338'. 06'095492

Library of Congress Catalog Card Number: 98-74507

ISBN 1 84014 970 1

Printed and bound by
Antony Rowe Ltd, Chippenham, Wiltshire

Contents

List of Figures

List of Tables

x

Foreword

This is an excellent piece of scholarly research, which poses an interesting and important question. Namely, why has manufacturing in Bangladesh shown disappointing performance even after implementation of economic reform measures. While many earlier studies have paid attention to the role of productivity growth in manufacturing industries, they do not find a link between productivity growth and economic reforms through the role of changing capacity realization.

Dr. Salim has surveyed the relevant literature in great detail and has used economic theory, econometrics and empirical information in an efficient way to examine the productive performance of the manufacturing sectors in Bangladesh. The careful overview of the history and structure of the manufacturing sector is important background for the analysis. The review of techniques for analyzing productivity is also unusually through and careful. The discussion of the model used and interpretation of the model results is very extensive and carefully done. A particularly valuable feature of this discussion for scholars in this area is the way in which the results obtained in this book are compared in detail with those obtained in earlier studies.

Another salient feature of this book is that Dr. Salim has drawn several policy conclusions based on the results from the analysis. These policy conclusions are important because these are derived from a proper econometric methodology of decomposing the total factor productivity (TFP) growth, technical progress and improvements in capacity realization. The traditional measures do not distinguish between these two components of TFP growth, rather TFP growth is often used synonymously with technological progress. Failure to take account of changes in capacity realization measuring TFP growth produces biased TFP estimates that would indicate that all firms are operating with full productive capacity realization. High rates of technological progress, on the one hand, can co-exist with deteriorating capacity realization performance. Relatively low rates of technological progress can also co-exist with an improving capacity realization performance, on the other hand. As a result specific policy actions are required to address the difference in the sources of variation in productivity. It is in this context that the book makes a valuable contribution by estimating the firm-specific productive capacity realization and its relationship to TFP growth.

In our view, the book is highly valuable to all students, scholars and practitioners of development and industrial economics. It illustrates how to use rigorous econometric techniques to decompose the growth experience in a developing country between the contribution of TFP and changes in capacity realization. It also provides important evidence on the nature of productivity growth in Bangladesh manufacturing and draws policy implications, which would have important relevance to other developing countries.

Professor Warwick McKibbin
Head of the Department of Economics
Research School of Pacific and Asian Studies
The Australian National University
Canberra ACT 0200

and

Dr. K. P. Kalirajan
Deputy Executive Director
Australia South Asia Research Centre
Research School of Pacific and Asian Studies
The Australian National University
Canberra ACT 0200

Preface

The impact of market oriented reforms on the productive performance of an economy remains contentious, as the theoretical literature does not yet provide a clear-cut conclusion regarding the direction on such association and, thus, it remains an empirical issue. The purpose of this book is to examine the impact of recent economic reforms on productive performance of Bangladesh manufacturing industries.

An analytical framework has been developed to measure the productive performance of manufacturing firms in terms of total factor productivity (TFP) growth before and after reforms. TFP growth is defined as the growth of output not accounted for by growth of inputs and it is traditionally measured as the shift of production frontier and identified with technological progress. Any kind of capacity underutilization is ignored in this approach and produces flawed TFP estimates. Therefore, the use of the available TFP indices to measure firms' productive performance invariably leads to incorrect policy implications. The problem is particularly important in view of recent efforts taken by many developing countries to restructure their economies. The success or failure of such policies will be very difficult to assess if some of the key indicators for measuring individual firm's performance (such as TFP) are not quite accurate.

This book argues that capacity realization is an important component of TFP growth and has relevance for resource poor countries, such as Bangladesh, where the high opportunity cost of holding unrealized productive capacity poses serious consequences for productivity growth. An attempt has been made to develop a methodology by using the random coefficient frontier production function to estimate firm-specific capacity realization indices in selected manufacturing industries. Further, TFP growth has been estimated as two components: changes in capacity realization and technological progress. These two TFP components are analytically distinct, and their measurement provides an added dimension in terms of deriving policy implications, particularly for developing countries. This approach has the advantage of estimating TFP growth, rather than obtaining it as a residual, as is the case in the conventional growth accounting and index number approaches, where TFP growth estimates are likely to be contaminated by various measurement errors inherent in the data.

I am greatly indebted to Drs. T. S. Bruesch and K. P. Kalirajan of the Australian National University who taught me econometrics and economic modeling. Kalirajan, the specialist in the area of production frontier introduced me to the field of efficiency and productivity measurement. His constructive guidance, valuable advice, and seriousness in academic research helped me in dealing with controversial, complex and difficult issues. I owe a special debt to Dr. R. T. Shand and Cristopher Manning for their constructive advice, meticulous and timely reading the manuscript and helpful criticism and comments during the writing of this book. I would also like to record my deep gratitude to Professor Warwick McKibbin who, despite his heavy engagements, found time to read, correct and give insightful suggestions, which will always be appreciated. I am also grateful to all those authors whose works are cited here.

My wife Shahnaj and our only daughter ILma missed me very often while working on this book, without their support and unfailing love this work would have taken much longer time to complete. I records special thanks to them.

She who would be the happiest at this occasion, my beloved mother, Mrs. Touhida Khatun, passed away from this world in 1992 (Peace be on her departed soul). In her life she endeavoured and sacrificed a lot to instill in me the value of learning and a sense of purpose in life. In her blessed memory I drew the inspiration that helped me to keep going, and I dedicate this book to the loving memories of my mother.

Ruhul A. Salim

List of Abbreviations

ADB	Asian development bank
BBS	Bangladesh Bureau of Statistics
BGMEA	Bangladesh garments manufacturers and exporters association
BIDS	Bangladesh Institute of Development Studies
BOI	Board of investment
BSCIC	Bangladesh small and cottage industries corporation
CES	constant elasticity of substitution
CMI	Census of manufacturing industries
COLS	Corrected ordinary least square
CR	Concentration ratio
DFIs	Development finance corporations
DI	Department of industries
DOT	Department of textiles
EPB	Export promotion bureau
EPZs	Export processing zones
ERA	Effective rate of assistance
ERP	Effective rate of protection
ESEPP	Employment and small scale enterprise policy planning
FDI	Foreign direct investment
GDP	Gross domestic product
GLS	Generalized least squares

HIID	Harvard Institute of International Development
HYV	High yielding variety
ICB	Investment Corporation of Bangladesh
IIS	Industrial investment schedule
ILO	International labour organization
IMF	International Monetary Fund
IPO	Import policy order
IS	Import Substitution
ISIC	International standard industrial classification
LM	Lagrange multiplier
MFA	Multi fiber arrangement
MLE	Maximum likelihood estimation
MNCs	Multinational corporations
NCBs	Nationalised commercial Banks
NIEs	Newly industrialized economies
NIP	New industrial policy
NPO	National productivity organization
OLS	Ordinary least squares
PCR	Productive Capacity Realization
RIP	Revised industrial policy
TFP	Total factor productivity
TK	taka, Bangladesh currency; US$1 = taka 36.14 in 1991
UPC	unrealized productive capacity
WES	Wage earner's scheme
XPB	Export performance benefits
XPL	Export performance license

1 Introduction

The Setting

During the 1980s, market-oriented economic reforms became the 'new' development strategy in many developing countries. Macro imbalances, such as balance of payment crises, and micro inefficiencies, combined to force reconsideration of policy towards an outward orientation, reduced government intervention, and allowing market forces to work (Papageorgiu, Choksi and Michaely 1990, Greenway and Morrissey 1992, Corbo and Fischer 1995). These policy reforms were often adopted as part of a structural adjustment effort, with various conditionalities attached by the World Bank and the International Monetary Fund (IMF).

Theoretical arguments in favour of outward oriented economic policies have rested on the quest of allocative efficiency, in that an open economy is more likely to allocate resources in line with the comparative advantage of a given country. However, a related argument for a more liberal economic system is based on the assumption that there is a positive association between outward orientation and the rate of productivity growth. It is also argued that liberal trade policies and the liberalization process enhance total factor productivity (TFP) growth through the appropriate allocation of resources and increased productive capacity realization[1] (Handoussa, Nishimizu and Page 1986, Tybout, de Melo and Corbo 1991). Consequently, trade and industrial policy reforms are the central features of the reform agenda in many countries including Bangladesh.

Following independence in 1971, Bangladesh pursued an inward looking development strategy with the emphasis on a leading role for the public sector in economic activities. This was reinforced by nationalization of all large industries, banks and insurance companies in 1972. As a result, 92 per cent of total industrial assets came under public ownership at that time. Private sector participation was limited by an investment ceiling and foreign investment was discouraged by complex administrative procedures and minority equity participation. A series of measures, such as quantitative restrictions, highly differentiated tariff rates (0 to 400%), and various licensing procedures along with an overvalued exchange rate and huge subsidization programs were put in place to protect domestic industries from competition. These policies benefited only producers and administrators through rent-seeking activities while hindering higher productive capacity realization and productivity growth of manufacturing units which resulted in a level of output below the country's potential (Khan and Hossain 1989, Ahmad 1993, and Ahammad 1995). Moreover, the economy experienced severe economic problems of mounting foreign debts, huge fiscal and current account deficits, coupled with high inflation in the 1970s. These problems were exacerbated by a worldwide recession (during the two oil shocks in the 1970s),[2] declining terms of trade and a stagnant flow of external resources. Finding a way out of these crises as well as the impressive success of outward-orientation in East Asian economies provided the impetus in Bangladesh for undertaking market-oriented reform programs in the early eighties.

Bangladesh has followed a gradualist approach in the process of economic reforms. The reform measures have included the partial replacement of quantitative restrictions by tariffs, reduction of tariff rates, an easing of complex administrative procedures, and the introduction of various incentives for promotion of exports and attracting foreign direct investment (FDI). Simultaneously, various programmes of deregulation, divestment and privatization of perennial loss-making public enterprises were launched to improve the management of state owned enterprises. Also included in the policy reform regime are the reduction of subsidies, deregulation and privatization, together with improved management of state owned enterprises, devaluation of the domestic currency and unification of dual exchange rates to acquire international competitiveness, all of which have affected the production environment under which production units operate. Therefore, an examination of the performance of production units and comparisons between pre and post reform periods will yield useful information about the effectiveness of the policy reform and provides guidance for the direction of further policy reforms.

Growth and Productive Performance

After a decade of implementation of economic policy reform, Bangladesh has not produced the expected result of high growth rates. Gross Domestic Product (GDP) has grown on average by about 4 per cent per annum from 1972/73 to 1993/94. But comparison of the average growth of GDP of 4.2 per cent in the post-reform period (1982/83 to 1993/94) with 3.9 per cent in the pre-reform period (1972/73 to 1981/82) indicates only a marginal improvement in growth (Bangladesh Bureau of Statistics (BBS), 1993, 1995). The slow growth of the economy has resulted from the sluggish growth of the key sectors, particularly manufacturing. The growth of manufacturing value added over the last two decades has been disappointingly low (only 3.5 per cent per annum) and its share of the country's GDP has stagnated at about 10 per cent per annum. After the implementation of economic reforms, a few sub-sectors of some industries (such as ready-made garments, fish and sea food, and leather) have achieved impressive growth but this was not sufficient to increase the contribution of the manufacturing sector to the country's GDP growth.

There is convincing evidence that Bangladesh has achieved macroeconomic stability in terms of a reduction in budgetary deficits, lower inflation rates and higher foreign exchange reserves through these policy reforms (Rahman 1992, Ahmad 1993, Reza and Mahmood 1995). Despite the commendable achievement of macroeconomic stabilization, the industrial sector's performance has been disappointing.[3] At micro level, poor performance in terms of capacity realization and productivity growth have been observed both in public and private manufacturing enterprises. Sahota (1991) argued that there is substantial unrealized productive capacity in the manufacturing sector in Bangladesh, even after several years of continued economic reforms. Krishna and Sahota (1991) computed technical efficiency and productivity growth for 30 industries, covering the period 1974/75 to 1985/86, and found that most of their sample firms were producing at less than 50 per cent of their full productive efficiency. They also found that fifteen out of thirty industries had experienced no significant improvement in technical efficiency or TFP growth, five sample industries had experienced accelerated TFP, while the remaining 15 industries experienced a deceleration in TFP during the sample period. The Harvard Institute of International Development (HIID) and 'Employment and Small Scale Enterprise Policy Planning' (ESEPP) project of Bangladesh Planning Commission (1988, 1990a) computed TFP indices for a large number of industries, both at the firm level and four digit industry levels for the period of 1975/76 to 1983/84. The overall results showed that only about 35 per cent of manufacturing firms experienced positive cumulative TFP growth over the entire sample period. Several other studies (1990b, c) within the HIID/ESEPP project investigated the relationship between economic policy reforms (in terms of incentive structures) and manufacturing value added growth and TFP growth and reported no significant relationship. Thus, none of the earlier studies found any systematic evidence of a positive impact from the economic reforms on productivity growth.

However, the assessment of these studies of the impact of policy reforms on industrial performance may not be fully valid because they used data at aggregate level (either at national or sectoral levels) and failed to analyze firm-specific micro-level characteristics that are influenced by reform measures.[4] These studies also used data from earlier periods when the time was not yet mature for studying the effectiveness of the reform measures. Moreover, the earlier studies applied the traditional methodology of productivity growth, which assumes away any kind of capacity under-utilization of production agents and thus provides incomplete and ambiguous conclusions. Therefore, it may be argued that the empirical evidence linking the economic reforms in Bangladesh with gains in productivity is both under-studied and inconclusive. Further empirical studies with appropriate data and methodology are warranted to examine whether the economic reform measures have improved the productivity performance of the industrial sector.

The industrial sector in Bangladesh remains narrowly based and is still at an early stage of development. Major industries include cotton and jute textiles, garments, food processing, chemicals, leather, steel and engineering and paper and paper products. Among these, textiles (both cotton and jute) and garments, food processing and chemicals are the three largest industry groups in terms of contribution to output; value added; employment and foreign exchange earnings. In 1991, these industries contributed about 64, 60 and 75 per cent to total manufacturing output, value added, and employment respectively, and earned 75 per cent of total export earnings (BBS 1995). Within each of these industry groups, there are both import substituting (generally slow growing) and export promoting (generally fast growing) industries, which carry significant weight in the industrialization process of Bangladesh. Given the importance of these industries and the availability of consistent data, this study has chosen these three industry groups for empirical analysis.

Issues and Questions

The sluggish performance of the Bangladesh industrial sector represents a continuation of a longer-term stagnation, which began in the early 1970s. However, a few sectors of certain industries (for example, ready-made garments in the textiles and garment industry group, fish and sea food in the food processing industry group and fertilizer in the chemical industry group) recorded impressive growth after the implementation of reforms. An understanding of the pattern of productive performance in Bangladesh's industries is critical for projecting both the production potential of manufacturing firms and the likely effects of policy reform on the overall growth of the manufacturing sector as well as the economy. This understanding is required to resolve the question of why so few sectors of Bangladesh manufacturing industries are growing after the implementation of economic reform. In other words, why have the reform measures, particularly the trade and industrial policy reforms been so ineffective in boosting growth for so many industries.

Though there is now an extensive literature assessing the impact of policy reforms on the performance of production units,[5] the findings of these studies are diverse. Thus, the linkage between policy reforms and productivity gains is still not properly understood. Rodrik notes that 'There is as yet no convincing empirical evidence for developing countries that shows liberalization to be conducive to industry rationalization' (1992 p:170). Similarly, Pack observes that '....to date there is no clear confirmation of the hypothesis that countries with an external orientation benefit from greater growth in technical efficiency in the component sectors of manufacturing' (1988 p:353). From what follows, the relationship between market oriented economic reforms still remains an empirical issue. Drawing on the arguments developed by Bhagwati (1988) and Havrylyshyn (1990) it may be inferred that the theoretical foundation for such linkages is not yet solid. However, the 'endogenous growth theory' which explicitly recognizes firm-specific behavioural characteristics, provides a basis for the link between reform and improved industrial productivity. For example, to analyze such a link, Krugman (1987) and Lucas (1988, 1993) exploit learning-by-doing and externalities, Grossman and Helpman (1991) use technological innovation, and Corden (1974) and Rodrik (1992) use organizational and managerial efforts.

Thus, the link can be established in terms of microeconomic aspects of the theory of firm. The microeconomic approach concerns firm-specific characteristics that have a direct bearing on its competitive behaviour, and X-efficiency, which are the prime targets of reform measures for improvement. However, macroeconomic environment strengthens the link by facilitating firms to increase exports and improve capacity realization through appropriate exchange rate and trade policies. Thus, one effective way of assessing the significance of reform on industrial productivity is equivalent to examining whether there have been any significant changes in firm-specific production performance before and after reform, over a sufficient period of time after reform. Given the availability of firm level data, and various distinct policy sequences in Bangladesh since the early to mid-eighties, the industrial sector in Bangladesh appears to be a suitable case study.

Generally, output growth is achieved by either inputs growth or total factor productivity (TFP) growth. Of these, TFP growth is obtained by either technological progress, improvement in the use of the chosen technology that leads to the full capacity realization or both of these factors. Particularly, from the reform point of view, productive capacity realization is an important source of output growth. Recent market-oriented economic reforms have changed the production environment at the firm level and are expected to influences firm-specific capacity realization. This leads to the next task of identifying the variables that influence firms in achieving or inhibiting maximum realization of productive capacity. A detailed examination of various determinants (including economic reforms, particularly trade and industrial policy reforms) of the observed differential in capacity realization rates may assist government in framing industrial policies. Again, empirical studies linking trade policy reforms with improvement in firms' capacity realization, whether in Bangladesh or elsewhere, are sparse. This study examines the various factors which cause differentials in firm-specific capacity realization in selected industries of Bangladesh.

Chapter Outline

The book is structured as follows:

Including this introductory chapter the book comprises eight chapters. Chapter 2 surveys the pre and post reform performances of the Bangladesh economy with emphasis on the manufacturing sector. It highlights major policies adopted by the Bangladesh government in the 1970s, and the major policy shifts in the 1980s that affected the pre and post reform performances of the manufacturing sector. This chapter concludes with an overall performance and policy evaluation.

Chapter 3 reviews the existing literature on the measurement of TFP growth and capacity realization of production units and emphasizes the need for alternative methodologies.

Chapter 4 discusses the analytical framework and develops new measures for capacity realization and TFP growth by using the random coefficient frontier production function approach. This chapter also discusses the sources of data for this study and identifies relevant variables for measuring PCR and TFP, and for examining variations in firm-specific capacity realization, if any.

Chapter 5 provides an overview of the structure and performance of the three selected manufacturing industry groups. It also provides the empirical estimates of firm-specific productive capacity realization indices for these selected industries. A summary of findings and policy implications is also presented at the end of the chapter.

Chapter 6 also provides empirical measures of sources of output growth (TFP growth and inputs growth) for these industry groups and compares the results with those from some other developing countries. These chapters also measure biases of technological progress at the firm level for the selected industry groups. Finally, there is a summary of major empirical findings. Policy implications and limitations are also discussed.

Chapter 7 develops a theoretical framework for explaining the determinants of capacity realization. It also explores several determinants of capacity realization, and develops several hypotheses for empirical investigation. Finally, a model is selected to show which particular factors influence capacity realization the most.

Chapter 8 provides a summary of the major findings and draws conclusions from the study. It also discusses policy implications and suggests directions for further reforms and presents limitations of the study and focuses for further research.

Notes

[1] In the literature, the term 'capacity utilization' is used to describe the most efficient output minimizing the present values of the cost stream given stock of capital and technology (Morrison 1985, 1988 and Kang and Kwon 1993), while this study uses the term 'capacity realization' to describe maximum possible output obtainable from a given set of inputs and technology by following Klein (1960) and Färe *et al* (1989). Clearly, capacity realization is a broader concept than capacity utilization. This distinction is made in Chapter 3.

[2] As Bangladesh has been a net importer of oil, the oil price hikes adversely affected the economy by drawing a huge sum of money from important development works to finance import bills.

[3] The industrial sector is a broader concept than the manufacturing sector and includes manufacturing plus mining and quarrying. Industrial and manufacturing sectors are used synonymously throughout this study as mining and quarrying have been very minor contributors to industrial output.

[4] Nelson (1981) argued that aggregate level analyses may provide useful indication of overall productivity change, but they fail to capture what is important for productivity growth altogether.

[5] See for example, Balassa (1978), Balassa and associates (1982), Bhagwati (1978), Krueger (1978), (1980), Riedal (1984), Chenery *et al* (1986), Garnaut (1991), Helleiner (1992), Williamson (1994). For a detailed review of earlier studies, see Pack (1988) and Rodrik (1995).

2 Policy Regimes and Development Experiences in Bangladesh

Introduction

East Asian countries have been enjoying spectacular growth performance during the past two decades, but the growth of South Asian countries, particularly that of Bangladesh remain sluggish. While the growth of real Gross Domestic Product (GDP) was, on average, almost double digit in the East Asian Newly Industrialized Economies (NIEs), it was only 4 per cent in the South Asian countries from 1971 to 1994 (World Bank 1995). In the same period, with only 3 per cent of average real GDP growth, Bangladesh remained one of the low income countries of the World. The question then arises: What factors contributed to such rapid growth in some of these Asian economies, and are those factors absent in Bangladesh? This question is pertinent, because, ironically, during the 1950s and 1960s Bangladesh[1] and other South Asian countries had been growing at much the same, or even at higher rates than these East Asian economies.

From the literature, it appears that sound macroeconomic policies, along with market-oriented export policies and an appropriate level of government intervention in economic activities, led to the spectacular success of the East Asian economies.[2] Stimulated by the success of these Asian economies, Bangladesh like many other developing countries, started implementing economic policy reforms at the beginning of the 1980s. Despite these reforms, economic growth in Bangladesh remains sluggish. This chapter analyses the economic policies and performance of Bangladesh, in an attempt to identify the important factors that have been contributing to the sluggish performance.

This chapter starts by focusing on Bangladesh's trade and industrialization record, then examines the policy regimes pursued by the government in the 1970s, major policy shifts during the 1980s, and assesses the impact of these policy changes on aggregate economic variables. Conclusions are then drawn at the end of the chapter.

Bangladesh Economy Pre-reform Era (1973-82)

Prior to economic reform, from 1973 to 1982, Bangladesh achieved moderate growth, with real Gross domestic product (GDP) increasing by about 4.5 per cent annually. Rapid population growth (over 2 per cent annually) resulted in per capita income growth of less than two per cent (Table 2.1). Although this GDP growth rate was not low by developing country standards,[3] it was well below that of East Asian countries. The gap between the growth rate of Bangladesh and these countries has widened over time, and Bangladesh has remained one of the poor countries in Asia.

Table 2.1: Macroeconomic Indicators, 1973-96*

	1973	1977	1973-82	1985	1993	1983-96
Population growth	2.93	2.10	2.33	2.36	1.62	2.27
GDP growth rate	-0.20	1.00	4.53	3.90	4.5	4.17
Per Capita GNP growth	-2.61	-1.76	1.82	1.28	2.92	1.82
Domestic savings as % of GDP	3.40	6.18	1.70	2.05	7.00	4.11
Investment as % of GDP	8.71	11.52	11.25	12.94	14.3	13.15
Budget deficit as % of GDP	-14.5	-12.9	-10.2	-6.9	-5.9	-7.4
Current account balance (% of GDP)	-6.2	-6.3	-8.6	-8.4	-2.6	-5.4
Real effective exchange rate	16.19	28.69	26.97	28.04	39.75	30.90
Foreign exchange reserve (US $m.)	143.2	232.7	227.3	336.5	2121	1148
CPI (% change)	49.01	16.81	19.50	10.70	1.40	7.52

* Values are at constant (1984/85) prices wherever relevant.

Source: Bangladesh Bureau of Statistics (BBS), *Statistical Yearbook of Bangladesh* (various issues) and Government of Bangladesh (GOB), Bangladesh Economic Review (various issues).

Throughout the seventies, Bangladesh experienced disequilibrium in both the internal (budget deficit) and external accounts (balance of payments gap). Domestic resource mobilization was highly inadequate compared to investment requirements, so the saving-investment gap remained as a chronic structural imbalance of the economy (Table 2.1).

The current account position was also precarious, due to the anti-export bias in trade policies. Bangladesh relied on traditional exports such as jute, jute goods, and tea - the international prices of which were subject to severe fluctuations. The situation was aggravated by rapidly rising import prices and a serious deterioration in the terms of trade. The export-import gap increased about three folds from US$555 million in 1973-74 to US$1645 million in 1979-80 in nominal terms (BBS 1982). As foreign exchange reserves were at a very low level, Bangladesh resorted to deficit financing and an increased money supply to fill the internal gap, and external resources to fill the foreign exchange gap. As a result, double digit inflation crippled the economy throughout the seventies (Table 2.1).

Structure and Growth of the Economy

While it is argued that structural transformation is one of the main characteristics of economic growth,[4] the development pattern in Bangladesh, before economic reform, indicates the economy experienced little structural change in the 1970s.

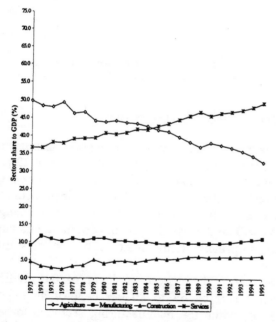

Figure 2.1: GDP at 1985 Constant Prices by Sector of Origin, 1973-95

Sources: BBS, *Statistical Yearbook of Bangladesh* (various issues).

Bangladesh remained overwhelmingly an agrarian country. Agriculture contributed about 50 per cent to GDP in the early 1970s. Agricultural productivity improved then with the introduction of new seeds, fertilizer and irrigation, but the spread of new agricultural practices was low. So its share of GDP fell to 44 per cent in 1982. The small decline in agriculture's share was accompanied by an increased GDP share of services in construction, trade and banking (Figure 2.1), increasing from 36 per cent in 1973 to 41 per cent in 1982. The share of the manufacturing sector in GDP remained virtually unchanged over this period. Despite the policy emphasis given to the development of this sector, its share remained low, at an average of 10 per cent from 1973 to 1982 (Figure 2.1).

Table 2.2: Sectoral Contribution to GDP Growth, 1973-96

	1973-78	1973-82	1983-88	1989-92	1993-96
GDP growth	4.12	4.53	4.10	4.21	4.40
Agriculture	27.40	21.86	24.07	25.75	26.05
Manufacturing	15.31	15.83	16.15	16.30	16.45
Construction	5.30	6.48	3.32	6.17	5.75
Services	52.01	55.83	56.46	51.78	51.75

Note: Figures are at 1985 constant prices. Sectoral contribution to GDP growth is calculated as a ratio of GDP growth and the sectoral growth weighted by its percentage share in GDP.

Source: BBS, *Statistical Yearbook of Bangladesh* (various issues).

From 1973 to 1982, the service sector was the highest contributor to GDP growth (exceeding 55 per cent) followed by agriculture (about 22 per cent), construction (7 per cent), and the manufacturing sector (16 per cent). The contribution of each sector to the growth of GDP remained virtually stagnant during this period indicating that very little structural change occurred in the economy. As will be discussed in the next section, this lack of structural change is not surprising in the light of the policies that prevailed.

Agriculture has been the single highest employer of the civilian labour force in Bangladesh absorbing 65 to 80 per cent of aggregate employment during the 1970s, while the manufacturing sector absorbed only around 4 per cent (Table 2.3). However, between 1974 and 1981, the labour force in agriculture declined in absolute terms. This dramatic change in the composition of labour force was not necessarily due to the dynamic diversification of the other sectors, but more to the fact that the growth of agriculture was labour displacing at the margin rather than labour absorbing (Khan and Hossain 1989).[5]

As a result, the labour pushed out from agriculture to various non-agricultural activities was mostly of a residual variety characterized by low productivity. These include petty trade, repairing shops, porterage, pushing cart and pulling rickshaws, etc. Labour absorption increased in the services sector and the share of manufacturing employment remained almost unchanged during the 1970s.

Table 2.3: Sectoral Distribution of Employment (selected years)

Year	Agriculture (million)	Manufacturing (million)	Services (million)	Total (million)
1974	16.8	1.0	3.6	21.4
1981	15.5	1.1	8.7	25.3
1986	17.5	3.0	10.1	30.6
1989	21.1	4.5	6.9	32.5
1991	33.3	5.9	12.0	51.2
Percentage distribution by sectors				
1974	78.5	4.7	16.8	100
1981	61.3	4.2	34.5	100
1986	57.1	9.9	33.0	100
1989	65.0	13.9	21.1	100
1991	65.0	11.5	23.5	100
Change between periods (million)				
1974-1981	-1.3	0.1	5.1	3.9
1986-1991	15.8	2.9	2.1	20.6
Percentage of total change between periods				
1974-1981	-33.33	2.56	130.77	100
1986-1991	76.70	14.08	10.20	100

Source: Government of Bangladesh (GOB), *Population Census* 1974 and 1981, BBS, *Labour Force Surveys* 1985-86, 1989 and 1990-91.

Industrialization and Industrial Performances

Bangladesh inherited a very small industrial sector. Jute and cotton textiles, food and beverages, drugs and chemicals, paper and newsprints, sugar, and leather were the major industries in terms of output and employment.

Except for jute goods and leather products, almost all industries were engaged in import substitute manufacturing and agro-processing activities. Despite the abundant labour force, and the agro-base, the pace of industrialization in the 1970s was very slow. For example, the number of manufacturing units increased only by about 4 per cent annually during 1973 to 1982 (Table 2.4).

Table 2.4: Growth of Manufacturing Sector, 1973-93[*]

	1973	1978	1982	1973-82	1985	1990	1983-93
No. of Establishments	-15.15	6.69	6.47	4.37	5.19	7.31	5.60
Fixed Assets	16.98	17.88	21.84	20.36	18.78	12.25	17.14
Employment	10.42	8.92	3.72	10.76	3.75	3.64	3.85
Output	32.25	20.62	-4.87	23.52	2.14	8.04	10.46
Value Added	23.41	24.74	-9.13	8.87	-4.67	6.45	3.64

[*] Figures represent the annual average growth rates (per cent). Caution should be given in analyzing these growth figures, because data are only for the reported establishments in the census of manufacturing industries.

Source: BBS, Report on the Census of Manufacturing Industries (CMI), (various issues).

Table 2.4 reveals that between 1973 to 1982 fixed assets, employment and output, on average, grew annually at about 20, 11, and 23 per cent respectively. The growth rates of these parameters appeared higher in the early 1970s compared to later years. The smaller base in the earlier years might have been partly responsible. In the early stage of import substitution, it may have been possible to divert demand from foreign to domestic suppliers and thus boost growth. However, in succeeding periods the limited size of the domestic market and the shortage of foreign exchange needed for raw materials and capital goods constrained growth.

During 1973 to 1982, there was strong capital-bias in Bangladesh in the process of industrialization. The average growth rate of fixed assets in the manufacturing sector had been growing as high as 20 per cent per annum during the pre-reform period. This growth was double to that of employment. Substitution of labour for capital in manufacturing production is crucial in a labour surplus economy, the opposite occurred in Bangladesh. Many earlier studies (Islam 1977, Rushdi 1982, and Ahmed 1984) examined the factor substitution possibilities in Bangladesh manufacturing sector, and found that there was ample scope for factor substitution. Consequently, an inappropriate input mix in the production process adversely affected the growth performance of the manufacturing sector.

Table 2.5: Real Growth of Manufacturing Output by Major Industry Groups, 1973-93

	1973	1977	1982	1973-82	1985	1990	1983-93
Food processing	8.47	4.32	3.25	4.16	1.31	13.15	6.32
Tobacco	17.32	12.15	8.43	11.76	13.78	-4.07	10.22
Textiles	3.72	6.12	3.35	3.55	3.15	9.95	4.86
Garments	0.0	0.0	5.48	4.01	10.69	32.35	21.66
Paper & paper products	15.32	8.56	5.62	10.25	11.37	5.03	5.21
Leather products	5.76	4.21	4.65	5.32	0.74	12.41	10.54
Chemicals	16.54	7.42	5.46	6.75	10.19	7.51	6.32
Basic metals	8.52	12.76	7.20	11.35	22.06	-7.46	5.12
Machinery	5.08	3.98	3.65	2.65	-7.56	5.65	3.70
Electronics	0.57	3.21	4.55	3.43	33.62	7.15	12.43

Source: BBS, Census of Manufacturing Industries (CMI), various years (Current Production).

Thus, the interesting results that emerge from Table 2.4 are that the manufacturing sector expanded inputs substantially during the 1970s and output growth was perhaps mainly from this increase in inputs, rather than from an increasing realization of production capacity, or an increase in total factor productivity growth. This situation is similar to what Krugman (1994), Young (1994) and Kim and Lau (1994) found in the case of East Asian countries. Krugman concluded that East Asian growth seems to be driven by extraordinary growth of inputs such as labour and capital rather than by gains in efficiency. His conclusion is supported by Young who claimed that while the growth of output and manufacturing exports in East Asia is unprecedented, the growth of total factor productivity is not. Kim and Lau, using a meta production approach found that the most important source of economic growth in the 'Four Tigers' is capital accumulation, accounting for between 48 and 72 per cent of their economic growth in contrast to the case of the Group of Five industrialized countries in which technical progress has played the most important role, accounting for between 46 and 71 per cent of their economic growth.

Manufacturing industry growth patterns changed little before economic reform (Tables 2.5 and 2.6). The relative share and rate of growth of individual industries in Bangladesh reflect an unbalanced industrial structure. Only three industries, tobacco, paper & paper products, and basic metal industries, recorded double digit growth from 1973 to 1982, while they together contributed only 17 per cent of total manufacturing value added and employed only 7 per cent of total manufacturing employment. Of the major industry groups, textiles & garments, food processing and chemical industries claimed more than two thirds of manufacturing value added and about 75 per cent of employment. These dominant industries grew relatively slowly and the faster growing industries did not expand sufficiently to alter the pattern of concentration.

Table 2.6: Annual Average Share of Output, Value Added and Employment by Major Industry Groups, 1973-93

	Output (%)		Value added (%)		Employment (%)	
	1973-82	1983-93	1973-82	1983-93	1973-82	1983-93
Food processing	12.47	14.61	10.75	12.19	9.07	11.36
Tobacco	9.33	6.14	10.35	11.56	2.59	2.27
Textiles	27.77	30.21	33.59	30.74	58.08	57.24
Garments	1.45	6.25	1.85	3.15	0.54	5.41
Paper & paper product	3.43	3.20	3.02	2.42	2.27	2.50
Leather products	3.44	5.32	1.63	1.77	0.70	0.78
Chemicals	10.55	12.19	17.41	15.24	7.23	7.32
Basic metals	6.80	5.21	3.08	2.87	1.77	2.01
Machinery	1.89	1.21	1.92	1.35	2.11	1.43
Electronics	1.76	2.49	2.24	2.54	1.07	2.48
Others	20.81	13.17	14.16	16.17	14.57	7.20

Source: BBS, *Statistical Yearbook* of Bangladesh, (various issues) and Report on the Census of Manufacturing Industries (CMI) (various issues).

The structural composition of manufacturing value added, in terms of end-use of products, also showed little change during 1970 to 1982 (Table 2.7).

The shares of both intermediate and capital goods remained almost unchanged during this period, indicating a less impressive performance from import substituting industries. Consumer goods industries remained dominant and accounted for 50 per cent or more of total manufacturing value added. Almost all large manufacturing enterprises were owned by government and accounted for 92 per cent of total industrial fixed assets. These enterprises were managed by a number of public sector corporations.[6]

Table 2.7: Structure of Manufacturing Industries by End-use Products (percentage), (selected years)

	Share in Manufacturing Value Added					
Type of Industries	1970	1980	1982	1986	1989	1993
Consumer goods	56	59	52	59	57	58
Intermediate goods	37	35	36	39	38	36
Capital goods	7	6	12	2	5	6
Total	100	100	100	100	100	100

Source: GOB, The Fourth Five Year Plan 1990-95; Planning Commission, Input-Output Table for Bangladesh, Dhaka, and Bhuyan and Rashid (1993).

Table 2.8: Financial Performance[a] of Public Sector Industrial Corporations[b], (selected years) (TK. Million)

	1974	1977	1982	1973-82	1985	1990	1983-95
BJMC	-355	-525	-234	-7354	-1462	-3709	-18426
BTMC	90	-132	23	-1021	42	-175	-3163
BSFIC	-42	149	218	167	-234	164	-2475
BSEC	-39	76	-273	-586	-135	-365	-4159
BCIC	-16	51	158	-105	131	455	1181
BFIDC	44	-4	-6	97	15	-40	-103
Total	**-318**	**-385**	**-112**	**-8802**	**-1643**	**-3670**	**-27145**

[a] Net profit before tax (negative sign denotes losses). [b] See endnote 7.

Source: Autonomous Bodies Wing, Ministry of Finance, GOB.

As these corporations owned such a high proportion of fixed assets of the industrial sector, they were the catalysts of the performance of the whole manufacturing sector. During the 1970s, employment and fixed industrial assets increased steadily in public sector enterprises, but value added remained constant at about 2 per cent (Bakht and Bhattacharya 1991). Inertia together with lack of governmental strategies in directing these industries were partly to blame. The cost effectiveness of public sector enterprises has been a perennial problem. The financial performance of these enterprises has been disappointing mainly due to complex management systems, inappropriate price policy, and frivolous use of productive resources.

Table 2.9: Structure of Merchandise Exports in Bangladesh, (selected years), (percentage)

	1973	1980	1985	1990	1993	1995
Total Exports (US $m.)	**354**	**722**	**934**	**1524**	**2383**	**3473**
Total Exports (%)	100	100	100	100	100	100
Traditional Exports	**97.3**	**87.8**	**71.8**	**44.0**	**23.42**	**13.43**
Raw Jute	37.8	19.9	16.1	8.2	3.11	2.29
Jute goods	52.3	54.3	41.7	21.5	12.25	8.38
Tea	2.7	4.6	6.5	2.6	1.72	0.94
Leather & Leather prodts.	4.6	9.1	7.5	11.7	6.34	1.82
Non-traditional Exports	**2.7**	**12.2**	**28.2**	**56.0**	**64.47**	**86.57**
Fish & Sea foods	1.3	5.2	9.6	9.5	8.65	8.97
Ready-made garments	0.0	0.1	12.4	40.0	52.04	52.85
Newsprint	0.7	1.1	0.9	0.2	0.13	0.04
Urea Fertilizer	0.0	....	0.5	1.1	2.14	2.96
Napta, Furnace oil, and Bitumen	0.0	3.2	2.2	1.1	1.51	0.39
All Others	0.7	2.6	2.5	4.0	12.11	21.4

Source: GOB, *Economic Survey* (various issues), Ministry of Finance.

The heavy losses were a huge drain on amount of government resources over this period. For example, from 1973 to 1982, the total loss incurred by six sector corporations amounted to about 9 billion Taka or approximately US$2.8 million (Table 2.8). Not only did they burden the budget directly by requiring periodic capital infusion from the government, but they were also a heavy load on the banking system because of loan write-offs, waiving of interest charges and bad debts.[7] Moreover, due to inter sectoral linkages the poor performance of the public enterprises had serious consequences for private enterprise performance.

Owing to its early stage of development and limited natural resources, Bangladesh was heavily dependent on imports in the 1970s, not only for raw materials but also for acquisition of foreign technology. As a result, Bangladesh has been a net importer in merchandise trade, and the gap between exports and imports has widened over the years. Exports as a percentage of GDP remained stagnant, at an average rate of 5 per cent during 1973 to 1982, while imports grew by 15 per cent per annum in the same period (EPB 1997).

Table 2.10: Structure of Merchandise Imports in Bangladesh, (selected years), (percentage)

	1973	1980	1985	1990	1993	1995
Total Imports (US $m.)	780	2372	2647	3759	3986	5834
Share of imports by end-use of products (% of total)						
Consumer goods (Food grains and Edible oil)	**46.6**	**29.1**	**23.6**	**16.6**	**8.38**	**11.93**
Other consumer goods	**25.8**	**21.9**	**27.7**	**36.0**	**41.3**	**42.44**
Intermediate goods	**14.8**	**26.0**	**25.4**	**22.3**	**19.06**	**16.71**
Petroleum	3.9	16.2	13.9	12.7	7.63	6.56
Fertilizer	3.1	5.6	5.2	2.4	3.29	2.43
Cement	0.9	1.5	1.2	2.4	2.89	1.98
Raw Cotton	5.1	2.2	4.0	3.3	2.06	2.31
Yarn	1.7	0.5	1.2	1.4	3.19	3.43
Capital goods	**12.8**	**23.0**	**23.3**	**25.1**	**31.26**	**28.93**

Source: GOB, *Economic Survey* (various issues), Ministry of Finance.

Bangladesh's export base was traditionally narrow and until 1980 there was no significant change in export composition, reflecting the slow pace and character of industrialization (Table 2.9). Since then, traditional exports have declined and non-traditional exports have increased sharply. During this period the pattern of Bangladesh's imports changed markedly. Between 1970 and 1980, the share of consumer goods to total imports fell from 72 per cent to 51 per cent. On the other hand, during the same period the proportions of intermediate and capital goods in total imports rose from

27 per cent to 49 per cent (Table 2.9). This rapid increase in capital goods was facilitated by import substitution.

Despite the emphasis on import substitution industrialization during the 1970s, Bangladesh remained a highly import dependent country for manufactured products with a large proportion of domestic absorption met by imported goods (Table 2.11). This paradoxical situation[8] in Bangladesh is consistent with the experience of many other developing countries at that time, and was created because of an anti-export bias and undue emphasis on import substitution. As a result, firms operated on a small scale in a sheltered environment, and as several studies have shown, many countries failed to achieved their objective of dynamic industrialization in terms of productive efficiency and technological catch up because of import substitute regimes (Little *et al* 1970, Bhagwati 1978, Krueger 1978 and Bautista *et al* 1981, Adhikari *et al* 1992).

Table 2.11: Export, Import and Domestic Absorption of Manufacturing Products, (selected years)

	1981	1985	1990	1993	1995
Domestic Production (million TK)	66251	101301	190254	236392	267618
Exports (million TK)	8103	18149	36683	88215	121147
Imports (million TK)	26556	42050	85803	138198	272279
Share of Export in Production (in percentage)	12.2	17.9	19.3	37.32	45.27
Share of Imports in Apparent* Domestic Absorption (%)	31.4	33.6	27.5	48.26	65.02

*Apparent domestic absorption is calculated as the sum of the domestic gross production and net imports.

Source: Stern, J. J., Mallon, R. D., and Hutcheson, T. L., (1988) and author's calculation from BBS (1997) *Statistical Pocketbook*.

As a small developing economy, Bangladesh not only maintained these import substituting industries and insulated them from the international competition but also provided them with cheap credit and concessionary imports of industrial raw materials and machinery. As a result, these industries failed to stand on their own feet and standardize their products, and there was a tendency to overcapitalize the production process. In order to qualify for concessionary imports, import substituting industries continued to build up excess capacity. Consequently, output per unit of input fell, while import content per unit of output increased. This explains the increase in the share of imports in the apparent domestic absorption over time in Bangladesh.

Bangladesh's manufacturing sector suffered heavily from factor bias leading to a major under-utilization of capital inputs. As a result, the sector remained undeveloped, bereft of dynamism or any diversification of output, and above all, with a level of output far below its potential.

Policies that Affected Industrialization in the 1970s

Many recent studies in development economics have emphasized the role of various policies.[9] Trade and industrial policies, in particular, have an important influence on the performance of economic decision-making units. These policies have essentially shaped the structure and pace of industrialization growth. Hence, an analysis of policy evolution in Bangladesh is important for an understanding of the pattern of resource allocation and efficiency in production.

Following independence in 1971, Bangladesh commenced industrialization with an inward-looking policy of import substitution (IS), which gave the lead role to the public sector. This IS strategy was supported by a plethora of protective and concessionary measures, mainly, quantitative restrictions and bans, coupled with import licences, high levels of effective protection along with differentiated rates of nominal tariffs, an overvalued domestic currency and exchange control, as well as *ad hoc* concessions and subsidised loans. With the ambitious objective of equity and social justice, the government proceeded to nationalise all large and medium industries,[10] banks and insurance companies, and exerted strict government control over international trade and payments. As a result, 92 per cent of industrial assets came under government control in 1972. This was the highest share of government sector for any Asian country except China. A moratorium on nationalization was declared for 10 years but there was no guarantee that those nationalized industries would be given back to private ownership after 10 years. On the contrary, government reserved the right to nationalize any enterprise, which was running losses or under-utilizing production capacity. Thus, Bangladesh became a command economy with almost all economic activities run by government.

Private sector participation in industrialization was constrained by an investment ceiling. Private enterprises were allowed an investment in initial fixed assets of up to 2.5 million Taka (TK) (equivalent to US $0.3 million), with growth in assets allowed of up to TK. 3.5 million (US $0.46 million) through reinvestment of profits. Foreign direct investments were discouraged, and foreign private investors were allowed to set up industries only with minority equity participation. These measures severely limited the role of the private sector and hindered development opportunities and entrepreneurship.

Over time, the private sector has gradually been given more opportunities by liberalizing these restrictions over the size and areas of investment. Various incentives, including liberal credit facilities have been given to private enterprise by the Nationalized Commercial Banks (NCBs) and Development Finance Institutions (DFIs). The Investment Corporation of Bangladesh (ICB) was set up to provide bridging finance and underwriting facilities for private entrepreneurs. By the end of 1978, the ceiling on private investment was completely abolished, and a compensation plan was set up for private firms which had earlier been nationalized.[11] The Dhaka stock exchange was reactivated to mobilize and channel private savings into industrial investment. A denationalization program was started in the mid seventies, but the pace of denationalization was slow, due to both strong trade union and political opposition. Up to June 1981, only 255 public enterprises (equivalent to 7 per cent of total fixed assets of the manufacturing sector) had been divested (Humphrey 1990).

Industrial investment in the economy was controlled through the Industrial Investment Schedule (IIS) in successive Five Year Plans. All investments require licenses, which entitle the investors to the allocation of foreign exchange. The IIS specified investment possibilities in various sectors in terms of aggregate investment allocations and also served as an instrument to restrict and regulate private foreign and domestic investment. As the private sector became more important over the years, the IIS remained as a guide to the sanctioning authorities for approving industrial investment projects.

The investment sanctioning procedures served as a deterrent to industrial investment growth in Bangladesh and was a cause of serious concern for many investors. Depending on the size and areas of investment to set up an industry, investors needed approvals from a plethora of government departments and agencies, like the Board of Investment (BOI), Department of Industries (DI), Bangladesh Small and Cottage Industries Corporation (BSCIC), NCBs, and DFIs, etc. Sanctioning also entailed additional bother and cost for investors as the sanctioning authorities frequently required extensive justifications in support of proposed investments.[12] Thus, the sanctioning process received by potential investors was unnecessarily complex, time consuming, and lacking in transparency.

From the early seventies, Bangladesh followed a stringent trade regime with massive import controls. The overriding principles behind these controls were to provide protection to domestic industry and conserve scarce foreign exchange to meet balance of payments problems. Traditional administrative instruments, such as discretionary quantitative restrictions, outright ban, etc. have been used through the Import Policy Order[13] (IPO) for this purpose. A so called 'positive list' of items eligible for import were included in the IPO. Until 1982, 735 4-digit items were subject to import bans or import restrictions.

Until the mid-eighties the government allocated scarce foreign exchange among users through a centralized import licensing procedure. Import licenses were allocated to firms according to a set of predetermined criteria. These included sanctioned productive capacity, import requirements per unit capacity, and the percentages of import entitlement eligible for cash licenses. This provided privileges to firms in acquiring industrial raw materials, including restricted items at the official exchange rate, and controlled entry into production and discriminated against small firms in favour of larger ones. Industrial units often inflated installed capacity, or exaggerated unused capacity to obtain more licenses. This arbitrary and complex system of licensing and foreign exchange allocation created excess capacity in industry and distorted industrial growth. The system encouraged lobbying and side payments to government officials, and created an unfavourable environment for industrial efficiency.

The government imposed high tariffs to obtain more revenue, as well as to protect domestic industries. Customs duties (tariffs), combined with sales taxes and development surcharges, constituted about 40 per cent of government revenue. Of these, tariffs were the most important. The government published a series of statutory rates, which were the highest that could be levied legally. The maximum tariff rate was 400 per cent and the rate actually applied varied widely across products in each sector. For many products, basic raw materials received higher protection than intermediate output, which were, in turn, more protected than final products. Special exemptions, and the existence of many transactions that bypassed official channels, created additional anomalies in the structure of protection. These anomalies created scope for widespread abuse in tariff assessment and rent-seeking by both importers and customs officials.

Tariff rates were also highly discriminatory. They varied not only among industries, but also between products in the same industry, depending on the type of importer, the end use of product, geographical location of firms, etc. As a result of these divergent nominal rates, the effective rates of protection (ERP) also varied widely and unsystematically. Hutcheson (1986) estimated ERP for selected industries of Bangladesh, and found that, although the overall level of ERP to manufacturing was only 114 per cent, there was a wide variation in these rates ranging from minus 90 per cent to as high as plus 995 per cent, showing that the existing system of protection gave uneven incentives to different industrial sectors. Such an outcome was the result of the series of *ad hoc* decisions taken in determining tariff rates by the government (Hutcheson and Stern 1986, Sood 1989).

There were provisions for a few incentives such as the export performance license (XPL), duty drawback, etc. for export development after 1972. Under the XPL scheme, exporters, particularly non-traditional item exporters, were given entitlement certificates allowing more Taka for each dollar of export than the official rate of exchange. These entitlement certificates were convertible and exporters were also allowed to exchange XPL at a premium with the central bank or in the secondary exchange market. But these were not enough to offset the various biases against exports, and had no real impact on export performance other than aggravating the import control regime, which added to the anti-export biases in Bangladesh, as in many other developing countries (Salma 1992, Ahammad 1995, Herderschee 1995).

Table 2.12: Official Exchange Rates, Secondary Market Exchange Rates and Exchange Rate Premium, (selected years)

	1978	1981	1984	1987	1990	1991
Official Exchange Rate	15.12	16.26	24.94	30.63	32.92	35.72
Secondary exchange rate	19.86	20.11	27.16	33.08	33.58	36.38
Exchange rate premium[*]	31.35	23.68	8.90	8.00	2.01	1.85

[*] Exchange rate premium is calculated on the basis the difference between the two rates as a percentage of the official rate.

Source: Bangladesh Bank, (1994).

Bangladesh pursued a fixed exchange rate regime from 1972 to 1979. The Taka was pegged with the Pound Sterling. Because of excessive trade controls, the exchange rate remained overvalued. To facilitate more exchange earnings, the government opened the Wage Earner's Scheme (WES), a legal secondary exchange market in 1975. Foreign exchange remittances of overseas Bangladesh nationals, tourists, and other service earnings, were channelled for sale through the WES. Initially, only a few items could be imported under the WES, so the importer had to pay a higher rate for foreign exchange than the official rate. Over time, the rules were simplified and more items could be imported, so importers were given greater access to raw materials and other goods (Mallon and Stern 1991).

In 1979, the government adopted a flexible exchange rate policy. The Taka was pegged to a basket of currencies of Bangladesh's major trading partners, weighted according to their bilateral foreign exchange transactions with Bangladesh. The aim of this change was to facilitate a gradual adjustment of the nominal exchange rate to the fluctuations in the currencies of Bangladesh's major trading partners. The WES rate was closer to the market clearing rate as it was determined through bidding. Besides, the Bangladesh Bank intervened from time to time to avoid sharp fluctuations in the exchange rate. Although the spread between the WES and the official exchange rate declined gradually (Table 2.12), the Taka remained overvalued throughout the 1970s because of the high degree of protection for import substitution and the complex system of rationing foreign exchange. While the overvalued exchange rate encouraged domestic producers to import more machinery and equipment, the minimum wage legislation together with periodic upward revisions of wages discouraged them from employing more labour. The result was the substitution of imported capital inputs for labour. On the other hand, the protection policies favoured capital intensive industries in which Bangladesh had comparative disadvantage, thereby reducing the capital available for other sectors and, by raising capital returns, encouraging capital intensity in manufacturing.

Price control of industrial output of public sector enterprises and imported inputs was prevalent in Bangladesh in the 1970s. The aim of price control was to supply cheap output to consumers and cheap inputs to public sector industries and government priority sectors. Arbitrary price fixing without considering the cost of capital encouraged managers of public enterprises and distributors of products to earn rents out of the system.[14] As a result, price increases and shortages of goods were common throughout the 1970s (Sobhan and Ahmad 1980). Most public sector industries suffered huge losses, which were covered by bank credit, straightforward grants, or subsidies. Price regulation together with this lavish assistance to the enterprises created distortions in the market. Dodaro (1991) examined the price distortion index developed by Agarwala (1983), and for those of the 41 countries covered by the World Bank, Bangladesh recorded the second highest value of this index. The only country with a higher value of this index was Ghana. Thus price regulation neither helped to exploit comparative cost advantage in production, nor provided the right type of incentive to firms for realizing full productive capacity.

The whole policy framework in Bangladesh in the 1970s was unnecessarily complex, relying heavily on discretionary decisions and lacking transparency. Therefore, rather than providing incentives to industrial efficiency and entrepreneurial development, the industrial policies created strong incentives for 'rent-seeking'. Taken together with the fact that Bangladesh recorded rates of economic growth which were low by international standards, this evidence presented a strong case for a major shift in economic policy.

Economic Policy Reforms in the 1980s and the Bangladesh Economy

Major Policy Shift

Bangladesh began to emphasize liberalization reforms in the late 1970s, but the reform process made little headway until 1982. It gathered momentum only with the promulgation of the New Industrial Policy (NIP), which aimed to develop private sector-led industrialization. Various promotional procedures, such as denationalization of public enterprises, relaxation of administrative procedures, etc. were introduced. The reform package included fiscal reform, financial liberalization, and the maintenance of a realistic and flexible exchange rate, together with trade liberalization, reduction of government intervention, and improved management of public enterprises. The economic reforms of the 1980s were designed to improve the productivity performance of manufacturing industries by encouraging competition from within the economy as well as from outside. The underlying objective was to strengthen growth capability as well as to attain international competitiveness for the Bangladesh economy.

Under the NIP, industries were categorized into three lists. The 'reserved list' of seven strategic industries: arms and ammunition, atomic energy, air transportation and railways, telecommunications, electricity generation and distribution, mechanized forest extraction, and currency printing and minting, which remained exclusively under public control. A 'concurrent list' comprised thirteen sectors: jute textiles, cotton textiles, sugar, paper and newsprint, minerals and oils and gas, cement, petrochemicals, heavy and basic chemicals and pharmaceuticals, shipping, and equipment and appliances for telecommunication, in which public and private investment could be made. The remaining industries made up the 'free list' which was thrown open to the private sector.

In 1986, a Revised Industrial Policy (RIP) was adopted by the government which laid further emphasis on the private sector, by extending and strengthening the incentive measures undertaken in the NIP and adding yet another dimension to the privatization process by way of selling up to

49 per cent of shares in selected public enterprises to private buyers.[15] The 'reserved list' of seven industries for public investment was retained while the 'concurrent list' was dropped. A 'discouraged list' of twelve industries was introduced for environmental reasons (e.g., deep sea trawling) or serious over capacity (e.g., white sugar). The most recent industrial policy of 1991 withdrew the 'discouraged list' but stated that certain industries could be regulated on the grounds of environmental degradation and public health. All industries, except those on the 'reserved list', are now open for private investment. So, the scope for private sector has been progressively increased over the years. The industrial policy of 1991 also deleted electricity generation and transmission and telecommunications sectors from the 'reserved list' opening these up for private investment.

The privatization process that started in the late 1970s was intensified with the adoption of the NIP. As a result, 609 public enterprises had been divested by 1990 (Humphrey 1990), and another 12 public enterprises were divested during 1990-93 (GOB 1995). Nevertheless, public enterprises still account for approximately 40 per cent of total fixed assets in the manufacturing sector.

Since 1982 the investment climate has gradually been liberalized, with the promulgation of the NIP. Under the NIP, the scope for private sector participation was encouraged by rendering the IIS 'indicative' for all industries except 'reserved sectors' for public investment, so that it no longer sets investment targets but serves as a 'guide' to private enterprises for the sectors where increased capacity is deemed to be warranted. Private investment ceilings have been abolished and the scope of so called 'reserved sectors' for government investment narrowed. Also, a number of special incentives were introduced in the RIP to attract foreign direct investment (FDI). More recently, the Taka has been made convertible on current account to relax foreign exchange control. On capital account, foreign exchange can be freely converted into Taka, but, except in a few cases, conversion of Taka into foreign exchange needs permission of the Bangladesh Bank.

The sanctioning procedure for investment has been simplified, and no formal approval is now necessary from government authorities, except for investments in the Export Processing Zones (EPZs). Even registration is not mandatory unless the investors wish to avail themselves of such benefits as import entitlements, concessionary duties on machinery imports, etc. To encourage new entrepreneurs and quicken procedures, a 'One Stop Service' (OSS) has been established within the Board of Investment. Along with liberalization of investment sanctioning procedures, directives have been given to NCBs and DFIs to pursue a liberal credit regime for private sector industries, and the limits below which NCBs and DFIs do not require government approval to make loans have been increased significantly. The investment environment has, therefore, become more liberal over time.

Since 1987, IPO listed only those items which were banned and restricted under the 'negative list' and 'restricted list'. Commercial and private industrial importers were entitled to import items provided in the 'pass book' issued to them by import control authorities. The government tried gradually to reduce the number of items in the two lists in line with its avowed intention of continuing a policy of liberalizing trade and industrial policies. More recently, IPO combined these into a single 'control list'. The import control authority also discontinued the pass book system and brought all importable items not included in the control list under the tariff structure to eliminate possible discrimination among importers.

Following the recommendations of the TIP (trade and industrial policy) reform program in 1986, there has been significant liberalization of import licensing with a view to eventual elimination of the system. Imports are now permitted through a letter of credit (LC) authorisation form to be accepted by banks designated by industrialists. The 'control list' has been reduced over the years. Under a 4-digit Harmonized System Classification, fewer than 50 items remain banned or restricted on security, health, social and religious grounds (World Bank, 1993b). All imports are now carried out through the LC system except those based on foreign aid and barter arrangement. These reforms have made industrial raw materials more accessible to private enterprise.

To facilitate export-oriented industrialization, various incentives, including Export Performance Benefits (XPB), access to restricted imported inputs, duty drawback system, bonded warehouse facility, easy access to industrial credit and subsidies, tax rebates on export and concessionary duties on imported machinery, were offered to investors. XPB replaced the previous XPL scheme to offer higher entitlements with less dispersion in the entitlement rates and with greater weight to export-oriented industries. Beneficiary exporters could directly cash XPBs in the secondary exchange market. In 1987, XPB coverage was extended to include indirect exports, i.e. domestic products used as direct inputs in the export industries to promote backward linkages. However, the benefit of XPBs was eroded over time as the differential between official and WES exchange rates continued to narrow, and the two rates were eventually unified in 1992.

Under the RIP, export industries were allowed to import any banned or restricted inputs with the permission of the Chief Controller of Imports

& Exports (CCI&E) and with the recommendation of the Export Promotion Bureau (EPB). They were also allowed to recover duties and taxes paid on imported inputs under the duty drawback scheme. Refunds were initially calculated on the basis of actual payments and the duties refunded on a case by case basis, and latter calculated at a flat rate system, in which refunds were made on the basis of predetermined input coefficients and periodic calculations of the average percentage of value of customs, excise and sales tax for a product or product group. In 1983, the notional system[16] was introduced exporters were exempted from paying duties and taxes on imports used in export production. This system is only valid for 100 per cent export-oriented industries.

Export-oriented industries enjoy a wide range of monetary and credit facilities introduced in the NIP and RIP. These are: (i) a back-to-back letter of credit facility for imported and domestic raw materials and inputs, (ii) a concessional rate of interest on working capital (8.5 to 11.5 per cent per annum compared to the commercial rate of 16 per cent per annum) (Rahman 1994), and (iii) export insurance, through the introduction of the Export Credit Guarantee Scheme (ECGS). Major fiscal incentives to support export-oriented industries include tax holidays and tax rebates, income tax exemption, and accelerated depreciation allowances, excise tax refunds on domestic intermediates, etc. Under the Industrial Policy of 1991, proportional income tax rebates on export earnings are allowed of between 30 and 100 per cent. Industries located in the EPZs are allowed an income tax exemption for ten years, and a proportional income tax rebate of between 30 to 100 per cent on exports after this period. These industries also enjoy a three year tax exemption on salaries of foreign executives and technicians, interest on foreign loans, royalties, technical know-how and technical assistance fees, and profits on account of transfer of shares by foreign companies.

All the above measures to promote export orientation are discriminating and based on discretionary decisions, leaving serious difficulties in the implementation of the proclaimed policies, which continue to undermine the credibility of the policy initiative (Rab, 1989).

Labour market remained almost untouched in recent liberalization reforms. Labour management, workers' relation, wage determination and workers' compensation, etc. have been maintained through age-old policies. However, recent trade and industrial liberalization program affected labour market. Then government declared redundancy package and introduced so called 'golden handshake' program to reduce already over-employed labour in the public sector enterprises. Further, government ordered not to retrench excess labour for one year from newly privatized enterprises. After one year of privatization even if new owners were allowed to retrench redundant labour, it involved high costs due to existing labour regulations.

Financial sector reforms that began in 1990 aim at bringing necessary changes in institutional lending and financial intermediary services. Under the provisions of these reforms, interest rates have been made flexible within certain bands and stringent terms and conditions for industrial lending have been withdrawn. Two nationalized commercial banks were denationalized and private sector's banks were allowed to enter the market to introduce competition in the industry.

Since the late 1970s, Bangladesh has maintained a dual exchange rate system. In 1983, the United States (US) dollar replaced the pound sterling as the intervening currency because of the US dollar's higher relative trade weight.[17] During the 1980s, the Taka was devalued several times in response to domestic inflation, and to attain international price competitiveness, so the nominal exchange rate depreciated. Over time the WES rate was also adjusted upward. The foreign exchange premium, defined as the difference between the WES and official exchange rates and expressed as a percentage of the official exchange rate, declined from 24 per cent in 1981 to 1.8 per cent in 1991, due to frequent exchange rate adjustments in this period (Table 2.12). As a result, the rationale for dual foreign exchange markets was weakened and in 1992 the two exchange rates were unified.

As part of economic liberalization, steps were taken to rationalize and reduce tariff rates. In 1986, the existing 24 tariff slabs were reduced to 12. The maximum tariff rate was reduced from 400 per cent in 1978 to 100 per cent in 1991, except for a few luxury goods. In 1989, the preferential rates for public sector enterprises were eliminated. As a part of the rationalization measures, tariff rates were limited to a maximum of 20 per cent on raw materials, 75 per cent on intermediate products and 100 per cent on final products. To assess the effects of trade policy reform relating to imports, Rahman (1994) compared statutory tariff rates in 1982-83 and 1989-90. He showed (Table 2.13) that, although the weighted average tariff rate increased over the period, the dispersion of the rates measured by the coefficient of variation decreased from 0.70 to 0.59, so that the distortionary tariff rates were reduced significantly. Tariff rates were further reduced drastically during 1992 to 1994. The top operating rate was brought down to only 60 per cent with 5 tariff slabs in place of 12 in 1991. In line with Rahman similar calculations were carried out in this study and found that the weighted average tariff decreased to 26 per cent and the coefficient of variation to only 0.19. So it may be inferred that major trade policy reforms have taken place.

The Harvard Institute for International Development (HIID) and the Planning Commission (PlanCom) of Bangladesh studied 21 major industries in Bangladesh and found that the average ERP received by these industries had steadily increased in the 1980s compared to the mid 1970s (Figure 2.2). Bhuyan and Rashid (1993), also showed that import substituting industries still enjoyed fairly high rates of ERP even after trade liberalization. Their estimates showed that while sugar had a 189 per cent ERP for domestic sale, the handloom industry produces had an ERP as low as 20 per cent.

Table 2.13: Tariff Structure of Bangladesh

Tariff rates (%)	Percentage of import items	
	1982-83	1989-90
20	13.21	10.38
40	5.66	28.30
50	18.87	31.13
75	6.60	a
100	27.39	22.64
150	18.87	1.89
300	5.66	4.72
Average Rate	92.88	103.11
Coefficient of Variation	0.71	0.59

[a] The 75 per cent duty slab was withdrawn. Note: Calculations are based on 106 imported manufactured products covering approximately 60 per cent of total imports and 95 per cent of manufacturing output.

Source: Rahman, S. H., (1994).

As mentioned earlier, generous incentives have been provided in the NIP and RIP to promote industrialization, so the HIID and PlanCom study estimated the effective rates of assistance (ERA) for a broad picture of the change in the magnitudes of effective assistance.[18] It found that the ERA to manufacturing increased by approximately 30 per cent due to NIP but declined by about 13 per cent from the peak of 1986 during the post 1986 period due to RIP (Figure 2.2). The index of ERAs stood approximately 17 per cent higher in 1986-88 than in 1979-80.

There has been little change in domestic policies and market structure during the ongoing economic reform in the 1980s. The market structure remained monopolistic and oligopolistic.[19] Output targets and output prices for public sector enterprises continued to be fixed by the authority as part of the Five Year Plan. Hardly any direction was given in the policy reforms to increasing efficiency and productivity, improving technology, and raising product quality. Entry and exit of firms is still limited by bureaucratic process, and the financing of all new industrial investments still requires government approval one way or another. Thus, excessive discretion of government officials, lack of predictability of taxes and codified rules and, above all, perpetual sustenance of depressed firms, both public and private, indicate that a 'soft budget constraint' (Kornai 1980, 1986) syndrome exists in Bangladesh (Khan and Hossain 1989, Ahmad 1993). Unprofitable firms have been sustaining because of the refusal to allow them to exit, like the 'sick' firms in India. This constraint is a major cause of enterprise inefficiency, and an overriding obstacle to reform initiatives.

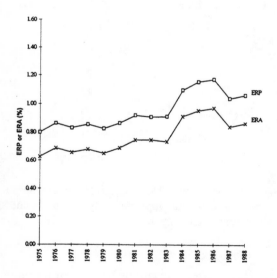

Figure 2.2: Effective Rate of Protection and Effective Rate of Assistance (percent)

Source: Sahota, Gian S. and Huq, Mainul, (1991).

In review, the removal of many bans and controls during the reform period has significantly reduced the role of government in investment and pricing decisions and made the economy more market oriented. However, lavish domestic assistance (e.g. subsidies and easy credits) to industrial firms have softened their budget constraints and still leave them uncompetitive and inefficient.

Performance in the Post-reform Era

While many countries, particularly in Southeast Asia, experienced spectacular growth in the 1980s, the growth of the Bangladesh economy, even after the implementation of economic reform, has remained alarmingly low. Average GDP growth declined to 4.2 per cent from 1983 to 1995, from 4.5 per cent from 1973 to 1982 (Table 2.1). Domestic savings and investment, as percentages of GDP, increased from 1.7 per cent and 11 per cent to 4 per cent and 13 per cent respectively during this period, indicating only a marginal improvement. The significant improvements were achieved in the current account balance and government budget deficit. On average, foreign exchange reserves increased to US$1148 million during 1983 to 1995 from a meager US$227 million during the 1970s. Inflation was reduced to a single digit figure (7 per cent per annum) after the reform period. Although all macro indicators show a positive response to economic policy reform, much of the gain has been eroded by high population growth (over 2 per cent annually). Therefore, a quarter of a century after independence, Bangladesh remains one of the poorest and least developed countries in the world.

In the 1980s, the structural changes that occurred in the economy did not assist the manufacturing sector. Although the share in GDP of the agriculture sector declined from 46 per cent in 1980 to 32 per cent in 1995, it still remained the economy's major employer, accounting for 65 per cent of the total labour force. The service sector enjoyed a high growth rate in the 1980s (averaging 5 per cent per annum) and become the dominant sector with 49 per cent of GDP in 1995, yet this sector accounted for only 21 per cent of total employment in 1992. The share of the manufacturing sector to GDP remained constant at about 10 per cent throughout 1980s, contributing only 13 per cent to total employment (Figure 2.1 and Table 2.3).

The market-oriented environment that developed with the gradual relaxation of import controls and the introduction of various export incentives led to an increase in two way external trade. Total foreign trade increased from US$ 2.5 billion in 1977 to US$ 4.4 billion in 1992, with an average growth rate of 9.5 per cent. Imports as a proportion of GDP increased from 12 to 18 per cent, and exports increased from 7 to 12 per cent during the same period. Despite these increases, exports remain highly concentrated. Dependence on jute and jute goods for foreign exchange in the 1970s has been replaced by dependence on garment exports in the 1980s (Table 2.9). Liberalization reforms have been partial so that anomalies still remained in the country's tariff structure. As explained above that Bangladesh, like many other developing countries introduced export incentives while maintaining protection in the import regime. So resources movement from the captive domestic market to a competitive international market remained limited. Therefore, exports did not grow as much as it was expected. The overall trade balance, though improved, has remained negative (Table 2.1).

Table 2.14: Indices of Industrial Production by Major Industry Groups, (selected years) (1981-82=100)

	1977	1980	1985	1987	1990	1993	1995
Food processing	83.3	84.1	81.1	106.0	145.2	134.4	172.2
Tobacco	93.2	90.5	91.2	93.6	77.9	71.5	110.1
Textiles	95.3	93.2	109.5	101.9	113.3	120.5	95.1
Ready-made garments	0.00	110.8	2274.8	4962.2	5464.7	10579.4	14079.4
Paper & paper products	97.7	78.4	119.2	128.5	130.4	125.7	115.9
Leather products	103.7	97.4	101.3	207.1	243.9	215.2	251.0
Chemicals	140.8	232.7	136.8	153.2	117.0	110.1	281.5
Basic metals	61.6	87.1	82.1	58.4	63.5	41.3	126.7
Machinery	144.0	136.1	166.7	135.8	103.2	114.1	69.8
Electronics	102.4	103.5	153.5	162.8	195.1	161.1	242.8
Total Manufacturing	96.0	98.0	124.8	145.0	170.0	210.0	262.1

Source: BBS, *Statistical Yearbook of Bangladesh* (various issues).

Despite the incentives provided by trade reform liberalization policies, manufacturing has shown little structural change (Tables 2.6, 2.7 and 2.14) or expansion relative to other sectors in the economy. Food, textiles and chemical industries have continued to dominate the sector while output has declined in tobacco, textiles, non-electronic machinery, and basic metal industries. Despite continued high protection and favourable government treatment, these industries have not established a strong footing in the international market, and their output has declined due to a failure to adjust to the opening of the economy. Phenomenal output growth was achieved by the garments industry in Bangladesh during the 1980s, due to the response to export-oriented policies and the captive international market under the Multi Fibre Arrangement (MFA). This industry along with other fast growing industries (electronics and food processing) did not expand fast enough to surpass the dominant traditional industries.

Table 2.15: Output, Employment and Wages in the Manufacturing Sector

	1973-74	1982-83	1987-88	1990-91	1992-93
Consumer goods					
Output	100	123	100	108	112
Employment	100	114	121	131	137
Real wages	100	138	136	138	142
Intermediate goods					
Output	100	134	252	263	287
Employment	100	90	99	102	108
Real wages	100	161	164	172	180
Capital goods					
Output	100	431	360	385	392
Employment	100	317	386	392	412
Real wages	100	143	163	185	196

Source: Calculated from 'Input-Output Table for Bangladesh', Planning Commission.

Output, employment and wage indices for three broad categories of manufacturing industries, namely, consumer goods, intermediate goods and capital goods (Table 2.15) reveal that output index for consumer goods declined in the early 1980s to the early 1990s while that of capital goods showed a sharp decline. However, there was an upward trend of output in intermediate goods over the years. Employment and real wages increased most in the capital goods industries relative to other two sectors. The point is that high protection did not result in high growth rates in the manufacturing sector. For example, the consumer goods and capital goods industries received the highest protection but exhibited poor output, employment, and wage growth compared to the less protected intermediate goods industries.

Expansion of the manufacturing sector has been limited by the poor rate of investment. Investment in manufacturing as well as in the whole economy is still disappointingly low (Figure 2.3). A World Bank study (1992) showed that Bangladesh has the lowest average investment-GDP ratio of the ten poorest countries in the world. Although efforts to increase domestic and foreign investments have been made through deregulation and streamlining administrative procedures and by providing incentives through policy reform, continuing red tape and a lack of adequate legal protection have deterred the flow of foreign funds as well as discouraging domestic private investment.[20]

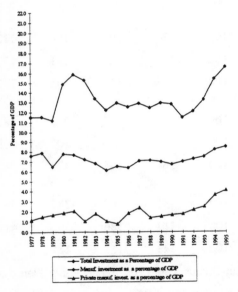

Figure 2.3: Investment Patterns in Bangladesh, (selected years)

Source: Board of Investment , GOB.

Moreover, there has been a lack of effective guidance to investors as to the direction and quantum of investment. The market information base is so weak and fragmented that no effective investment planning is possible for the promising investors. Other causes of low investment include corrupt and insincere administration, and the continued political crises of recent years. Because of severe resource constraints public investment has also been low. Figure 2.3 shows that, after economic reform, investment as a percentage of GDP stagnated, if not declined, both in manufacturing sector, and in the economy as a whole. However, it shows upward swing after the introduction of 1991 industrial policy.

As it was found that macroeconomic stabilization has achieved in terms of the reduction of current account and budgetary deficits and inflation rate but such stabilization failed to provide any charge manufacturing investment and production activities. Partial or half-hearted nature of liberalization reforms could be one of the reasons for such poor results. Lack of commitment of the political regimes and bureaucrats inhibit the process of implementation of policy reforms. It is true that Bangladesh initiated liberalization reforms in line with the prescription of donor agencies to get various soft loans and aids but not because of conviction to globalization. Not until the declaration of 1991 industrial policy, efficiency and productivity in production have not been emphasized in any stage of reform. Enterprises' output target continued to be set by the Five Year Plan even after the implementation of reforms. Present policy structure is such that investment in construction (of shopping complex), trading and indenting become more rewarding than investing in manufacturing firms. Policy regimes created a profiteering and rent-seeking class rather than an entrepreneurial class who can bear risk in manufacturing investment.

Table 2.16: Capacity Utilization in Major Manufacturing Industries, (selected years)

Industry	1977	1985	1989	1991*
Jute Goods	0.68	0.49	0.48	0.52
Cotton Yarn	0.67	0.66	0.70	0.63
Sugar	0.82	0.45	0.57	0.45
Cement	0.80	0.56	0.80	....
Fertilizer	0.62	0.48	0.68	0.68
Steel	0.40	0.40	0.35	....
Paper & Newsprint	0.37	0.97	0.96	....
Chemicals	0.54	0.68	0.75	0.72

Source: GOB (1990), The Fourth Five Year Plan 1990-1995 and * Salim (1997).

In addition to the low rate of investment, the Fourth Five Year Plan document (1990-95) indicated that the low rate of capacity utilization was one of the major causes of poor performance of the manufacturing sector (Table 2.16). Steel, the most capital intensive industry in Bangladesh, had the lowest rate of capacity utilization. Industries like jute goods, sugar, and steel which largely dominate public sector enterprises, had relatively low rates of capacity utilization. ADB (1987) also showed that capacity utilization varied only 40 to 73 per cent in public sector enterprises in 1984-85. Some other empirical studies found low rates of capacity utilization both in public and private manufacturing enterprises. For example, (Rahman 1983) showed that the unweighted average rate of capacity utilization of public enterprises in 38 industrial activities was 43 per cent compared to that of 58 per cent in 22 private industrial activities in 1979-80. Control of foreign exchange and important imported inputs has encouraged the creation of excess capacity. Decline in import control and domestic industrial licensing policies has protected the high cost industries from domestic and foreign competition, blunting the incentive for high productivity growth. Inadequate infrastructural and other operating constraints such as uncertainties of power supply, shortages of, raw materials, fuels and transport facilities and deteriorating labour relations had significant effect on capacity realization of industries. Thus, the low rate of capacity utilization undermines total factor productivity in manufacturing enterprises, and therefore, continues to retard overall industrial growth.

Conclusion

During the 1970s, trade and industrial policies were highly restrictive and less than transparent. The economy was *autarkic* (e.g. inward looking) and government intervention was prominent. Although the 1980s witnessed an overhaul of trade and industrial policies, complex and interventionist policies still remain which encourage continuation of rent-seeking activities and fail to provide incentives to producers to utilize their full production capacities and therefore improve the overall productivity of the manufacturing sector.

After more than two decades of industrialization, the manufacturing sector in Bangladesh still remains small and undiversified, with sluggish output and value added growth. The industrial sector accounted, on average at constant 1984-85 prices, for only 11 per cent of GDP and absorbed only 7 per cent of total employment from 1983 to 1995. The real growth of manufacturing value added was only 3.6 per cent per annum during the same period, because the dominant industries, including textiles, food processing and chemicals, either stagnated or experienced only modest growth. A few sectors, mainly garments and paper and paper products, have grown strongly during the 1980s in response to the policy reforms. Most other key industries have not been able to attain international competitiveness or utilize their full production capacity because of their long time and continuous dependence on protective regime that was established in the 1970s. The degree of production capacity that remains unutilized in individual firms and the extent to which it is associated with the above policy regimes are key issues to be discussed in subsequent chapters.

Notes

[1] Bangladesh became independent on 16 December 1971, after nine months long liberation war with the then West Pakistan (now, Pakistan). Prior to 1971, Bangladesh as an eastern wing of Pakistan had been growing at almost equal or even higher rates than those of East Asian economies.

[2] Many of the studies were conducted under the sponsorship of international agencies, particularly the World Bank and the International Monetary Fund (IMF) which vigorously promote economic liberalization in the developing countries. See, for example, Papageorgiou, *et al* 1990, World Bank 1993, Hughes 1987 and Garnaut, *et al* 1995.

[3] While all low income countries were growing on average by 4.7 per cent per annum, South Asia was growing at only 3.5 per cent per annum in the 1970s (The World Bank, 1993a, World Tables 1993).

[4] Resource movement from low productivity sectors to a high productivity sectors increases the average productivity levels of the economy, and therefore, makes a positive contribution to growth.

[5] The decline of absolute employment in agriculture can also be explained by data deficiencies and the change in the definition of economically active labour force between the 1974 to 1983/1984 surveys. Besides these problems there was a genuine shrinking of the forestry and livestock sub-sectors as well as some late labour displacements (exceptionally women labour) in various post-harvest operations. This particular phenomenon and a stagnant demand for labour in the crop sector led to an absolute decline in employed labour force in agriculture (Abdullah and Rahman 1989).

[6] These were: Bangladesh Jute Mills Corporation (BJMC), Bangladesh Textiles Mills Corporation (BTMC), Bangladesh Sugar and Food Industries Corporation (BSFIC), Bangladesh Steel and Engineering Corporation (BSEC), Bangladesh Chemical Industries Corporation (BCIC), and Bangladesh Forest Industries Development Corporation (BFIDC).

[7] A detailed analysis of financial losses and debt defaults of the public sector corporations was given in Sobhan, R. (ed.) 1991.

[8] The paradox of import substitution generating increased pressure for imports has gained wide and well-evidenced discussion in the literature (Little *et al* 1970, Balassa *et al* 1971 and others). Import substitution 'which was rationalized in many countries as a means of reducing dependence on the international economy, actually seems to increase it as import substitution activities are import-intensive and

require imports of both intermediate and capital goods to sustain production and growth' (Krueger 1982 p:5).

[9] See, for example, Nishimizu and Robinson 1984, Helleiner 1994 and Kalirajan and Shand 1994a.

[10] Apart from political commitment, other reasons for the nationalization movement were the dearth of businessmen/entrepreneurs and the lack of a well-developed capital market.

[11] For details on the privatization process in Bangladesh, see Humphrey 1990, Sen 1991 and Reza 1993.

[12] For example, when submitting an application for industrial investment, investors were expected to provide documentary support relating to draft loan agreements where foreign loans were involved, bank certifications of solvency, income tax payment certificates, and evidence of bank commitments if any bank loans were involved, etc.

[13] The Import Policy Order (IPO) specified all permissible importable items and documented procedures and conditions for imports. IPO, however, did not include importable items financed by project aid, barter and special trading arrangements, or commodity aid.

[14] Government claimed that the price of output was determined on the basis of the cost plus principle, i.e. average cost of product plus some percentage of capital cost. Apart from measurement problems of capital, government sometimes deliberately set the price of certain products below cost (for example, newsprint and cotton yarn).

[15] A study conducted by USAID noted that 'the government seems to feel that the 51-49 plan is more palatable to the general public...than outright divestiture' (Humphrey 1988 p:119).

[16] This system requires recording item-wise imports and establishment of a suspense account for all duties and taxes payable thereon. Liability to pay the amount of these taxes and duties is removed on the proof of export.

[17] About one third of total Bangladesh exports are to the United States.

[18] The concept of effective rate of assistance (ERA) is an extension of the conventional measure of effective rate of protection (ERP). ERP accounts only trade assistance. The ERA treats both trade and domestic assistance.

[19] This issue has been clearly explained in Ahmad 1993.

[20] The weak and outdated business laws such as a 1861 Admiralty law, a 1911 Patent Law, a 1933 Patent and Design Rule and a 1962 Copyright Ordinance, delays in settling legal disputes and faulty accounting systems are some areas which all need urgent change and updating.

3 Productive Performance Measures: Total Factor Productivity (TFP) Growth and Productive Capacity Realization

Introduction

In the literature, productive performance of economic agents is measured in a number of ways. Traditionally, it is measured by indices of profitability, labour productivity, capital utilization, technological change, capacity realization, and above all, by total factor productivity (TFP) growth. Some of these measures, such as labour productivity and capital utilization are partial productivity measures, the limitations of which are well known.[1] This book focuses on total performance measures in terms of capacity realization and total factor productivity growth of production agents. These two measures are related, but are conceptually different.

Total factor productivity growth (TFP) is an important indicator of sustained growth and structural change in an economy. In many recent empirical studies, economists have used TFP growth as a yardstick in evaluating the impact of market-oriented economic reform on the performance of firm, industry, or any other production units.[2] Though capacity realization and technological progress are two important components of TFP, these studies have concentrated on technological progress, with the implicit assumption that productive capacity is fully realized. Capacity realization refers to the ability and willingness of the production agent to produce the maximum possible output from a given supply of inputs, and production technology and technological progress refers to the innovation and diffusion of new technology. Researchers with few exceptions have ignored capacity realization in measuring the performance of production agents so TFP has been synonymously equated with technological progress. However, identifying TFP growth solely with technological progress and ignoring capacity realization measures leads to incorrect conclusions. The importance of capacity realization has been emphasized in several empirical studies which show that the excessive controls of protective regimes in the 1960s and 1970s have led to a high degree of unrealized productive capacities in industrial sectors, particularly in developing nations.[3]

Further, there is a very high opportunity cost of not realizing the full production capacity in developing countries where resources are scarce. On the other hand, the rapid growth of the Newly Industrializing Economies (NIEs) has encouraged developing countries to emulate their dynamic growth path. Again, theoretical and empirical studies in production and development economics demonstrate that maximum realization of production capacity relaxes both supply and demand side constraints on industrial expansion.[4] So, policies should be directed to achieve the realization of maximum productive capacity, in order to acquire a level of output that is closer to a country's full potential. Recent trade and industrial policy reforms in many countries has validated such efforts. Bangladesh is a resource poor country and has hardly any alternative option other than to realize its maximum production capacity in order to achieve industrial expansion and overall economic development. Therefore, it becomes important to evaluate the performance of the manufacturing sector in terms of the above two components of TFP growth.

This chapter reviews the concept of TFP, the basic notion of the growth of productivity measurement of economic agents, reviews different approaches to the measurement of capacity realization, one of the two important components of TFP growth, and finally, suggest an alternative methodology for measuring TFP and capacity realization based on a modified neo-classical production economics.

Total Factor Productivity Growth: Theories and Methodologies

Productivity measurement consists of a variety of measures that reveal various aspects of the input-output relation. Of these, the TFP growth is measured as the difference between the growth of output and the growth of inputs. In other words, it is the growth of output not attributable to the growth of inputs. Measurement of TFP growth goes back to the pioneering works of Abramovitiz (1956), Solow (1957), Swan (1957) and Fabricant (1959). Latter, Griliches (1960), Kendrick (1961), Denison (1962) and Jorgenson and Griliches (1967) made important early contributions to the literature.[5]

Recently, another class of methodologies for measuring productivity growth has been developed based on the 'frontier approach'. In this approach, productivity growth is defined as the net change in output due to change in technical efficiency and to technical changes (Nishimizu and Page 1982, Bauer 1990, Fan 1991, Färe *et al* 1994 and Perelman 1995). While the former methodologies for measuring TFP growth are directly based on the neoclassical framework, the later approach is based on a modified neo-classical framework.

These methodologies can also be categorized into two groups: (1) Growth accounting approach, and (2) Econometric approach. The growth accounting approach for measuring TFP growth can further be subdivided into two groups: (a) the arithmetic index number approach which does not require any explicit functional specification between inputs and outputs, and (b) the geometric index number approach, which requires the specification of a production function. The econometric approach can also be subdivided into (a) the deterministic and (b) the 'best practice' or frontier approach.

Growth Accounting Approach

On the basis of the neoclassical theory of production and distribution the growth accounting approach states that payments to factors exhaust total product under the assumption of competitive equilibrium and constant returns to scale. However, with the presence of technological advance, payments to factors would not exhaust total production and a residual output remains not explained by total factor inputs. This residual output is used as the basis for measuring and explaining productivity growth.

Arithmetic Index Number Approach: The arithmetic index number approach was introduced by Abramovitz (1956) and Kendrick (1961) in which TFP is measured as the ratio of output quantity index to an index of all inputs weighted appropriately. The productivity index **Q** with two inputs can be defined as

$$Q = \frac{y/y_0}{\left(\frac{P_{k0}K_0}{y_0}\right)\left(\frac{K}{K_0}\right) + \left(\frac{P_{l0}L_0}{y_0}\right)\left(\frac{L}{L_0}\right)},$$

or
$$Q = \frac{y}{P_{k0}K + P_{l0}L} \qquad (3.1)$$

where y/y_0, K/K_0 and L/L_0 represents indices of output, capital and labour respectively; P_{k0} and P_{l0} are base year prices of capital and labour; and the weights used for capital and labour are their respective base-year shares in output. The most commonly used indexing formulae in practice involving the arithmetic index are the Laspeyres index and the Paasche index. The Laspeyres index uses base year quantities as weights in its calculation and thereby permitting more meaningful comparisons of outputs over time since these quantities will not change from one calculation to the next. The Paasche index uses current year quantities as weights and thereby reflecting producers' behaviour patterns with response to consumers' demand for output.

The Laspeyres index is more popular than the Paasche index in empirical studies. One reason is the computational simplicity of the Laspeyres index. The Paasche index has a tendency for upward bias in measures of output per unit of input (Ruttan 1954). However, the popularity of the Laspeyres index has diminished recently, due to the implicit assumptions regarding the underlying production function (Christensen 1975). A Laspeyres index assumes that the production function is linear, which implies perfect substitutability of factors of production. That is, the elasticity of substitution between two factors in any input pair is considered to be infinity. Moreover, marginal productivities remain constant for a linear function, regardless of how fast one input is growing in relation to the other (Yotopoulos and Nugent 1976). Hence, the procedure for measuring productivity growth based on this index is likely to produce biased results. Caves, Christensen and Diewart (1982) argued that this formulation may be a useful conceptualization, but it is not convenient for actual measurement of productivity growth, using index numbers.

Another commonly used index number for measuring the TFP growth is the Törnqvist index number, whose underlying functional form is a translog production function[6] at two points in time, say t and $t-1$. The TFP growth over the period $t-1$ to t can then be expressed as the difference between the successive logarithms of total output less the weighted average of the differences between successive logarithms of input shares:

$$TI = \left[\ln y(t) - \ln y(t-1)\right] - \sum_i \frac{1}{2}\left[S_i(t) + S_i(t-1)\right]$$

$$\left(\ln x_i(t) - \ln x_i(t-1)\right) \qquad (3.2)$$

where TI refers to the Törnqvist index and S_i represents the input shares, i.e. $S_i = \dfrac{p_i x_i}{\sum_i p_i x_i}$ of a particular time period, where p_i represents the prices of inputs.

It appears from Equation (3.2) that a Törnqvist index number measures the average contribution of technical change to output growth. It can be measured in terms of price and quantity data at each point in time. When using quantity data, this approach is attractive intuitively, even in the face of so called market imperfections.

The Törnqvist productivity index, corrected by a scale factor, is equal to the mean of two Malmquist indexes, the latter index being defined for production structures with arbitrary returns to scale, elasticity of substitution, and technical change biases (Caves, Christensen, and Diewert 1982). Diewert (1976) has also shown that the Törnqvist index is 'exact' for the homogeneous translog technology and the index is 'superlative' since the functional form is flexible. If the aggregate functions are nonhomothetic, the Törnqvist index is still attractive, since the translog function can provide a second-order differential approximation to an arbitrary twice-differentiable function (Diewert 1981). However, Fuss (1994) has demonstrated that this index yields flawed TFP estimates, if the assumption of output prices' approximation to marginal costs does not hold. The Törnqvist index is approximately consistent in aggregation, i.e. an overall Törnqvist index of a Törnqvist indexes of subaggregate groups is approximately equal to a Törnqvist index of all the basic components within those subaggregate groups (Diewert 1975). However, Christensen and Jorgenson's (1973) claim that the Törnqvist index is consistent in aggregation is not universally correct.

Geometric Index Number Approach: Solow (1957) pioneered this index to measure technical change in productivity analysis. Compared to the arithmetic index, the geometric index is a more appropriate procedure to measure technical change, in that it allows for prices and thereby their marginal productivities vary, unlike the Laspeyres and the Paasche indexes. Ruttan (1957), Chandler (1962), and Lave (1964) were among the earliest users of the geometric index for studying productivity and technical change in U. S. agriculture. The geometric index can be derived by assuming an aggregate production function of the following form:

$$y = \alpha(t) f(x) \qquad (3.3)$$

where y, x are output and inputs. The technology function $\alpha(t)$ indicates that technology is a function of time, which means that $\alpha(t)$ captures shifts in the production function over time. So, the technology is independent of factor inputs. Therefore, the technology is both disembodied and Hicks-neutral. That is technical change does not affect the marginal rate of substitution between factors of production. Again,

Solow assumes that $f(\bullet)$ is homogeneous of degree one and those inputs are paid the value of their marginal products. This assumption indicates that producers maximize profit, implying no technical or allocative inefficiency.

Totally differentiating Equation (3.3) with respect to time and division by y yields

$$\frac{\dot{y}}{y} = \frac{\dot{\alpha}}{\alpha} + \sum_{n=1}^{N} S_n \left(\frac{\dot{x}_n}{x_n} \right) \tag{3.4}$$

where 'dot' connotes the time derivative and

$$S_n = \left(\frac{\delta y}{\delta x_n} \right) \left(\frac{x_n}{y} \right)$$

or

$$= \frac{w_n x_n}{py} = \frac{w_n x_n}{\sum_{n=1}^{N} w_n x_n}$$

where p and w represent the prices of output and inputs respectively. Now rearranging the terms in Equation (3.4) gives the fundamental growth accounting Equation:

$$\frac{\dot{\alpha}}{\alpha} = \frac{\dot{y}}{y} - \sum_{n=1}^{N} S_n \left(\frac{\dot{x}_n}{x_n} \right) \tag{3.5}$$

This is Solow's geometric index of productivity, which measures productivity, as the residual growth in output not accounted for by growth of inputs. Therefore, it is popularly known in the literature as Solow's 'residual' approach of productivity growth. Under the assumption of constant returns to scale, and Hicks-neutral technology, TFP growth based on this residual method is equivalent to the technical change (i.e. the vertical shifts of the production technology).

Solow made the assumption that the time derivatives could be approximated by discrete changes while calculating Equation (3.5). The resulting index number is time invariant only under a very restrictive assumption of approximation of time. Jorgenson and Nishimizu (1978) and Denny and Fuss (1981) discussed the problems of using index numbers for measuring productivity growth with discrete data. Using continuous time formulation, calculation of Equation (3.5) yields an index reflecting the changes in output arising from changes in inputs, i.e. a movement along the frontier is given by:

$$\left(\frac{y_t}{y_0}\right)' = \exp\left[\int \sum_{n=1}^{N} S_{nt}\left(\frac{\dot{x}_{nt}}{x_{nt}}\right)\right] \qquad (3.6)$$

This formulation is equivalent to the *Divisia* index of productivity growth. Like other productivity indexes, this index has the advantage that it can be evaluated directly from the pertinent data, without econometric estimation, but it is preferable to other indexes since it is less restrictive. Diewert (1976) showed that the *Divisia* index is 'exact' for the case of the translog aggregate production function. Also, Solow (1957), Richter (1966), and Hulten (1973) proved that this index is 'exact' for any functional form subject to satisfying general regularity conditions on Equation (3.3). However, in a case of a production function with more than two inputs, this index is computationally difficult, and more data demanding. Another disadvantage of this index, as in the case of other index number approaches of TFP measurement is that the calculations are not based on statistical theory so statistical methods cannot be applied to evaluate their reliability. Moreover, since this index is a line integral, its value depends on the path of integration, leading to the problem of cycling (Hulten 1973, Sudit and Finger 1981).

Solow's 'residual' approach has been widely used in empirical studies including, Krueger and Tuncer (1980), for Turkey, and Denison and Chung (1976) and Nishimizu and Hulten (1977), for Japan, Nishimizu and Rabinson (1984), for semi-industrialized countries, and more recently, Perkins (1996), for China. This is probably because of its computational ease, since no parameter estimation is required. However, this approach is based on some very strong assumptions, such as constant returns to scale, a competitive market, Hicks-neutral technology, etc. In many cases, these assumptions may not hold. So measuring productivity growth of economic agents using this approach may be misleading. Abramovitz (1956), a noted pioneer in this field has argued that TFP growth is really a 'measure of ignorance'. Domar (1961) maintained that, 'it absorbs, like a sponge, all increase in output not accounted for by the growth of explicitly recognized inputs'(p:712). Indeed, if inputs are measured properly, and the function governing their interactions is correctly specified, the residual TFP growth should be zero (Nadiri 1970). So there is a tendency to view TFP growth as 'manna from heaven' (Capalbo and Vo 1988). 'Despite all that, the procedure still is followed in numerous studies; the change in 'total factor productivity' (TFP),....has been and continues to be calculated again and again. Yet, if I am right, there should be no residual and no change in TFP' (Scott 1993, p:421). Naturally, the thrust of the intellectual effort in recent years has continued toward better measurement of inputs and a more precise estimation of the production function itself.

Econometric Approach

The econometric approach to productivity measurement is based on the estimation of either production or cost functions. The econometric approach assumes technological change can be described by shifts in a production function (or cost function), so that if scale and efficiency effects are assumed to be constant at a certain level, the shift in the production function (or cost function) associated with technological change can directly be used as a measurement for productivity. The attractions of the econometric approach are that, unlike index number and non-parametric approaches, it provides 'goodness of fit' measures, and allows an examination of important aspects of technological change, and the demand for inputs.

Assuming a production function with time as an argument,

$$y^t = f(x^t, t) + u \tag{3.7}$$

where u is disturbance term and $t = 1, 2, 3, \ldots \ldots T$.

The estimated parameters are then used to solve for technical change as $\delta \ln f(x^t, t)/\delta t$. Assuming no slack in capacity realization or technical efficiency, the measure is equivalent to TFP growth.

Following Ohta (1975) and Chambers (1988), the duality between cost and production functions can be exploited to formulate technical change using a cost function. The cost function which is a dual of a production function is given by

$$C^t = C(y^t, w^t, t) \tag{3.8}$$

Writing Equation (3.8) alternative way:

$$C^t = \sum_{n=1}^{N} w_n^t x_n^t$$

where x_n^t are chosen to minimize cost at t given output, input prices w^t and technology. Assuming constant returns to scale, perfect competition and Hicks-neutral technical change and following Grosskopf (1993), the cost function may be written as

$$C^t = \beta(t)C(w^t)y^t \qquad (3.9)$$

where $\beta(t)$ is the efficiency function which captures technical change. Totally differentiating the above equation (3.9) with respect to time, and using *Shephard's* lemma, gives

$$\frac{\dot{C}}{C} = \frac{\dot{y}}{y} + \frac{\dot{\beta}}{\beta} + \sum_{n=1}^{N} S_n \left(\frac{\dot{w}_n}{w_n} \right) \qquad (3.10)$$

Rearranging the terms of Equation (3.10) we get

$$\frac{\dot{\beta}}{\beta} = \frac{\dot{C}}{C} - \frac{\dot{y}}{y} - \sum_{n=1}^{N} S_n \left(\frac{\dot{w}_n}{w_n} \right) \qquad (3.11)$$

This shows that technical change is the residual change in average cost, not accounted for by the change in the index of input prices. In other words, it is the shift in the average cost curve over time. Numerous factors can cause the average cost curve to shift, even though researchers often tend to identify TFP growth, so measured, with technological progress. Clearly, under the constant returns to scale, $py = \sum_{n=1}^{N} w_n x_n$, from whence it follows that $\dot{\beta}/\beta = -\dot{\alpha}/\alpha$ (from Equation 3.5), so technical change is again equivalent to TFP growth, assuming no technical or allocative inefficiency is present in the production process.[7]

The implicit assumption in both the growth accounting and conventional econometric approach is that production agents are in long-run equilibrium in that inefficient firms exit, and only the firms which are efficiently utilizing resources continue to operate. In other words, production always takes place on the frontier, so the shift of a production frontier measures technical change. Then, given the assumption of 100 per cent efficiency, or full realization of capacity in the production process, the shift of production frontier also measures productivity growth. So, technical change is synonymous with TFP growth. This is not correct, since the shift in production frontier may not only be due to technical change but also to an improvement in the utilization of productive resources (i.e. to an increase in technical efficiency as the production takes place below the frontier).[8] So, if unrealized capacity or technical efficiency exists, and that is ignored in measuring TFP growth, the TFP estimates will be biased.

Reliable estimates of TFP growth are important from a policy perspective, for policy prescriptions based on unreliable estimates of TFP growth can lead to misleading results. A slowing of productivity growth, due to increased unrealized productive capacity calls for different policies than a slowdown due to lack of technical change. Slowing of productivity growth due to unrealized productive capacity may be due to institutional barriers, or structural bottlenecks, and policies to remove these may be more appropriate in improving productivity than policies directed towards innovation and diffusion of new technology. However, both types of policies may be needed. In this context, it may be argued that opting for new technology without fully utilizing existing productive capacity is a suboptimal policy strategy.

Several methods have been suggested in the literature to correct TFP estimates:

Explicit Incorporation of Capacity Realization: In this approach, the capacity realization index is explicitly used as an argument of production function along with other inputs. This method is well described in Kim and Kwon (1977). They argued that productivity growth depends on the stock of factor inputs and the extent of realization of that stock. Accordingly, the rate of growth of output becomes:

$$\frac{\dot{y}}{y} = \frac{\dot{\alpha}}{\alpha} + \sum_{n=1}^{N} S_n \left(\frac{\dot{x}_n}{x_n}\right) + \sum_{n=1}^{N} \phi_n \frac{\dot{U}_n}{U} \qquad (3.12)$$

where U is the rate of capacity realization.
Now, rearranging Equation (3.12):

$$\frac{\dot{\alpha}}{\alpha} = \frac{\dot{y}}{y} - \sum_{n=1}^{N} S_n \left(\frac{\dot{x}_n}{x_n}\right) - \sum_{n=1}^{N} \phi_n \frac{\dot{U}_n}{U} \qquad (3.13)$$

where ϕ represents the elasticity of output with respect to change in capacity realization.

Clearly, the growth of the residual falls, due to the incorporation of the capacity realization index in the production function, as does productivity growth. The same conclusion can be reached by putting U in the cost function as well, i.e.

$$\frac{\dot{\beta}}{\beta} = \frac{\dot{C}}{C} - \frac{\dot{y}}{y} - \sum_{n=1}^{N} S_n \left(\frac{\dot{w}_n}{w_n}\right) - \sum_{n=1}^{N} \lambda_n \frac{\dot{U}_n}{U} \qquad (3.14)$$

where λ is the cost/capacity realization elasticity.[9]

The major problem with this model is to find a good measure of the capacity realization index. Kim and Kwon (1977) used the ratio of actual consumption of electricity to the maximum possible consumption by installed electric motors as a proxy. Traditionally, peak-to-peak, shifts over time, energy use, and others have been used as proxies to derive the capacity realization index. As will be shown, most alternative approaches are *ad hoc* rather than based on an explicit theoretical foundation.

Implicit Accounting of Capacity Realization: Due to the existence of un-realized production capacity, or other distortions in the production process, the standard residual understates productivity growth. Berndt and Fuss (1986) provided a shadow valuation of capital stock for correcting biased TFP estimates. They argued that bias in the estimate of TFP growth is due to mismeasurements of the weights in the calculation of the flow of capital services. They maintained that the value of services from stocks of capital should be altered by using a shadow price instead of a rental price for the quasi-fixed input.

In empirical research, Berndt and Fuss (1986) suggest alternative approximations of the shadow price of capital, such as the internal rate of return, or the rental price of capital multiplied by Tobin's-q. Unfortunately, these measures are not readily available for developing countries. Morrison (1986) suggests a production model with dynamic optimization incorporating non-stochastic expectations. However, data requirements preclude applying this approach to developing countries.

The limitations of the traditional approaches of TFP measurement provides impetus for a frontier approach based on the work of Farrell. According to Farrell, both technological progress and the utilization of production capacity are continuous processes, and firms neither function at a technical optimum, nor at full production capacity level. It takes time for a firm to become familiar with the new technology and to utilize its full potential. Also, firms vary in the vintages of capital they can deploy and in their level of organization skill. Thus, the average level at which firms operate is typically below feasible best practice. This led to a new measure of TFP growth.

'Best Practice' or Frontier Approach

This approach is based on the well known frontier production function relating input quantities to the maximum possible output, as opposed to the realized output which is used in conventional empirical work on productivity growth. It is more in accord with the theoretical definition of a production function. The production frontier, embodying an idea of maximality, serves as a standard against which actual performance of an economic agent can be compared. There have been many extensions of the frontier approach of productivity measurement since the pioneering work of Farrell.[10] These can be grouped into deterministic and stochastic approaches. Both approaches have advantages and limitations. The deterministic approach lumps noise and inefficiency together while the stochastic approach confounds the effects of misspecification of functional form with inefficiency. However, in recent years, the stochastic approach has gained popularity in empirical work. Estimation of TFP growth applying this approach provides components of TFP growth (i.e. improvement in capacity realization, or increase in efficiency and rate of technical change) and does not require further correction. This book applies this technique for estimating capacity realization and TFP growth and detailed discussion of the technique is given below.

Clearly, total production growth results from total input growth and productivity growth. In traditional theory and in almost all empirical work cited above, productivity growth is explained as resulting from technological progress, assuming that the production unit is operating with full capacity realization. This is a restrictive assumption and does not reflect reality, particularly in developing countries. In the methodology of this study, this restrictive assumption is relaxed in order to measure total factor productivity growth. There are a few *ad hoc* methods of relaxing this assumption, but this study employs a method with a strong theoretical basis and validity. Basically, the approach used in this study incorporates the fact that firms may not be operating with full capacity.

Productive Capacity Realization: Theories and Methodologies

Capacity realization (traditionally, utilization) can generally be in estimated two ways: one involves an engineering approach, in which capacity is decided based on technical data and is measured deterministically, and the other is estimated based on economic principles.

Engineering Approaches

Engineering approaches comprises two further subcategories; survey based and conventional methods. In survey methods, direct questions (e.g. 'What are your firms' production capacities and realization rates?') are asked of proprietors, or of managers of businesses. Most respondents' replies to those questions are based on their machines' output per hour, or targeted output set earlier, i.e. based on their preferred output (which may not be possible in practice). There are various ways to collect survey data and interpret them (see Christiano 1981). In the United States (US), the Federal

Reserve Board uses McGraw Hill Book Company survey data on operating output to estimate PCR, and generates a series of 'long term trends' of realization rates.

Other survey-based measures for US industries include surveys of the Bureau of Economic Analysis and the US Census Bureau. These compile realization rates simply by asking 'at what percentage of manufacturing capacity did your company operate (month and year) ?' While respondents are not given the precise definition of capacity, most respondents reply to this question on the basis of practical machine capacity. Many countries in the world have their own surveys of realization rates: the MITI index of operating rates for Japan, the manufacturing operation ratio index for Korea, the Swedish Business Tendency survey and the Confederation of British Industries (CBI) survey for British industries.

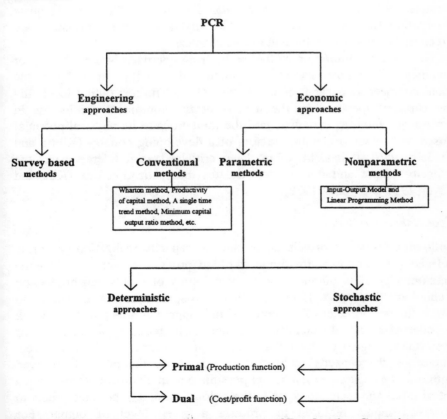

Figure 3.1: Approaches for Measurement of Productive Capacity Realization: Schematic Presentation

These survey-based methods of capacity realization measures have the obvious advantage of compilation of direct information from production units, including entrepreneurs' expectations, which would not be possible using a specific economic model. Also, this requires no specific functional form to estimate. However, the realization rates of these methods contain a critical weakness in that their measurement is based on the judgement and discretion of the respondents. Therefore, their application and interpretations remain ambiguous.

Conventional approaches to the measurement of capacity utilization comprise four methods: the Wharton index, Capital Productivity Method, a single time trend method and Minimum capital-output ratio method. Among these measures, the Wharton index has been popularly used in the literature. There are two other measures of capacity realization, viz. the shift measure and the electricity based measure. Conventional measures of capacity utilization indices are *ad hoc* measures without an adequate foundation from economic theory. The analyses of these measures are given in the appendix at the end of this chapter.

The chief limitation of the engineering approach is the arbitrary or technically determined nature of estimation of capacity output. Again, the rated engineering capacity is not a uniquely determined output level, and the capacity specified by the makers of the equipment for its use in developed countries may disregard the limitations to its physical potential posed by the socioeconomic factors of a developing country (Kibria and Tisdell 1986). It has, therefore, been criticized as it overestimates the capacity output and thus, underestimates the realization rate (Kim and Kwon 1977 and Forest 1979).

Economic Approaches

Following economic principles, productive capacity realization (PCR), is defined as the ability and willingness of any production unit to produce the maximum possible output from a given supply of inputs and production technology (Färe *et al* 1989). In other words, it expresses the degree to which the performance of a production unit approaches its potential, which is otherwise called technical efficiency. It requires a standard of performance against which the success of economic units is assessed. Therefore, the capacity realization rate refers to the ratio of observed output to the capacity or maximum possible output obtainable from a given set of input and technology, or to the ratio of minimum possible inputs to observed inputs required to produce a given level of output. For quantitative measurement, productive capacity realization (PCR) is simply defined here as the ratio of the actual to a measure of the capacity or maximum possible output, i.e.

$$U = \frac{y}{y^*} \qquad (3.15)$$

where U is a measure of PCR, y is actual output and y^* is a measure of capacity output. In this equation the numerator is observable but the denominator is not. It then becomes necessary to find a way to determine the denominator. An economic estimation of the denominator can be carried out in several ways. One common approach is to consider the capacity output to be the economically optimal output that guarantees efficient resource allocation in the Paretian sense of economic welfare (Phillips 1970). It is calculated when a firm is operating at a level where its long run average cost curve is minimum (Cassel 1937). Sometimes such capacity output has also been estimated from the point of tangency between the short and long run average costs curves of a firm (Chenery 1952 and Hickman 1964).

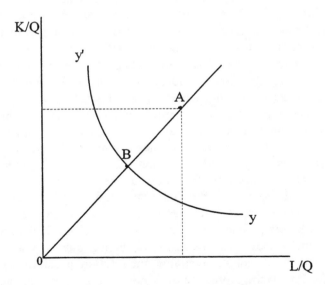

Figure 3.2: Farrell's Measure of Potential Output and Capacity Realization

Again it might be the firms' desired output that is 'the production flow associated with the input of fully utilized manpower, capital and the relevant factors of production' (Klein 1960:275). This, in a sense, is the firms' potential or maximum possible output that would have been produced from the existing bundle of input and technology. This leads to another approach. In this regard, Farrell's concept of potential output is central to the measurement. He defines it as a level of output where the firm is on a 'unit isoquant' that cannot be increased with existing inputs and technology (Farrell 1957). So this is a firm's frontier output when it follows 'best practice' technology. This potential output of firms may or may not be realized.

Let a production frontier be $Q = f(L , K)$ with constant returns to scale, i.e. $1=f(L/Q, K/Q)$. The isoquant yy' in Figure 2.1, represents the various combinations of two inputs that a best practice firm may use to produce output level y. Points to the south and west of yy' are not feasible. Firms which lie to the north and east of yy' are underutilizing productive capacity. Firms producing with full productive capacity will fall on the yy' isoquant.

Consider two firms A and B, both producing y units of output, using inputs L and K in the same relative proportions, with different absolute quantities. Firm A gets less output per unit of variable input on average than B. The distance OA, relative to OB, measures the extent to which the same amount of output could be produced with fewer inputs used in the same proportion. Slack or excess resource consumption, is depicted by the distance of A from the frontier along the axes. Slack represents excess expenditures which could have been avoided while realizing the same output. So firm B is successful in producing maximum possible output, with minimum input, while firm A is not. Capacity realization may, therefore, be measured in Farrell's framework as the deviation of A from best practice firm B, i.e. OB/OA. This definition is broader than an ordinary measure of capacity realization, in the sense that the realization rate is measured from the observed input and output, rather than by considering a single input, while assuming all firms in the sample are producing with best practice technique.[11] Färe *et al*, in their recent book, highlighted that: 'Best practice may be better than average practice precisely because it exploits available substitution possibilities or scale opportunities that average practice does not' (Färe, Grosskopf and Lovell 1994 p:3).

The essential and critical aspect of the unit isoquant, described above, is the existence of interior points. Different quantities of output yielded from identical inputs and technology explains the existence of interior points to a unit isoquant for a given level of output. Without interior points to the unit isoquant for firms producing the same output, there is no need for the concept of a frontier production function (Berkley 1987). So the production possibility set is used as an alternative description of maximum possible output and input combinations (keeping one input constant). This type of production function clearly represents a production set that is solid, rather than the surface that one ordinarily associates with a production function in traditional production theory. In Figure 3.2, points *B* and *B'* show maximum output with given input levels and technology. There is no way to increase output without increasing the input set, or these levels of output could have not been obtained with less input. However, at point A, a firm is producing at less than its productive capacity, as it could get the same level of output, i.e. y_1 by using less input (L_1). Alternatively, it could produce more output, y_2, with the same input level, L_2.

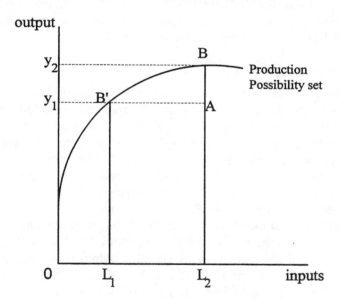

Figure 3.3: Production Possibility Set and Production Points of Full Productive Capacity and Non-full Capacity

It is implicit that, in both cases, neither the total input bundle nor the technology changes, only the degree to which the productive capacity (or technology) is utilized. So firms' maximum possible output is in the production possibility set in which points *B* and *B'* lie. In practice, however, there are deviations between realized and maximum possible output which Morrison (1988) termed as the *'disequilibrium gap'*. The larger the gap, *ceteris paribus*, the lower is the realization of productive capacities. The PCR index measures this gap of firm's output.

The objective is to measure PCR. It is estimated by first calculating the capacity output. The accuracy of the measurement of PCR depends on the accurate measurement of capacity, or maximum possible output, because this output cannot be observed. Production, or cost function approaches from neoclassical theory have been used extensively for estimation of maximum possible output and thereby for measuring PCR. These approaches addressed the first category of measuring capacity output (as defined above) in accordance with economic principles. Empirical research using this first category of measure for capacity realization is discussed below.

The recently developed frontier approach, based on Farrell's 'best practice' principle, has also been used for estimating maximum possible output in measuring technical efficiency. This study suggests a methodology for measuring PCR based on this principle, and applies it to firm level data of selected manufacturing industries below.

Non-parametric Approaches

Nonparametric and parametric types of methodologies have been developed in the literature. Nonparametric approaches include the input output model and linear programming methods. The input output model is developed from observed output and inputs of industries while then changes output towards full capacity which satisfying the equation systems. From these changing output levels, an overall picture of national capacity can be estimated (Klein 1960). However, severe aggregation problems occur in estimating PCR using this model.

Another measure of PCR uses the linear programming technique. Maximum possible output is subject to resource constraints. Malenbaum (1964) pioneered the estimation of capacity output using this approach, which was followed by the work of Griffin (1971). In studies of chemical and petroleum refining, Malenbaum and Griffin measured capacity as the bottleneck point in expansion, along a given ray corresponding to a fixed product mix. When one product hits such a bottleneck, all others dependent on it for intermediate inputs are restricted at less than full capacity realization. This provides a maximum output point while preserving a given product mix (Klein and Long 1973).

Recently, Färe *et al* (1989) developed a linear programming approach based on the Johansen's (1968) definition of plant capacity.[12] Realization rates are determined after the estimation of maximum possible output from observed output and input. This approach is in line with the Farrell measure of technical efficiency. The basic idea of this approach is:

Let there be $k= 1, 2, 3, \cdots\cdots, K$ activities or firms in an industry producing a scalar output $y^k \in R_+$ by using inputs $x^k \in R_+^N$. The maximum output of firm k can be estimated from the linear program as[13]

$$\emptyset(x^k) = \max_z \sum_{k=1}^{K} z^k y^k \qquad (3.16)$$

Subject to

$$\sum_{k=1}^{K} z^k x_n^k \leq x_n^k, \ n= 1, 2, \cdots, N, \ z \in R_+^K, \ z= z^1, \cdots\cdots, z^k$$

where z is a vector of intensity variables. The only restriction on the intensity vector z is that it be nonnegative, which implies that technology exhibits constant returns to scale. Now the technology set containing observed inputs and outputs (x^k, y^k), $k= 1, 2, \cdots\cdots, K$ is formed as

$$S= \{(x,y) \in R_+^{N+1} : y \leq \sum_{k=1}^{K} z^k y^k, \ \sum_{k=1}^{K} z^k x_n^k,$$

$$n= 1, 2, \cdots\cdots, N, z \in R_+^K \} \qquad (3.17)$$

One can now easily compare $\emptyset(x^k)$ and observed output y^k and get the realization rate by defining as

$$\emptyset(x^k)/y^k, \ k= 1, 2, \cdots\cdots K.$$

Since the authors followed Johansen's definition of plant capacity, their ultimate measure of realization rate becomes

$$PCR = \phi(x^k) \Big/ \hat{\phi}(x_f^k),$$

that is the ratio of maximum possible output, when inputs are given as observed over maximum plant capacity when fixed inputs are given as observed, and all other factors are allowed to vary freely. This nonparametric programming technique can easily be applied where the underlying function is linear homogeneous. The major advantage of this approach is that there is no need to impose a specific functional form on the data set. Rather, this method envelops the observed data points and reveals the technology as practiced in the industry (Färe *et al* 1989).

Färe (1984) has shown that certain functional forms, for example Cobb Douglas, are inconsistent with the existence of plant capacity as defined by Johansen. Another advantage of this approach is that it does not require price variables, and therefore provides one way of estimating PCR indices when prices of inputs and outputs are unavailable or unreliable.

However, this approach has limited applications because of its many serious shortcomings. The principal of these is the assumption of constant returns to scale. The extension of this method, for example, to increasing or non-increasing returns to scale, as followed by Grosskopf (1986), is far more cumbersome. Again, in this approach, the production possibility set is so arranged that it stands deterministic in nature. The resulting measures of PCR, therefore, incorporate 'noise' from the data. Consequently, the analysis focuses on the average performance, rather than an efficient measure for individual observations. Another problem is the complexity of estimating PCR for multi-product firms. There is also general equilibrium problem in making sure that the capacity points for all sectors are mutually compatible. Finally, it does not provide any information to enable statistical tests (of errors) to be carried out.

Parametric Approaches

For convenience's sake, parametric methods of economic measures of PCR can be divided into two groups: deterministic and stochastic approaches. Estimates of potential output are calculated from the exact relationship of relevant variables in the former approach, while estimates of the same are calculated from the stochastic relationship of variables in the latter approach.

The deterministic production function has rarely been used for estimating PCR index, in contrast with the deterministic cost function. Cassell (1937) and Klein (1960) measured the PCR index through the cost framework. However, their methods have not been empirically examined until the recent development of modern duality theory and the short run specification of firms' short run temporary equilibrium. In the last decade, a number of studies based on the duality theory have evolved in the literature. These studies have recently begun to incorporate short run quasi-fixed inputs. To name a few, Berndt and Morrison (1981) Morrison (1985), and Berndt and Hesse (1986) are important. They argue that a firm's short term production is conditional on the quasi-fixed inputs and therefore, there is a gap between current output and long run output. So, the firm's long run or capacity output is obtained through minimization of variable cost, rather than through the competitive way as suggested by Klein (1960). Consider a typical firm which minimizes cost in producing a certain level of output y with variable inputs x_j and a quasi-fixed input K that is the stock of capital.

The firm's short-run variable cost function is
$$F(y, p_j, t, K) \tag{3.18}$$

where p_j and t are the price of variable inputs and disembodied technical progress respectively. The short-run total cost function of that particular firm is then

$$F + p_k K \text{ or } C = C(y, p_j, t, p_k, K) \tag{3.19}$$

where p_k is the prices of K. If the firm is producing with constant returns to scale (CRTS), the firm's capacity output y^* will be at the minimum point of the short-run average cost (SRAC) curve. So, differentiating the short-run cost function with respect to output y, one can solve for that level of y which minimizes short run average cost, i.e. $y^* = y^*(K, p_j, p_k, t)$.

However, if the firm is producing at nonconstant returns to scale (NCRTS), capacity output is then obtained from the tangency point between the short and long run average cost curves. This can be found by differentiating C with respect to K and solving for y^*, i.e. y^* solves

$$F_k(y, p_j, t, K) + p_k = 0. \tag{3.20}$$

Given the capacity output, realization rates are then defined as $PCR = y/y^*$. Two important points for this measure of realization rates are:

- The PCR index can be greater than unity and therefore, is able to provide indicators for investment allocations (for detailed analysis see Morrison 1985 and 1988, Berndt and Hesse 1985 and Segerson and Squires 1990).
- This method can incorporate changes in p_j due to external shock and is able to quantify such impacts (see Berndt and Morrison 1981 and Berndt and Hesse 1985).

For all of these, estimating realization rates using a cost function may be a good step, 'but there is a problem in obtaining a sharply defined minimum point for empirical average cost function' (Klein and Preston 1967 :35). The problem is further accentuated when estimating realization rates, particularly when using data from a developing country.

There is an alternative dual *PCR* measure in terms of the cost gap (when $y \neq y^*$) developed by Morrison (1985) and extended by Segerson and Squires (1990) for estimating PCR for regulatory industries. Suppose the firm is in the long-run equilibrium, then $y = y^*$.

In that case one can write from equation (3.20)

$$-F_k(y, p_j, t, K) = p_k \qquad (3.21)$$

Now, $-F_k(y, p_j, t, K)$ can be interpreted as a shadow value of $K(Z_k)$, so that when the firm is in the long-run equilibrium, the shadow value of capital is equal to the price of capital. Therefore, if y is the long-run output then the firm's cost would be given by the shadow cost, i.e.

$$C^* = C(y, p_j, t, Z_k, K) = F(y, p_j, t, K) + Z_k K \qquad (3.22)$$

So, the cost gap gives us the new PCR measure, i.e.

$$PCR_{c.gap} = \frac{C^*}{C} = \frac{(y, p_j t, Z_k K)}{(y, p_j, p_k, K)} \qquad (3.23)$$

where PCRc.gap is the productive capacity realization index in terms of the cost gap and C^* and C are shadow and actual costs respectively. This is a single product measure of PCR. Segerson and Squires (1990) extended this measure for a multiproduct firm. In a similar fashion they also recently derived a profit gap measure of PCR to analyze the impact of output quotas on the US marine fishing industry (Segerson and Squires 1993).

Deterministic approaches provide PCR indices without incorporating random 'noise' (i.e. measurement errors) into the production or cost function. So statistical inferences and hypothesis testing are not possible. It is likely that these approaches overestimate the capacity output and, therefore, underestimate the realization rates.

The deficiencies of deterministic approaches led to the specifications of stochastic models which take account of statistical errors, i.e. measurement errors in estimating PCR indices. These approaches include conventional production and cost functions. The pioneering work was done by Klein and Preston (1967), using the Cobb-Douglas form of production function, which was followed by many studies, including, Macmahon and Smyth (1974), Artus (1977), O'Reilly and Nolan (1979), and Harris and Taylor (1985). Some studies also used the Constant Elasticity of Substitution (CES) production function as well (Harris and Taylor 1985). Theoretically, both primal and dual methods provide the same estimates of PCR indices, however, data limitations constrain the choice of one over the other.

These approaches are obvious departures from the above deterministic and conventional approaches to the measurement of PCR.

However, all these approaches are based on neo-classical theory of the firm, and explicitly or implicitly assume the following:

(i) The production decision maker is rational. In neo-classical theory, this implies that agents are profit maximizing or, at least loss avoiding.

(ii) The market exists to direct efficient allocation of productive resources. Therefore, there are no constraints or intervention from any quarter on demand and supply of inputs and output, and an 'invisible hand' automatically clears the market.

(iii) The decision-maker has all information regarding input and output markets, and technology.

(iv) The individual production firm is capable of generating financial resources internally, or can borrow from other firms or sources under certain regular rules, which are to be followed strictly. In Kornai's terminology, the budget constraint is not soft.[14]

Given these assumptions, firms are producing on the frontier by realizing full productive capacity. In other words, a firm's actual and potential output are the same and may not follow the best practice techniques of production. However, in reality, firms will be operating below frontiers at varying levels of capacity realization, due to various non-price and organizational factors such as, excessive controls, 'soft-budget' constraint, lack of information about modern techniques of production, slow and arbitrary government decisions, work stoppages, material bottlenecks, and management inefficiency.[15] In this context, the conventional production function approach cannot model the production behaviour of firms and will provide flawed estimates of PCR indices. Policy applications based on these misleading indices may have unintended and undesirable results (for details see Alauddin *et al* 1993). The development of the frontier production function concept developed by Farrell, facilitates such a modelling.

Frontier Production Function and Productivity Measures

In recent years, the use of the stochastic frontier model for measuring productive performance of economic agents has become increasingly widespread. The main reason is that the notion of a frontier is consistent with the underlying theory of optimizing behaviour (Kumbhakar and Hjalmarsson 1996). To elaborate, it allows for underrealization of productive capacity, or inefficiency, while modelling productive performance of economic agents.

The stochastic frontier production function with a composite error term, popularized by Aigner *et al* (1977) and Meeusen and van den Broeck (1977a) can be written as:

$$y = f(X, \beta)exp(v_i - u_i) \tag{3.24}$$

where y is realized output from the input level X, β's are unknown parameters to be estimated, and the first part of the composite error term, v_i, represents stochastic error, which is expected to capture noise beyond the firm's control, such as luck, weather conditions, or unpredicted variation in machine or labour performance, that cause firm's output to vary around some mean level (Aigner *et al* 1977, Schmidt and Sickles 1984). It is assumed that v_i is normally distributed with mean zero and variance σ^2 (i.e. $v_i \sim N(0, \sigma^2)$. The second part of the composite error term, u_i, is a non-negative random variable, which takes account of the combined effects of all non-price and institutional factors which cause underrealization of production capacity, i.e. inefficiency in resource use. The actual shape of the distribution of this part of the composite error term is open to debate, and there are several suggestions about the shape of the distribution. Aigner, Lovell and Schmidt offered half-normal, Meeusen and van den Broeck suggested exponential distributions for u_i, while Greene (1990, 1993a) proposed a gamma distribution. However, both parts of the error term, v_i and u_i, are independent.

The specification of the above model implies that a firm is able to produce its potential output if, and only if, u_i equals zero, which means that there are no distortions in the production environment (due to successful policy reform). Hence, it can be argued that a firm cannot produce more than a theoretically possible level of output, which is why the above model is consistent with economic theory, unlike the conventional average production function approach. The greater the value of u_i, the further the firm is from the production frontier. If policy reform is successful, the firm will be able to utilize more of its productive capacity and move progressively closer to the frontier.

Firm-specific capacity realization rate is defined, as before, as the ratio of the observed actual output to the corresponding frontier output, conditional on the levels of inputs used by the firm. Given the stochastic production frontier (3.24), the frontier output denoted by y^* can be estimated by using the Corrected ordinary least squares (COLS) or the Maximum likelihood estimation (MLE) methods.

The PCR for the ith firm is then given as:

$$PCR_i = exp(-u_i) = \frac{y_i(given \ u_i \geq 0)}{y_i^*(given \ u_i = 0)} \qquad (3.25)$$

where PCR_i is firm specific productive capacity realization rate, y_i is the realized or observed actual output and y_i^* is the maximum possible output evaluated at the input level X. PCR varies from 0 to 1.

Following Perelman (1995), Equation (3.24) is written slightly differently by incorporating a time subscript and putting time (t) as an argument:

$$y(t) = f(X(t),t)exp(-u_i) \qquad (3.26)$$

where $f(X(t),t)$ is the frontier output.

The derivative of logarithm of Equation (3.26) with respect to time, divided by y_t gives:

$$\frac{\dot{y}(t)}{y(t)} = f_x \frac{\dot{X}(t)}{X(t)} + f(t) + (-\dot{u}) \qquad (3.27)$$

This is a familiar growth accounting equation. Equation (3.25) thus shows that output growth can be decomposed into three components: (i) the growth of inputs weighted by their respective output elasticities; (ii) the rate of technical change corresponding to shifts of the frontier; and (iii) rate of change of PCR. Following Nishimizu and Page (1982), the rate of growth of TFP can be defined as

$$T\dot{F}P = f(t) + (-\dot{u}) \qquad (3.28)$$

the sum of technical change and the rate of PCR change.

Once Equation (3.24) is estimated by using the COLS or MLE methods, TFP growth can easily be computed following (3.26) and (3.27). Thus, estimating TFP growth, using the stochastic frontier production function, yields more reliable estimates than with the traditional index number or growth accounting approaches (Kalirajan *et al* 1996 and Coelli and Rao 1997).

However, the above cited conventional stochastic frontier production function model is based on the assumption that the frontier production coefficients differ from the average production function coefficients only by intercepts. This means that both firms following best practice techniques of production and firms not following the best practice techniques have the same response from each individual input to output. This is an unrealistic assumption, because firms following best practice techniques will logically have higher input response coefficients to output than firms following inferior techniques of production.

Due to this important aspect of production, it is necessary to redefine the conventional production frontier models. The varying coefficient frontier production model introduced by Kalirajan and Obwona (1994) based on the random coefficient regression popularized by Swamy (1970, 1971), offers an alternative way of defining the frontier production function in which all production coefficients, including the intercept terms, can vary across firms and over time for the same firm. Thus, this methodology facilitates taking care of quality variations in inputs. This approach is explained in the next chapter.

Conclusion

This chapter has reviewed various approaches for measuring PCR and TFP growth rates. Every method has its nobility and limitations. The above analysis showed that some of these limitations are very serious, consequences of which produce bias estimates and cause policy makers to become confused and adopt wrong policies. Estimation of PCR and TFP growth rates in almost all earlier approaches are based on the assumption that production units are always operating on the frontier. In other words, earlier approaches assumed way any kind of inefficiency or under-utilization of capacity in production. This is unrealistic. Firms are producing far below their frontiers because of various non-prices and organizational factors. Therefore, this chapter concludes the need for the development of alternative methodologies for measuring PCR and TFP growth rates.

Appendix

Conventional Measures of Capacity utilization

Conventional approaches to the measurement of PCR include four methods namely, the Wharton indices, the capital productivity method, a single time trend method, and a Minimum capital output ratio method. These are explained below:

Wharton Method: The simplest in the class of conventional approach is Wharton's 'trend-through-peak' method. Until the early seventies this was widely used. This method is based on output series data, worked out by Klein. The basic principle underlying this approach is that capacity grows at a constant absolute amount for several periods, switches to growth by a different constant amount for another set of periods, and so on, so that 'trend-through peaks' of actual output indicate the full capacity output. Therefore, fitting a straight line through the successive peaks of actual output by linear interpolation produces capacity output. So the PCR index of any time is

$$W_t = \frac{y_t}{y_t^w} \qquad\qquad (A3.1)$$

where W_t is Wharton index of realization rates, y_t is actual output and y_t^w is capacity output taken from Wharton trend output.

This method has been widely used in earlier studies (Klein and Summer 1966, McMohan and Smyth 1974, O'Reilly and Nolan 1979, Sastry 1986, Harris and Taylor 1987 and others). However, it has been criticized for several reasons. First, selection of series- monthly, quarterly or yearly series is difficult, as is identification of peaks and piece-wise linearization. Second, it does not take into account the growth of inputs in estimating capacity output.

The Productivity of Capital Method: This is an extension of the Wharton method. Since output is constrained by stock of plant and machinery, estimates of capacity output can be obtained by fitting a straight line through the peaks of the output-capital ratio and then realization rates can be estimated by the following:

$$MW = \frac{Y}{K} \bigg/ \left(\frac{Y}{K}\right)^* \frac{Y}{n} \qquad\qquad (A3.2)$$

where MW is a modified Wharton index, Y/K ratio of output to capital and $(Y/K)^*$ estimated full capacity levels of Y/K, obtained by interpolating between selected peak levels of Y/K.

The advantage of this method is that, unlike the Wharton method, capacity output is subject to capital constraint. However, the disadvantages are many, most importantly, its ignorance of non-capital inputs and its inability to allow for factor substitution.

Single Time Trend Method: This method involves regressing actual output over a time variable, i.e. $y = \alpha + bt$ and using this estimated output as capacity output, obtaining the realization rates in the usual manner. This method is very simple and takes account of endogenous factors that affect the realization index. However, capacity output is underestimated and hence realization rates are overestimated, since capacity outputs are taken from the regression, which provides only average performance over the year.

Minimum Capital Output Ratio Method: In this method, capital output ratios are estimated with constant prices. A benchmark year is chosen, on the basis of a low capital output ratio, and considered as the capacity output. The estimate of capacity is obtained from real fixed capital stock, deflated by the minimum capital output ratio, and utilization rates are then obtained using the following formula:

$$CU = \frac{Y}{\hat{K}} \tag{A3.3}$$

where

$$\hat{K} = \frac{K}{(K/Y)\,\text{min}}$$

CU = Capacity utilization
Y = Real output (gross value added)
$\hat{K}$ = Estimated capacity
K = Real fixed capital
$(K/Y)_{\text{min}}$ = Minimum of capital output ratio

This is an alternative measure of capacity realization. However, the usefulness of this approach depends on the accuracy of the measurement of capital.

Time Based Method: This is the crudest of all measures of realization rates using the engineering approach. In this method, capacity output is obtained by taking the hourly output at 100% efficiency and multiplying it by the period of observation, i.e.

$$C_u = \frac{Y}{T.X_K} \qquad (A3.4)$$

where Y actual output, X_K is hourly output at 100% efficiency, T is the period of observation (8760 hours = 365×24). So $T.X_K$ is the theoretical maximum output. However, in practice, it is neither possible, nor feasible, for a machine to work for 24 hours of each day with 100% efficiency, owing to maintenance requirements, industrial practices and holiday closures, etc. So instead of T, t can be considered as the maximum feasible hours of work. Further, for empirical work, t' can be used as the actual number of hours worked. A machine will seldom reach an engineering maximum of 100% efficiency, due to wastage in process, machine breakdown, lack of proper labour training and supervision, etc. A standard norm of efficiency is selected on the basis of the existing condition of the machinery, and other environmental factors of the plant. Equation (A3.5), therefore, can be rewritten as

$$C_F = \frac{Y}{t'.X_K} \qquad (A3.5)$$

where CF feasible capacity utilization, t' is actual number of hours worked, a is the proportion of X_K considered to be attainable under prevailing conditions.

This method is complex and is rarely used in empirical studies. Ahmed (1973), Islam (1976), Rahman (1983) and Afroz and Roy (1978) applied this approach for selected manufacturing industries in Bangladesh.

Two other measures of realization rates in the literature are *shift measure (U_t)* and *electricity (U_E) measure*. In the shift measure, the actual number of shifts worked in a year is compared with the available number of shifts, on the assumption that a certain numbers of shifts can be operated daily. Marris (1964), Winston (1974) and others applied this approach. In the electricity measure, the actual consumption of electricity in kilowatt-hours used by electric motors in a plant is compared with their rated capacity, after allowing for some dissipation of power in the form of heat. Foss (1963) pioneered this method, which was latter used by Jorgenson and

Griliches (1967) and Christensen and Jorgenson (1970) for American industries, by Heathfield (1972) and Bosworth (1985) for British industries, by Bautista (1974) for the Philippine manufacturing industry, and by Kim and Kwon (1971) and Kwon (1986) for South Korean industries. However, this measure has a downward bias in realization rates.

Notes

[1] There are many studies which discuss the limitations of partial factor productivity measures, See for example, Craig and Harris 1973, Mehta 1980, McIntire 1980, Gold 1981, and Link 1987.

[2] Even though empirical research on the consequences of economic reforms is substantial, little work has been done on measuring TFP growth using firm level data. Most studies have dealt with either industries, or sectors, or even multi-country data. See for example, Krueger and Tuncer 1982, Nishimizu and Robinson 1984, Chen and Tang 1990, Dollar and Sokoloff 1990, Jefferson 1990, Nishimizu and Page 1991, Lee 1992, Jefferson, Rawski and Zeng 1992, Urata and Yokota 1994, Aw and Hwang 1995. Most of these studies used 2 or 3-digit industry level aggregate data and none of these studies corrected TFP growth by measuring the variation in capacity realization at firm level.

[3] See for example, Hogan 1967, Little *et al* 1970, Steel 1972, Kemal and Alauddin 1974, Paul 1974, Krueger 1978, Bhagwati 1978, Islam 1978, Bautista *et al* 1981, Islam 1981 and Rahman 1983.

[4] For elaboration of this point, see Betancourt and Clgaue 1981, Goldar and Renganathan 1991, Lieberman 1989, Scherer 1990, Srinivasan 1991 and 1992.

[5] This review section heavily dependent on the work of Grosskopf 1993. For further excellent surveys of productivity measures, see Nadiri 1970, 1972, and Nelson 1981. The most recent surveys were provided by Link 1987, Diewert 1992, and Felipe 1994.

[6] Everything required to estimate TFP growth through this index is observable so no estimation of the underlying production function is needed.

[7] For the case of non-constant returns to scale, Ohta 1974 has shown that $\dfrac{\dot{\alpha}}{\alpha} = -\varepsilon_y . \dfrac{\dot{\beta}}{\beta}$, where ε_y is the scale elasticity. Denny, Fuss and Waverman 1981 argued that if ε_y is known a *priori*, either the primal or dual method can be used in the measurement of TFP growth.

[8] There are other factors which also cause a shift in a production frontier such as non-constant returns to scale, change in scale of production, etc. These issues are discussed in Morrison and Diewert 1990. This study focuses on capacity realization because it has relevance for analysing productivity growth using data from developing countries, for example, Bangladesh.

[9] This is (λ) defined in Kwon 1986.

[10] For recent surveys on the frontier approach of productivity measurement, interested readers are referred to Bauer 1990a, Lovell 1993, Greene 1993a and Kalirajan and Shand 1994a.

[11] To determine how much productive capacity is realized by a production unit, it is necessary to ascertain what constitutes efficient production at the level of inputs. This could be a reflection of the *best* performance actually achieved in a production unit, or it could be a construct of the maximum output theoretically attainable based on the technology of the production process. Clearly, capacity realization measured in this approach is a broader measure than the ordinary measure of capacity utilization in that capacity output is described as the most efficient output minimizing the present values of the cost stream given stock of capital and technology (Morrison 1985, 1988, Kang and Kwon 1993).

[12] Johansen defines the plant capacity as '.... the maximum amount that can be produced per unit of time with existing plant and equipment, provided that the availability of variable factors of production is not restricted' 1968 p:52.

[13] The formulations follows Färe *et al* 1989.

[14] Kornai (1986) introduced the concept of 'soft budget constraint' in his book Economics of Shortage 1980, and in an expository article to analyze the characteristics of state owned enterprises of socialist economies. Later, Kornai and Weibul 1983, formalized this concept to examine state subsidies to firms subject to stochastic events.

[15] This refers to so called X-inefficiency (Leibenstein 1966).

4   Suggested Measures of Productive Capacity Realization and Productivity Growth

Introduction

Measurement of total factor productivity (TFP) growth has received considerable attention from theoretical and applied economists in recent years, particularly after the 'globalization' and 'restructuring' of many centrally planned and developing economies. From a theoretical stance, there has been a spirited exchange about the relative importance of various components of TFP (change in capacity realization, technological change, etc.) (Comanor and Leibenstein 1969, Nishimizu and Page 1982). From an applied perspective, measuring productivity is important, as it serves as a guide for investment planning and resource allocation. Also, the measurement of productivity growth can help to gauge the impact of recent economic reform on the performance of economic agents in developing countries, particularly Bangladesh, and has important implications for further policy formulation. However, little work has been done in developing more accurate and reliable measures for capacity realization and TFP growth, making the assessment of the success or failure of policy reform difficult. This chapter discusses the use of the preferred econometric approach and develops the methodology used in this study.

The use of the econometric approach of measuring of TFP, as well as PCR, has spread rapidly in the last decade.[1] Though these measures follow neoclassical theory, using either the cost or production functions in empirical research, they are usually estimated by allowing the functions to pass through the mean of the data set which provides average output and does not theoretically determine either the maximum possible output or the minimum cost. Estimation of production (cost) functions using the ordinary least squares (OLS) technique provides unbiased estimates from a statistical perspective, but any such estimates must be biased downward (upward for cost function) in terms of the underlying economic theory that motivated them. So the indexes of PCR are overestimated for some observations and underestimated for others, which in turn produce biased estimates of TFP growth.

There are five other potential limitations to the cost function approach. First, cost functions presume continuous adjustments of the factor mix to minimize cost (Tybout and Westbrook 1995). For various reasons, such as institutional barriers, the adjustment of factor mix may be delayed. So using cost functions to measure PCR indices may not give accurate results. Second, cost functions require output and factor price data; simultaneity between output and the error term is a problem with cost functions (Tybout and Westbrook 1995). Third, it is difficult to measure firm output and input absolutely correctly, but measuring firm costs is even more susceptible to measurement error. Similarly, measurement error in factor prices or output can bias the cost function estimates. Measurement errors may occur in the case of production function as well. However, the production function does not require any price data and is less prone to measurement error.

Fourth, capacity output is defined as the output corresponding to the minimum point on the average cost curve, empirical determination of which is indeed difficult especially in the context of multi-product firms. Klein and Preston (1967) rightly pointed out that determination of 'sharply defined minimum point' of cost curve is impossible. Moreover, if most cost curves are L-shaped, as Johnston (1960) found in a number of cases, the determination of capacity output becomes ambiguous. Fifth, data on cost and factor prices may not be available in developing countries, or, even if available, may be distorted. Hence, reliable estimates of PCR and TFP cannot be expected using a distorted cost function.

The framework developed here for measuring PCR, as well as TFP, is based on the production frontier, in the light of Farrell-type efficiency discussed in the previous chapter. The technique applied here is the random coefficient frontier production function introduced by Kalirajan and Obwona (1994). This analysis is both consistent with the definition of productive capacity and its realization, and is helpful in gauging performance of firms operating under different production environments. This approach allows much more realistic measures of the realization rate and TFP growth than was possible before and, hence, represents a significant methodological improvement.

Measurement of Productive Performances: The Random Coefficient Production Frontier Approach

Choice of the Random Coefficient Production Frontier

There has been a long-standing recognition of parameter variation in modelling economic activities since the Keynes' introduction of disequilibrium economics.[2] In modelling economic activities, a functional form is usually specified which may not be true if some relevant variables are excluded, and proxy and policy variables are used. The use of such variables may fail to reflect unobserved characteristics of production agents. Therefore, a fixed parameter stable econometric relationship is not valid. Despite theoretical recognition of a random coefficient model, it was not until Hildreth and Houck (1968) that empirical analysis used a random coefficient model. Swamy (1970, 1971) popularized this model in applied works, and there has been increased interest in the estimation of a random coefficient model.[3] However, in measuring the productive performance of economic agents, at the micro level in particular, application of this model has been lacking. On the basis of supporting arguments, this study has applied a random coefficient model for measuring TFP growth and capacity realization index of manufacturing firms of selected industries in Bangladesh.

The conventional stochastic frontier production function approach of Aigner *et al* (1977) and Meeusen and van den Broeck (1977) of measuring capacity realization implicitly assumes that the production frontier shifts in such a way that the marginal rate of technical substitution (MRTS), at any input combination, remains unchanged. In the literature, this is referred to as a 'neutral' shift of the production function. This does not hold true in practice. Firms may use the same levels of inputs with a given technology, but the method of application of inputs may vary across firms. Equal amounts of labour and capital in a particular production process may yield different levels of output from different firms, owing to variations in technical progress, labour efficiency and managerial ability. In the words of Stigler, '....two farmers with reasonable homogeneous land and equipment, who nevertheless may obtain substantially different amounts of corn..... The observed variation is due, perhaps, to differences in knowledge of technology or the knowledge of how far to carry the application of each productive factor....' (1976 p:215).

Moreover, although all firms in an industry use the same technology[4] some are more successful than others in utilizing it effectively. This implies a real variation in productive capacity realization. It can be argued that such differences in capacity realization across firms in the same industry are not accidental, but natural, due to the presence or absence of some additional economic factors, which affect the frontier. Stigler (1958) maintained that individual firms with similar fixed resources and technologies operate at different levels because of limitation of other resources,[5] or of risk and uncertainty. Market imperfections in developing economies and the heterogeneity [6] among manufacturing firms also cause productivity differences so that there must be differences in actual production among firms from given inputs and technology. The conventional frontier approach does not deny the existence of productivity variations across firms, but offers little explanation for these differences.

In the conventional frontier production function literature, it has been necessary to arbitrarily impose a particular distribution for the firm-specific performance related error term u_i (as explained in the previous chapter), especially with cross-section data. Schmidt notes that '....the only serious intrinsic problem with stochastic frontiers is that the separation of noise and inefficiency ultimately hinges on strong (and arbitrary) distributional assumptions' (1985 p:291). This has been restrictive, although there are numerous statistical tests to validate such distributions. However, there is no economic reasoning, or theoretical justification for the assumption of a particular distribution of the error term.

In measuring PCR, this analysis involves some policy variables. In conventional measures, such policy variables enter the model in an additive fashion, and the effects of policy changes are analyzed within the framework of the model. This is unrealistic in measuring producer behaviour to policy changes, as Maddala pointed out, '.....if economic agents are indeed maximizing, they would be taking these policy variables into account in their decisions and thus the variables would be entering the model not in an additive fashion but as determinants of the parameter of the model' (1977 p:403). Therefore, a varying parameter model is appropriate in evaluating the effects of policy changes.

There is no reason to believe that recent economic reform would have influenced each firm's production behaviour equally, so different levels of output may be obtained by different production agents, *albeit* using the same set of inputs. In other words, firms' maximum output varies regardless of input levels, since, response from each input varies from firm to firm. Hence, the conventional varying intercept and fixed slope production frontier may not be appropriate for measuring a firm's performance, and particularly for measuring firm specific capacity realization, as has been pointed out by Kalirajan and Obwona (1994), Kalirajan and Shand (1994b) and more recently, by Salim and Kalirajan

(1995). Rather, while modelling firms' behaviour, the slope coefficients should be allowed to vary in the production function to take into account of different input responses to output.

Lucas (1981) provides further justification for not using the conventional frontier production function model. In his study of econometric policy evaluation, Lucas argued that

> "....the standard stable parameter view of econometric theory and quantitative policy evaluation appears not to match several important characteristics of econometric practice. For example, fixed coefficient econometric models may not be consistent with the dynamic theory of optimizing behaviour (of firms); that is, changes in economic or policy variables will result in a new environment that may, in turn, lead to new optimal decisions and new economic structures" (1981 p:109-10).

Drawing heavily on the discussion of Hildreth and Houck (1968), Swamy (1970, 1971) and Kalirajan and Obwona (1994), this study adopts the following varying coefficient frontier production approach:

$$y_i = \alpha_i \prod_{j=1}^{k} x_{ij}^{\beta_{ij}} \qquad i = 1, 2, 3, \text{---------} n \quad (4.1)$$

where y_i and x_{ij} are the ith firm's output and jth input respectively. It can be seen from (4.1) that the output response coefficients with respect to different inputs vary across firms (implying variation in input application), as do the intercept terms (implying heterogeneity across firms). However, it is important to note that the performance related error is captured by the random coefficients α and βs, and that the 'white noise' term cannot be distinguished from the random error of the varying intercept term (Hildreth and Houck 1968). The PCR indices, which are estimated using the above model, can now be interpreted more consistently with firms' behaviour and economic theory.

Description of the Model

Let the production function parameters describing the production technology be random. Assuming Cobb-Douglas technology, the random coefficient frontier production function can be written as:

$$\ln y_i = \beta_{1i} + \sum_{j=1}^{K} \beta_{ij} \ln x_{ij} \qquad (4.2)$$

$$i = 1, 2, 3, \text{---------} n$$

where y refers to output, the x's are inputs and βs are the response coefficients for the ith firm. The above model requires $nK+n$ coefficients to be estimated with the help of only n observations. Since intercepts and slope coefficients can vary across firms, we can write:

$$\beta_{ij} = \beta_{ij} = \bar{\beta}_j + u_{ij}$$

$$\beta_{1i} = \beta_{1j} = \bar{\beta}_1 + v_i \qquad (4.3)$$

where $\bar{\beta}_j$ is the mean response coefficient of output with respect to the jth input, and u_{ij} and v_i are random disturbance terms. Indeed, u_{ij} is a crucial variable in this study, as it reflects the policy issues which govern the firms' output (Maddala 1977). Therefore, if the relation in Equation (4.2) is obtained by the maximization behaviour of firms, then it is not appropriate to include u_{ij} additively in Equation (4.2). Rather, it is appropriate to include u_{ij} as a determining variable for the parameters of the model as in Equation (4.3). This is one of the strong arguments in favour of applying this model in analyzing the performance of production units.

Equations (4.2) and (4.3) imply that the random coefficients (β_{ij}) are varying and depend on some explanatory variables. Combining equation (4.2) and (4.3) yields a single linear equation, which can be written as:

$$\ln y_i = \beta_1 + \sum_{j=1}^{K} \left(\bar{\beta}_j + u_{ij} \right) \ln x_{ij} + v_i \qquad (4.4)$$

In matrix format, equation (4) can be written as:

$$Y = X\beta + D_x u + v \qquad (4.4a)$$

where Y is a ($n\times1$) vector, X is a ($n\times K$) matrix of the stacked x_i', Dx is a ($n\times nK$) diagonal matrix of the x_i', u is a ($nK\times1$) vector of u_i's, v is a ($n\times1$) vector and βs are unknown parameters to be estimated.

The underlying assumptions of the above model are:

(4.5.1) $E(v_i) = 0,$

(4.5.2) $E(v_i v_i') = \sigma^2$, if $i = i'$.

(4.5.3) $E(v_i v_i') = 0$ if $i \neq i'$ \qquad (4.5)

(4.5.4) $E(v_i x_{ij}) = 0$, for all i and j

(4.5.5) $E(v_i u_{ij}) = 0$ for all i and j, i.e. the elements of u_{ij} and v_i are mutually independent.

(4.5.6) $E(u_{ij} u'_{i'j}) = \Gamma_u$, if $i = i'$

and   (4.5.7) $E(u_{ij} u''_{i'j}) = 0$ for $i \neq i'$ and $j \neq j'$

The last assumption implies that the variation of output response from inputs set in a particular firm is independent of that of another firm in the industry. Again, variation of output response, from any combination of any pair of inputs for a given firm, is uncorrelated.

In addition to the above classical assumptions, the following assumptions are also made:

(4.6.1) $E(\beta_{ij}) = \bar{\beta}_j$

(4.6.2) $Var(\beta_{ij}) = \sigma_j^2 > 0$ (4.6)

(4.6.3) $Cov(\beta_{ij}, \beta_{im}) = 0$ $j \neq m$

and   (4.6.4) $Cov(\beta_{ij}, u_{ij}) = 0$ $i = 1, 2, 3, \ldots\ldots n;\ j = 1, 2, 3, \ldots K$

These imply that the random coefficients β_{ij} are independently and identically distributed with fixed mean $\bar{\beta}_j$ and variance σ_j^2.

Given these assumptions, the composite disturbance vector,

$$w = D_x u + v$$

will have a mean vector of zero and covariance matrix:

$$\Delta = \begin{bmatrix} x_1' \Gamma x_1 + \sigma_1^2 I & 0 & \cdots & 0 \\ 0 & x_2' \Gamma x_2 + \sigma_2^2 I & \cdots & 0 \\ \vdots & \vdots & \ddots & \vdots \\ 0 & 0 & \cdots & x_n' \Gamma x_n \sigma_n^2 I \end{bmatrix}$$

or more compactly, $\Delta = X_i' \Gamma_u X_i + \sigma_i^2 I$ (4.7)

where x_i is the vector of observations on the *i*th cross-section production unit (or firm). This model is essentially in the spirit of the Hildreth and Houck's model and is a special case of Swamy's panel data model (1970).

So, it is apparent that the error structure of the above model violates the basic assumptions of the linear regression model, i.e. $\Delta \neq \sigma^2 I$. The

Hildreth-Houck random coefficient model belongs to the class of heteroscedastic error models, where error variances are proportional to the squares of a set of exogenous variables x. So the random coefficient regression model reduces to a model with fixed coefficients, but with heteroscedastic variances. This heteroscedasticity will remain, even if σ_i^2 = σ^2 values for all j values so long as the square of the explanatory variables is present. Since the above model is heteroscedastic, the ordinary least squares (OLS) method yields unbiased and consistent but inefficient estimates of mean response coefficients. This conclusion was formalized by *Aitken's theorem* (Aitken 1935).

Estimation Procedures for the Coefficients and Covariances

The parameters to be estimated are mean response coefficients $\bar{\beta}$ and σ_i^2 which obtain predictions for the actual coefficients β_{ij} of the above model. If the elements of Γ_u are known, the Generalized Least Squares (GLS) technique provides efficient estimators of β_{ij} and σ_i^2. However, in empirical studies, Γ_u is likely to be unknown so ways must be considered to estimate its elements. To that end, let $\hat{\Gamma}_u$ contain the unique elements of Γ_u. Several techniques are suggested in the literature to estimate Γ_u, [7] so, a number of methods can be employed to estimate Γ_u before estimating the slope coefficients. It may be necessary to restrict $\hat{\Gamma}_u$ to be positive semi-definite depending on which particular method is used, because, in some of these methods, there is no assurance that $\hat{\Gamma}_u$ will be positive semi-definite.

This is required for the covariance matrix. For the case where Γ_u is known to be diagonal, Hildreth-Houck (1968) suggest changing the negative estimate to zero in their method which uses the Ordinary Least Squares (OLS) to estimate the components of Γ_u. When Γ_u is not diagonal, Judge *et al* (1980) suggest making an *ad hoc* adjustment to the variances in estimating Γ_u such that it is non-negative definite. For example, Schwaille's (1982) method of reparameterization could be used to produce a positive semi-definite Γ_u. Although this method leaves doubt about the sampling properties of estimators, Judge *et al* (1980) argued that this is the best currently available methods to researchers.

Swamy and Mehta (1975) suggested four other methods to estimate βs and σ_i^2. The first two methods are based on *a priori* information about Γ_u. The third is based on the 'initial guess' about the elements of Γ_u. The fourth method, also suggested by Belsley (1973), Harville (1977), Raj and

Ullah (1981) and Srivastava *et al* (1981), the Maximum Likelihood Estimator (MLE), is based on the normality assumptions of the disturbance term. It is very difficult to get prior information about the elements of Γ_u and guessing good initial values for the elements of Γ_u is equally difficult. Therefore, the first three methods of Swamy and Mehta (1975) are not relevant for this study. The fourth method, i.e. the MLE could be used.

However, since the elements of variance-covariance matrix Δ must obey the constraint that the Γ_u is positive semi-definite and such constraints are nonlinear, some kind of iterative search technique must be used in order to get maximum likelihood estimates. This approach may fail, because the likelihood functions may be nearly flat in the neighbourhood of the optimum and therefore, there would be convergence problems. There might be local maxima (Maddala 1971). It is important to use an efficient search procedure that distinguishes local maxima from the global maximum. In such circumstances parameter estimation become burdensome. In this study, the parameters to be estimated are relatively large, so it could be difficult to obtain the maximum likelihood estimates. Furthermore, Froehlich (1973) found the GLS estimator was better (in the mean-square-error sense) than the ML estimator. Therefore, this study will use the Aitken's iterative Generalized Least Squares (GLS) technique.

Generalized Least Squares Method

Knowledge about the elements of Γ_u, as indicated above, is required to apply the GLS technique, in order to estimate the desired parameters of the random coefficient model. As there is no prior knowledge regarding the elements of Γ_u, the approach followed in this study to estimate Γ_u is the one employed by Swamy and Tinsley (1980) that estimates all the unique elements of Γ_u using the OLS. Swamy and Tinsley's suggested technique is iterative. The initial estimate of Γ_u is the identity matrix, used to obtain GLS estimates. Their residuals are also computed and are used to reestimate Γ_u. This process is repeated using the squared residuals and a new Γ_u continues to be estimated until the estimates of βs are stabilized, i.e. the estimates of βs and Γ_u do not change in repeated iterations.

However, there are three potentially damaging limitations for the above estimation procedure. First, there is no guarantee the estimated Γ_u would be positive definite in each iteration. Second, there is no guarantee the estimates will not cycle. Third, there is a possibility of producing unrealistically low variance estimates compared which observed variance for the data. This problem arises particularly for cost data. As output (value added) data are used, this problem will be minimal. If the second problem arises, a different procedure can be implemented, i.e. by replacing Γ_u with its corresponding *Cholesky* factorization and then entering the *Cholesky* variates in squared form to assure positive definite Γ_u. For the first problem, an adjustment is needed as suggested in many studies (Judge and Takayama 1966, Schmalensee 1972, Johnson 1977, Mehta *et al* 1978, Lee and Griffiths 1979, and Swamy and Havenner 1981) to make sure that the estimated Γ_u would be positive definite at every iteration.

In this study, as in Kalirajan and Shand (1994b), the method suggested by Judge and Takayama (1966) has been followed to avoid such problems. The structure of the variance coefficients can be written as:

$$w = z\Gamma + r \tag{4.8}$$

where w is the vector of the square of the estimated OLS residuals, z is the vector of the square of the explanatory variables, Γ is the matrix of the variance of the random coefficients and r is the vector of the random disturbance term. The following method is adopted to avoid negative estimates of Γ. Minimize $r'r$ subject to $\Gamma \geq 0$ which is also equivalent to maximizing $(-r'r)$ subject to $(-\Gamma) \leq 0$, i.e.

$$(-r'r) = -w'w + 2\left(\Gamma'z'w - \frac{1}{2}\Gamma'z'z\Gamma\right) \tag{4.9}$$

is maximized subject to condition that $(-\Gamma) \leq 0$.

Because $w'w$ is a scalar constant, maximization of $(-r'r)$ is equivalent to maximizing

$$\Gamma'z'w - \frac{1}{2}\Gamma'z'z\Gamma \tag{4.10}$$

subject to $C\Gamma \leq d$ where $\tag{4.11}$

$$C = \begin{pmatrix} -1 & \cdots & 0 \\ 0 & -1 & 0 \\ \vdots & \vdots & \vdots \\ 0 & \cdots & -1 \end{pmatrix}, \qquad d = \begin{pmatrix} 0 \\ \vdots \\ \vdots \\ 0 \end{pmatrix}$$

Following the suggestions of Theil and de Panne (1960), it can be argued that maximizing a quadratic function subject to linear equations is much simpler than maximizing subject to linear inequalities such as $C\Gamma \leq d$. First, the unconstrained maximization is considered to see whether the resulting solution does or does not satisfy the constraints, and this information is used as a basis for further computations. The vector which maximizes $(-r' r)$ in (4.10) without regarding the constraints is

$$\hat{\Gamma}_u = \left(z'z\right)^{-1} z'w \qquad (4.12)$$

So, if $\hat{\Gamma}_u$ satisfies the constraint $CT \leq d$, then $\hat{\Gamma}_u$ is the required solution, because a constrained maximum can never exceed an unconstrained maximum. However, if one or more constraints are violated, Theil and de Panne suggested maximization subject to each of the constraints in (4.12) written in the form of an equation instead of inequality. The procedure then involves successively adding the constraints, which are violated in equational form. Theil and de Panne showed that under certain general conditions the procedure leads to the required optimal vector $\hat{\Gamma}_u$ in a finite number of steps.

The GLS estimators for the mean response coefficients can be written as:

$$\hat{\bar{\beta}} = \left(X'\hat{\Delta}^{-1}X\right)^{-1} X'\hat{\Delta}^{-1} y$$

whose variance and covariance is $\left(X'\Delta^{-1}X\right)$.

Now, the predictions for the actual response coefficients β_i can be obtained as:

$$\hat{\beta}_i = \hat{\bar{\beta}} + \hat{\Gamma}_u X' \left(X'_i\hat{\Gamma}_u X_i + \sigma_i^2\right)^{-1} \left(y_i - X_i\hat{\bar{\beta}}\right) \qquad (4.13)$$

Hence, for known $\hat{\Gamma}_u$, $\hat{\beta}_i$ s are minimum variance, linear and unbiased estimators of the actual response coefficients β_i which were realized over the sample (Rao 1965, Zellner 1970, Griffiths 1972, and Lee and Griffiths 1979).

Testing Randomness of Regression Coefficients

In addition to estimation, the applied researchers are likely to test for the presence of randomness of regression coefficients. In this context, a wide variety of testing procedures has been proposed in the literature. In particular, Breusch and Pagan (1979), Chow (1984, section 10), Judge *et al* (1985 Chapter 11), Godfrey (1988, section 4.5) and Davidson and MacKinnon (1993 section 11.5 to 16.5) are relevant for this purpose. Since the Hildreth-Houck random coefficient model is a class of heteroscedastic model, the test for varying parameters is equivalent to the test for heteroscedasticity of the regression model. Hence, the appropriate null hypothesis to be tested is Ho : $\Gamma_u = 0$.

Swamy (1970) suggested a test statistic assuming the asymptotic normality of the maximum likelihood estimator of the elements of Γ_u. According to him, the use of a quadratic form of these elements of Γ_u weighted by the inverse of their covariance matrix, approximates Γ_u's distribution as χ^2 distribution. Since this approximation is crude, this test statistic has rarely been used by applied researchers.

The Likelihood Ratio (LR) test is also not a proper statistic in this case. The distribution of $-2\log\lambda$ (where λ is the ratio of the maximum likelihood function) under the null hypothesis $\Gamma_u = 0$ is not well approximated by the χ^2 distribution. Since there is a density mass $\hat{\Gamma}_u = 0$ with the assumption that the maximum likelihood estimates of the diagonal elements of Γ_u are non-negative. The distribution of $-2\log\lambda$ is more concentrated toward the origin than the χ^2 distribution. Therefore, the null hypothesis is less frequently rejected than the stated level of significance when the χ^2 distribution is applied.

The Breusch and Pagan (1979) test is likely to be satisfactory in this case. Recognizing the fact of different variances of the *i*th unit of the dependent variables, while introducing the random coefficient variation in the model, Breusch and Pagan suggested a test statistic within the framework of heteroscedasticity. They proposed the Lagrange Multiplier (LM) test which satisfies all the asymptotic properties of the Likelihood Ratio test, but is computationally simpler than the Likelihood Ratio test and will approximate the χ^2 distribution, unlike the LR statistic $-2\log\lambda$.

The Breusch-Pagan test statistic for testing the null hypothesis Ho: $\Gamma_u = 0$ is as follows:

$$LM = \frac{1}{2} \left| g'\dot{X}' \left(\dot{X}\dot{X} \right)^{-1} \dot{X}'g \right| \qquad (4.14)$$

where $\dot{X}$ is an independent variable X with each of its elements squared and g is the vector of observations on

$$g_i = \frac{e_i^2}{e'e/N} - 1; \qquad i = 1, 2, \ldots\ldots\ldots, N \qquad (4.14a)$$

with e_i^2 as least square residuals, $\dfrac{e'e}{N}$ is $\hat{\sigma}^2$

and
$$e = \left(I_N - X(X'X)^{-1}X' \right)y = My \qquad (4.14b)$$

So, this test statistic is simply one half of the explained sum of squares in the regression of g_i on $\dot{X}_i$. The LM statistic is asymptotically distributed as $\chi^2_{(k-1)}$ with degrees of freedom equal to the number of variables in $\dot{X}$ minus 1 when the null hypothesis $\Gamma_u = 0$ is true and will yield an asymptotically efficient test.

The Breusch-Pagan test is criticized for its dependence on the normality assumption. It has been argued by Koenkar (1981), and Koenkar and Bassett (1982), that the Breusch-Pagan LM test is quite sensitive to the normality assumption. Without the assumption of normality they suggest a more robust form of the LM test statistic which is as follows:

$$LM = N\left[\frac{g'\dot{X}(\dot{X}'\dot{X})^{-1}\dot{X}'g}{g'g}\right] \qquad (4.15)$$

which also follows a $\chi^2_{(k-1)}$ distribution with (K-1) degrees of freedom. Like the Breusch-Pagan LM statistic, this test also converges to an asymptotic distribution but without the assumption of normality, there is some evidence that it has been a more powerful test (Greene 1993b).

Measuring Firm-Specific PCR

There are two assumptions underlying the above model:

(i) The maximum possible output stems from two sources. First, by following the 'best practice' technique which involves the efficient use of inputs without having to increase their levels, the efficient use of each input contributes individually to potential output, and can be measured by the magnitude of the varying random slope coefficients (β coefficients) which differ between individual observations. Second, when all inputs are used efficiently, the combined contribution may exceed the sum of the individual contributions. This latter 'lump sum' contribution, if any, can be captured and measured by the varying random intercept term (α coefficient).

(ii) The highest magnitude of each response coefficient and the intercept term from the production coefficients of equation (4) constitute the production coefficients of the frontier production function showing the maximum possible output.

To elaborate, let β_1^*, β_2^*, β_3^*, ... β_K^* be the estimates of the parameters of the frontier production function yielding the potential output. The frontier coefficients β^*s are chosen so as to reflect the condition that represents the production responses from following 'best practice' techniques. These are obtained, by following Griffiths (1972), from the above input-specific response coefficients as follows:

$$\beta_j^* = max \; \{\beta_{ij}\} \qquad i= 1, 2\text{----------}n \qquad (4.16)$$
$$j= 1, 2\text{--------}K$$

The key points to note here are first, that these frontier coefficients need not necessarily correspond to the response coefficients for any single individual observation. They may represent the best combination of response coefficients derived from different individual observations. For example, β_1^* may come from the 7th observation while β_4^* may come from the 16th observation, and so on. This supports the earlier assertion that not all firms use each input efficiently. Second, the possibility of obtaining all β_j^*'s from a single observation cannot be ruled out. Human capital theory literature argues that a firm which uses some inputs efficiently may also use all inputs efficiently (Kalirajan and Obwona).

When the response coefficients are selected by using (4.16), potential output for the ith firm can be worked out as:

$$\ln y_i^* = \beta^* + \sum_j \dot{\beta} \ln x_{ij} \qquad (4.17)$$

where the x_{ij}'s refer to actual levels of inputs used by the ith firm. Subsequently, a measure of PCR can be defined as follows:

$$PCR_i = \frac{realised\;Output}{potential\;Output}$$

$$= \frac{y_i}{exp(lny_i^*)} \qquad (4.18)$$

where y_i and y_i^* are actually realized and potential output of the ith firms respectively. The PCR varies between 0 to 1. Thus, the varying coefficient regression model approach provides a realistic approach for estimating the PCR over a large number of firms using only cross-section data. Based on the above theoretical measures of potential output as well as PCR, empirical estimates of TFP growth will be calculated in later chapters.

In addition to estimating the PCR rates, applied researchers may be interested to explain the distribution of PCR rates. PCR rate variations across firms can be explained using second-stage regression analysis. Results of this analysis may assist managerial decision making (Sexton *et al* 1991) and can guide public policy (Caves and Barton 1990). Second-stage analysis of explaining technical efficiency variations started from the work of Timmer (1971) and is now commonly used in empirical studies. Variations in firm performances may be associated with such policy sensitive variables as, trade orientation, sources of finance, and gender composition of work force (Hill and Kalirajan 1993), or firm-specific characteristics as, age, size and ownership (Pitt and Lee 1981). This study takes the following three classes of variables for second-stage analysis: firm-specific variables (age, size, and ownership), a technology related variable (capital intensity), a market structure related variable (concentration ratio), and trade policy variables (effective rate of protection and openness). Construction of these variables is discussed below.

Measuring the Sources of Output Growth

Measurement of the sources of output growth has advanced since the pioneering works of Abramovitiz (1956), Solow (1957), Swan (1957) and Denison (1962). The main objective has been to estimate the relative contribution of factor inputs and technological progress in output growth. When firm behaviour is considered in line with the traditional view that firms are producing on the production frontier, the problem becomes simply one of decomposing the sources of growth between changes in factor endowments and improvements in technology. However, firms in reality are producing under the frontier, at varying level of capacity realization or technical efficiency for various reasons (discussed in Chapter 3). This encourages the application of the frontier approach in measuring the sources of output growth. The pioneering study in this respect was done by Nishimizu and Page (1982). They used a non-parametric linear programming technique to decompose TFP growth into the change in technical efficiency and technological progress. As this approach is highly sensitive to extreme observations, there is a danger that purely random components may lead to spurious identification of 'best practice' firms and provides biased estimates.

Fan (1991) and Lin (1992) examined the relative contribution of input growth, technological progress and technical efficiency changes to output growth in Chinese agriculture using the stochastic frontier production function. According to Kalirajan *et al* (1996), there are three limitations of Fan's (1991) approach in that his specification of the frontier production function implicitly assumes: (i) in a given period, the production frontier is neutrally shifted from the 'average' and the realized production functions; (ii) over time, the production frontiers themselves shift neutrally, implying that the technological progress is also the neutral type; and (iii) the rate of technological change over time is constant among firms. These assumptions are unrealistic.

None of the earlier studies in Bangladesh has attempted to decompose the sources of output growth into technological progress, improvement in capacity realization and growth in inputs. There are a few studies (Kim and Kwon 1977, Kwon 1986 and Callan 1986) in the literature which empirically estimate these components of output growth. However, all these studies followed an index number approach to explore the relationship between changes in productivity growth and technological progress and changes in capacity realization. Limitations of the index number approaches was discussed in detail in the previous chapter.

This book suggest a methodology, in the spirit of Kalirajan *et al* (1996), to empirically examine the sources of output growth using the random coefficient frontier production function discussed in the previous section. By following the random coefficient model the restrictive assumptions of the earlier methodologies can be eliminated. For example, the random coefficient frontier production function shifts non-neutrally so technological change is also of the non-neutral type. Secondly, in the earlier studies, technological progress, one of the components of output growth, is not estimated but is obtained as a residual while estimating the sources of output growth. In contrast, the methodology described below, estimates technological change as a shift of the best practice frontier and treats total input growth as a residual, while accounting for output growth. The chief advantage of not computing input growth but obtaining as a residual is in the avoidance of the problems usually encountered such as omission of some important inputs and adjustment of input quality changes.

The following diagram demonstrates the different sources of output growth, viz., improvement in capacity realization, technological progress and input growth. In Figure 4.1, a typical firm faces two production frontiers, the 'efficient production technologies', as characterized by Farrell (1957), for two periods, T_1 and T_2 respectively. At period 1, if the firm is producing with full productive capacity, its realized output will be y_1^*. However, because of various constraints, the firm may be producing at somewhere less than full capacity, which means that the realized output is y_1. So, there is a gap between realized and maximum possible outputs, i.e. there is unrealized productive capacity; $UPCR_1$ measures this gap by the vertical distance between y_1 and y_1^*. Now suppose there is technological progress, due to the improved quality of human and physical capital, induced by policy changes, so that a firm's potential frontier shifts to T_2 in period 2. If the firm keeps up the technological progress, more output is produced from the same level of input. So, the firm's output will be y_1^{**} from X_1 input shown in the figure. Technological progress is measured by the distance between two frontiers (T_2-T_1) evaluated at x_1.

Now the firm is generally induced to increase its levels of input in period 2. Its maximum possible output is y_2^* for new levels of input X_2, and its realized output is y_2. Again, the gap is measured by $UPCR_2$, the vertical distance between y_2 and y_2^*. So, the improvement in capacity realization between the two periods is measured by the difference between $UPCR_1$ and $UPCR_2$. The traditional source of output growth, i.e. output growth due to input growth between the two periods, can be measured by the distance between y_2^* and y_1^{**} along the frontier 2. Referring to Figure 4.1, the total output growth can be decomposed into three components: input growth, changes in capacity realization and technical progress.

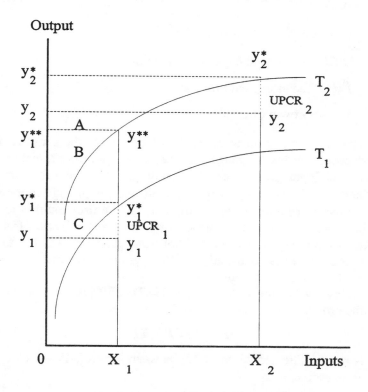

Figure 4.1: Sources of Output Growth

In accordance with the figure the decomposition can be shown as follows:

$$
\begin{aligned}
(y_2 - y_1) &= A + B + C \\
&= (y_2 - y_1^{**}) + (y_1^{**} - y_1^*) + (y_1^* - y_1) \\
&= (y_2^* - y_2^*) + (y_2 - y_1^{**}) + (y_1^{**} - y_1^*) + (y_1^* - y_1) \\
&= \{y_1^* - y_1 - y_2^* + y_2\} + (y_2^* - y_1^{**}) + (y_1^{**} - y_1^*) \\
&\quad \{(y_1^* - y_1) - (y_2^* - y_2)\} + (y_2^* - y_1^{**}) + (y_1^{**} - y_1^*) \\
&= (UPCR_1 - UPCR_2) + (y_1^{**} - y_1^*) + (y_2^* - y_1^{**}) \\
&= (UPCR_1 - UPCR_2) + TP + \Delta y_x \\
&= \Delta PCR + TP + \Delta y_x
\end{aligned}
\tag{4.19}
$$

where

$y_2 - y_1$ = Output growth

ΔPCR = Change in capacity realization

TP = Technological progress

Δy_x = Growth of inputs

This decomposition in Equation (4.19) yields the intuitive results that advances in both changes in capacity realization, technological progress and input growth lead to output growth. The first component ΔPCR captures the change in capacity realization implying the movement of firms towards or away from the frontier, i.e. the firm's ability to 'catch up'. The second factor (TP) represents the shift of production frontier at each firm's input mix, known as 'technological progress'. The last factor of (4.19) accounts for the contribution of input growth to output, which refers to a movement along its frontier.

Following Nishimizu and Page (1982), TFP growth not accounted for by the growth of input is:

$$
\Delta TFP = \Delta PCR + TP
\tag{4.20}
$$

Now, the TFP growth in (4.20) between period (t-1) and t for the ith firm can be estimated as:

$$\Delta \text{TFP} = \ln\left(\frac{TFP_{i,t}}{TFP_{i,t-1}}\right)$$

$$= \left\{\left(y^*_{1i,t-1} - y_{1i,t-1}\right) - \left(y^*_{2i,t} - y_{2i,t}\right)\right\} + \left(y^*_{1i,t} - y^*_{1i,t-1}\right) \tag{4.21}$$

where $y^*_{1i,t}$ and $y^*_{2i,t-1}$ (in logarithms) are the frontier outputs (or maximum possible output) with input level X_1 and X_2 in periods 1 and 2 respectively (see Figure 4.1).

Substituting Equation (4.21) into Equation (4.19)

$$y_{2i,t} - y_{1i,t-1} = \Delta TFP + \dot{y}_x \tag{4.22}$$

where $\dot{y}_x$ represents the growth of inputs which can be obtained as a residual. This Equation (4.22) is used to estimate the components of output growth empirically in the following chapter. This procedure is adopted in this study, first, because, it is practical, and second, because it is believed the resulting figure will be closer to what TFP growth is meant to be in economic theory.

While the foregoing analysis provides a method for allowing the decomposition of TFP growth to be made, it is also important to emphasize that unlike conventional procedures, the estimates of input growth are determined by a residual, and thus other qualitative factors that may affect inputs are taken into account. It is also important to note that the opening of the domestic economy enables firms to achieve new gains from trade and may cause productivity growth through technological progress. Institutional changes due to economic policy reform may also cause improve productivity. The above model is, therefore, realistic as it takes account of all the above effects on output growth.

Conclusion

This chapter developed a framework for measuring PCR and TFP growth rates. Since firms are not producing in equilibrium (on the frontier) the conventional varying intercept and fixed slope frontier production model is not appropriate for measuring firms' performance. This chapter developed methodologies for measuring firm-specific capacity realization and factor productivity growth applying the stochastic coefficient frontier production function model introduced by Kalirajan and Obwona and Kalirajan *et al.*

There are a number of sources of manufacturing data in Bangladesh. Since data from most of the sources cannot be used for comprehensive analysis this study found CMI data are useful for empirical measurement. Several explanatory variables were constructed using the most up to date formulae from the literature for second stage analysis. This chapter concludes that the nobility of the developed framework is to make allowance for random errors in data measurement.

Notes

[1] See for example, Kim and Kwon 1977, Harris and Taylor 1985, Nelson 1989a, 1989b, Berndt and Morrison 1981, Morrison 1985, 1988, Berndt and Hesse 1986, Segerson and Squires 1990, 1993, 1995.

[2] The standard neoclassical theories rest on the assumption that equilibrium conditions hold for every data point, while Keynesians argue that the market does not always clear, due to sticky wages and prices. Recently, Schultz 1975 remarked that firms could hardly, if ever, stay in a state of equilibrium, due to technological, market-resourced, or institutional changes.

[3] Theoretical and applied works are expanding rapidly. See, for example, Roenberg 1972, 1973, Belsley 1973a, 1973b, Swamy and Mehta 1975, Brown *et al* 1975, Harvey 1978, Pagan 1980, Raj and Ullah 1981, Swamy and Tavlas 1994 for theoretical works. See, for example, Fiege and Swamy 1974, Dixon and Martin 1982, Kniesner and Smith 1989, Kalirajan 1990b, Hoque 199, 1992, Kalirajan and Obwona 1994, Kalirajan and Shand 1994b, and Kalirajan and Salim 1997 for applied works. There is also a number of survey works on the random coefficient model, see, Nicholls and Pagan 1985 and Swamy and Tavlas 1995 for the most recent surveys.

[4] Production technology may differ from firm to firm only in the long run.

[5] For example, factors such as, information, access to credit, etc. vary from firm to firm.

[6] Firms' size, location, and quality differences of owners or managers cause manufacturing firms heterogeneous.

[7] For comprehensive analysis about various techniques, see the work of Rao 1970.

5 Measuring Productive Capacity Realization in Selected Manufacturing Industries

Introduction

Productive capacity realization (PCR) has been regarded as an important indicator for measuring economic performance of any production unit. While PCR indices are important for investment planning and resource allocation, the methods of measurement of PCR developed in the literature are not quite accurate at least for two reasons. As discussed in Chapter 3, these measures do not take into account differences in individual input response, arising from the different methods of application of inputs to output and disentangling the 'random noise' from measurement while measuring PCR. Therefore, the use of the available PCR indices invariably leads to incorrect policy implications. The problem is particularly important in view of recent efforts taken by many developing countries to restructure their economies. The success or failure of such policies will be very difficult to assess if some of the key indicators for measuring individual firms' performance (such as PCR) are unreliable. Drawing on the arguments of Klein (1960) and Färe et al (1989), an alternative methodology, which overcome these stringent limitations, was developed in the previous chapter. This method can also be used without having to know specific details about economic reform measures; the combined effect of all reforms is represented in the model by random variables, which is ultimately captured by the varying coefficients of the production frontier.

The framework developed in Chapter 4 is used here to estimate productive capacity realization (PCR) indexes of selected manufacturing industries in Bangladesh. First, this chapter highlights the structure and development performance of selected industries. The econometric model is then specified followed by a description of data sources and variables construction. Empirical estimation and interpretations of results are then arranged followed by summary and conclusions at the end of the chapter.

Structure and Performance of Selected Industries

A broad-based dynamic manufacturing sector is generally considered to be the key to economic development. Despite two decades of industrialization, Bangladesh's manufacturing sector remains small and narrowly based. A dominant portion of available investment funds has traditionally been channeled into existing rather than new industries. There are other significant barriers to entry in addition to limited access to capital as discussed in Chapter 2. Most of the industries are involved in agro-processing and import substituting activities, except for jute textiles, ready-made garments, and fish and seafood. So the pace of diversification and growth of manufacturing cannot be accelerated by relying on the domestic market, because, although the population is large, the disposable income of most individual consumers is exceptionally low.

The industrial sector accounted, on average at constant 1984/85 prices, for only 10 per cent of GDP and absorbed only 7 per cent of total employment during 1980-81 to 1989-90. The real growth of manufacturing value added was only 3.6 per cent per annum during the same period (World Bank 1992), because the dominant industries, including textiles, food processing and chemicals, either stagnated or experienced only modest growth. A few sub-sectors, such as ready-made garments, fish and seafood, fertilizers and industrial chemicals experienced rapid growth (Table 5.1). Achievement of international competitiveness by increasing efficiency and productivity has become a top priority in most of the world economies, so it is a matter of concern that most of the Bangladesh manufacturing sector remains under-performed. An investigation of the performance of major industries in Bangladesh is essential to determine the sources of growth, which could enable policy makers to target policies in order to achieve competitive advantage in manufacturing production.

Industries selected for this study are textiles and ready-made garments, food processing and chemicals. These are the three largest industry groups in terms of contribution to output, value added, employment and foreign exchange earnings. In 1991, these three groups contributed 64, 60 and 75 per cent to total manufacturing output, value added and employment respectively and earned about 75 per cent of total export earnings (BBS 1995). The structure and development performance of these industries are discussed below.

Textiles and Ready-made Garments

There are mainly three sub-sectors of this industry group, viz, jute textiles, cotton textiles and ready-made garment or apparel industries. Jute and cotton textiles are the country's oldest industries, started in the mid 1950s.

They are, in a sense, a mirror image of each other; the jute industry using local raw materials, produces mainly for export, while the cotton textile industry, using imported raw materials, produces for the domestic market. In the late 1970s and the beginning of the 1980s, a greater emphasis on food self-sufficiency reduced the supply of local raw materials for the jute industry and the slow growth of international demand for jute goods due to synthetic and other substitutes combined to retard the growth of the industry. Despite high protection policies, the cotton textile industry failed to achieve high growth. From 1977 to 1993, production indexes for both of these industries were well below the production indexes of the industry group and of the whole manufacturing sector. Both industries are plagued with a host of problems, such as a high incidence of sickness, low labour productivity and overstaffing, increasing obsolescence and low levels of modernization. Many firms, both public and private, have little or no chance of catching up technologically in an industry where change and innovation are extremely rapid (World Bank 1992b). These industries never experienced take-off and consequently, failed to be the engine of growth as occurred in some of the rapidly growing industrialized countries.

However, the ready-made garment industry, a sub-sector of the cotton textiles industry, experienced phenomenal growth from the beginning of the 1980s through the 1990s. Facilitated by liberal trade policies, a huge supply of cheap but trainable labour, preferential tariffs for imported inputs, MFA status, ready availability of credit and international environment, the number of firms in this industry grew by an average rate of 52 per cent per annum during 1978 to 1991 (World Bank 1992b). The share of ready-made garments in manufacturing output increased from virtually nothing in 1980 to 1 per cent in 1985, 10 per cent in 1990 and 15 per cent in 1993 (BBS 1988, 1996). The industry's exports (less than US$ 8 million in 1980) grew rapidly throughout the 1980s, and even faster in the early 1990s. The value of exports of garments increased from US$0.87 billion in 1990/91 to 2.23 billion in 1994/95 (Islam and Chowdhury 1996). Its share in the country's total exports also rose dramatically, from 1 per cent in 1980 to 12 per cent in 1985, 40 per cent in 1990 and 52 per cent in 1993 (see Table 2.9 in Chapter 2). Bangladesh's ready-made garment industry surpassed the traditional leading export-oriented industry (jute textiles) to become the largest industry in the late 1980s.[1] However, the success of ready-made garments has made only a limited contribution to industry's total value added and foreign exchange earnings because production has so far relied almost entirely on imported materials.

The competitive edge for Bangladesh lies primarily in low wages rather than high productivity (Alauddin 1995).[2] Rapid growth of domestic and external demand, relatively simple techniques, low capital requirements and government promotional policies, along with an abundant supply of cheap labour, has been the main strength of the textiles and ready-made garment industries. There is great potential for these industries in Bangladesh. All successful East Asian NIEs, such as Japan, Hong Kong, South Korea, and Taiwan, enjoyed this success during the 1960s and 1970s. However, in Bangladesh, the realization of this potential largely depends on government policies, modernization of textile mills and the creation of appropriate backward linkages with local textile industries as input suppliers.

Food Processing

Food processing is one of the important agro-based industries in Bangladesh. The industry is still in the development stage. Using largely local raw materials this sector is geared mainly to meet the domestic needs. Food manufacturing covers a wide variety of products among which dairy products, edible oils, grain milling, fish and seafood, hydrogenated vegetable oils, sugar, and tea and coffee processing are important.[3] This industry represents a very broad and diverse sector in terms of the nature of industries, size of investment, levels of technology, raw materials used and manpower employed. All food processing industries, except sugar factories, are the country's small and medium scale enterprises.

Food processing is one of the vital sectors of the national economy in terms of employment, contribution to GDP and foreign exchange earnings. This sector is second only to textiles in terms of value of output, accounting on the average for 24 per cent of total industrial output and 21 per cent of total manufacturing employment over the period from 1983 to 1992. The rate of growth of output has, however, been lower than that of manufacturing as a whole in some years within this period. For example, manufacturing output growth in 1991 was about 4.9 per cent, while that of the food processing sector was about 3 per cent (BBS 1995). With an abundant labour force and an overwhelmingly agrarian base, this sector should have been growing faster than the current stagnant and moderate rate of 3 per cent.

Fish and seafood processing, the lead sector of this industry group, is partly geared towards export. The production of fisheries products has increased significantly since 1978-79, and exports have fared even better. The production index for these products increased sharply from 102 in 1977 to 461 in 1993 at constant 1981-82 prices (Table 5.1). The value of exports was less than US$38 million in 1980 and rose to US$206 million in 1993 (see Table 2.9 in Chapter 2) and has become the second largest export item, after ready-made garments, replacing processed tea and coffee. Export earnings from this sub-sector have been increasing steadily since then. Total export earnings were recorded US$211.8 million in 1994, which was around 3 per cent higher than the previous year. As an export item, its importance has increased over the years. Exports of fish and food products (at current price in US dollars) grew at an average rate of 39 per cent per annum from 1979 to 1994 (Export Promotion Bureau 1995).

Table 5.1: Quantum Indices of Total and Selected Manufacturing Industries (1982=100)

	1977	1981	1985	1989	1991	1993
All manufacturing	**96**	**98**	**125**	**148**	**189**	**214**
Food Processing	**78**	**82**	**81**	**110**	**147**	**134**
Fish & Sea food	102	115	159	366	480	461
Edible oil	81	77	59	97	114	132
Grain milling	96	102	112	169	145	174
Sugar	47	48	44	59	122	92
Tea & Coffee Process	102	112	109	107	114	126
Textiles & Ready-made Garments	**98**	**105**	**133**	**167**	**206**	**273**
Jute Textiles	97	94	89	87	74	78
Cotton Textiles	103	106	110	119	120	121
Ready-made Garments	....	....	2275	4046	6894	10579
Chemicals	**102**	**124**	**137**	**162**	**174**	**230**
Drugs & Pharmaceuticals	110	108	98	128	98	150
Fertilizers	118	156	195	389	369	493
Industrial Chemicals	129	164	192	204	329	434
Soap & Detergent	114	132	158	137	110	128
Matches Mfg.	121	112	113	125	92	115
Petroleum Products	96	91	83	92	96	116

Sources: Bangladesh, Government of, *Statistical Yearbook of Bangladesh* (various issues), Bangladesh Bureau of Statistics, Planning Commission, Dhaka.

Overall, the food processing sector has great potential with the abundant labour force, an ample domestic supply of raw materials, growing urban demand and development of the transport network. But despite this potential, the overall productivity and performance of the food processing sector is far from satisfactory (ILO 1991). This could be due to old and obsolete technology used, managerial inefficiency, lack of trained and innovative entrepreneurs, and above all, government regulatory policy regimes.

Chemicals

Chemical is the third largest industry in Bangladesh. Growth of output in this sector has increased steadily since 1977 (Table 5.1) and in 1984, became the second largest, replacing the food processing industry, and accounting for 25 per cent of total industrial value added. Drugs and pharmaceuticals, fertilizers, industrial chemicals, perfume and cosmetics, matches, soap and detergents are important components of this industry group. All components of this industry group, except matches, are at an early stage of development and production is primarily for domestic consumption. Multinationals Corporations (MNCs) own a majority of enterprises in this industry group, particularly in drugs and pharmaceuticals, perfume and cosmetics, matches and soap and detergent sectors. MNC subsidiaries are well placed to withstand import competition and a handful of MNC subsidiaries contribute a substantial portion of this industry's total output.

Fertilizer is the single largest sub-sector of this industry group in terms of volume of output. The presence of an abundant supply of natural gas, the principal raw material has supported the development of this industry. The production index for fertilizer increased from 118 in 1977 to 195 in 1985, 389 in 1989 and 493 in 1993 (Table 5.1). The expansion of HYV technology in agriculture and its impact on fertilizer demand have played an important role in this buoyant growth. Recently, Bangladesh started exporting chemical fertilizers. Export earnings from fertilizers increased from a paltry US$ 4 million, in 1985, to US$ 51 million, in 1993 (Table 2.9 in Chapter 2). The growth rate of fertilizer exports has been 24 per cent per annum during 1985 to 1993 period (Export Promotion Bureau 1995).

Many sub-sectors of the chemical industry group are potentially promising such as fertilizers, paints and varnishes, industrial chemicals, dyes, colour and pigments, pesticides and insecticides. A study under TIP [Trade and Industrial Program (1985)] shows that most of these industries are producing at sub-optimal size owing to inefficient power supply, lack of raw materials and excessive government protection. This study also indicates that removing these bottlenecks with efficient management and further investment in these sectors could contribute to meeting domestic needs as well as exports.

The structure and development patterns of all these three industries reveal some interesting patterns. Although these are the three largest industries in Bangladesh, one or two sub-sectors within each dominate the volume of output and value added, e.g. fish and seafood in the food processing industry group, ready-made garments in the textiles and ready-made garments industry group, and fertilizers and industrial chemicals in the chemicals industry group. Table 5.1 reveals that the production index for food products has been lower than that for the whole of manufacturing during 1977 to 1993. The production indexes for textiles and garments, and chemicals, are larger than the production index for the whole of manufacturing and have become the dominant sub-sectors. Other than these two or three sub-sectors, most sub-sectors within the industry groups are not performing well and have remained relatively small within the manufacturing sector as a whole. This raises the question of why a few sectors of these manufacturing industries in Bangladesh are fast growing and most others are not with the implementation of economic reform? The resolution of this question involves the measurement of the sources of output growth, as explained below.

Model Specification and Estimation

According to neoclassical economics, specifying a functional form in empirical analysis is tantamount to an assumption that the underlying technologies are wholly consistent with that form. Economists have applied a variety of functional forms, such as Cobb-Douglas, CES (Constant Elasticity of Substitution), Translog (Transcendental Logarithmic), and so on, in empirical analysis. Each has its merits and limitations. For example, while the Cobb-Douglas production function is increasingly recognized as a restricted type of production function, the Translog form of production function is overparameterized and inflexible in representing separable technologies. Unfortunately, economic theory offers little guidance as to the best functional form for analysis. However, there have been numerous statistical test procedures introduced in the literature to identify the suitability of a specific functional form for a given data set in empirical analysis.

The reliability of estimates of TFP growth, and capacity realization indexes hinges crucially on the specification of the model. The Cobb-Douglas functional form has been extensively used in stochastic frontier production function analysis as this affords maximum flexibility in dealing with data imperfections (Tybout 1990). Although it is argued that the Translog production function is a more general type of production function, it may not provide efficient estimates, because collinearity among the explanatory variables cannot be avoided. Moreover, estimation of the Translog production function consumes many degrees of freedom, which can cause another inefficiency in the estimators when the number of observations is small. The Translog flexible functional form is often questioned for over parameterization (see Goldberger 1967). It is therefore not surprising that recent surveys of empirical applications of frontier production functions by Battese (1992), Bravo-Ureta and Pinheiro (1993) and Coelli (1995) revealed that the Cobb-Douglas technology specifications still continue to dominate.

Narasimham, Swamy and Reed (1988) demonstrated, in line with Zellner (1969), that the Cobb-Douglas production function is less restrictive when all coefficients are allowed to vary. Moreover, it has been demonstrated that the Cobb-Douglas functional form fits Bangladesh manufacturing data reasonably well (Hossain 1984, Krishna and Sahota 1991). Nevertheless, the Translog and the Cobb-Douglas specifications for annual data and selected industries are sequentially tested here and Ramsey's (1969) RESET test is used as an important decision-making tool when theoretical considerations do not suggest correct functional specifications. Statistical results support the Cobb-Douglas functional form in each case.

Accordingly, the following the Cobb-Douglas production function is used to estimate the maximum possible output of individual firm and the resulting estimates are then used to estimate firm-specific capacity realization and TFP growth:

$$ln\, y_i = ln\, \alpha_i + \sum_{k=1}^{2} \beta_k\, ln\, X_{ki} \qquad (5.1)$$

$$i = 1, 2, 3, \ldots\ldots\ldots\ldots n$$

where y refers to value added and X's are core inputs, namely, capital and labour respectively.

The Breusch-Pagan's LM test was used to test the randomness of coefficients of the specified model and the test results are given in Appendix Table A5.1. The results rejected individual heteroscedasticity in favour of vector heteroscedasticity, lending support to the random coefficient model specification. But this test cannot provide any indication of the exact form of randomness of coefficients. So this study used one class of random coefficient model, in which it is assumed that the coefficients vary unsystematically, i.e. the response to a change in one explanatory variable is different for different observations (firms).

The computer program *TERAN*[4] was used to estimate the unconstrained variance-covariance matrix of the random coefficients (Schwallie, 1982) to obtain the GLS (Generalized Least Squares) mean estimator and individual response coefficients (Griffiths, 1972). These estimators were used to estimate the empirical model (5.1) for selected manufacturing industries in Bangladesh.

Data Sources and Variables Construction

Bangladesh's main official source of data is the Bangladesh Bureau of Statistics (BBS). The Bureau's industrial division conducts a yearly census across the country's manufacturing industries, known as the 'Census of Manufacturing Industries' (CMI). The CMI covers all public enterprises and privately owned enterprises with 10 or more employees. A number of other organizations and agencies including the Bangladesh Institute of Development Studies (BIDS), Metropolitan Chamber of Commerce and Industry (MCCI), Department of Industries, National Productivity Organization (NPO), the World Bank resident mission and Bangladesh Garments Manufacturers and Exporters' Association (BGMEA) also collect data on manufacturing firms. However, these organizations only collect data which is either sector specific or on an occasional basis. So, to evaluate the comprehensive performance of selective industries, these data have limited use. The CMI is the principal source of data for this study.[5] Since each member garment industry has to keep its accounting balance sheet in the BGMEA, it is typically by researchers that data on garments' factories are well documented in the BGMEA. Therefore, data for the garments' factories are taken from this source. Since the CMI and the BGMEA provide only raw information at the establishment level, adjustment of data and construction of different variables required for this study are made using formulae taken from the literature. This section describes the coverage of industries in this study and the construction of variables. Finally, data limitations are also discussed.

Coverage of This Study

Based on availability and reliability of data, this study selected three industries for analysis: textiles, (including ready-made garments), food processing, and chemicals. These are the largest three industries in Bangladesh in terms of value added and contribution to total industrial employment (about 60% of total industrial value added, and about 65% of industrial employment). It can generally be argued that food processing is a labour intensive and domestic resource based industry group. High growth in these industries is needed to create employment opportunities, which can contribute to overall economic growth. Textiles is labour as well as material intensive, while chemicals are a capital intensive group.[6] This study is, therefore, able to analyze all three types of industry, namely, labour intensive, material intensive and capital intensive, or in a further classification, domestically consumed, export oriented, and import substituting industries, respectively.

Unlike most earlier studies on capacity realization in Bangladesh, and elsewhere, this study uses 4-digit industry level data, classified according to the 'Bangladesh Standard Industrial Classification' (BSIC), which corresponds to the 'International Standard Industrial Classification' (ISIC). This level of disaggregation is in line with the suggestion of Meeusen and van den Broeck (1977b) that two-digit industries are too heterogeneous and that at least three-digit and preferably four-digit observations are required. There are at least two advantages of using firm level data: they avoid aggregation problems[7] and have the theoretical justification that, for example, decisions regarding target level of production and expansion of capacity are taken at the firm level and not at industry level. So research using firm level data can give a sharper focus to the mix of policy measures for better realization of productive capacity.

Table 5.2: Sample Industries for Empirical Analysis

	CMIreorted firms			Sample firms for the study
	1981	1987	1991	
Food Processing Industries	167	196	245	93
Cotton Textiles	76	102	124	48
Jute Textiles	67	82	110	51
Garments[a]	....	140	515	62
Chemical Industries	94	93	134	58

Source: BBS, CMI master-tape (for selected years), [a] Data on garments' industries were taken from BGMEA.

Cross-section data for the above mentioned selected industries for three intertemporal years, (i.e. 1981, the year before reform; 1987, the year during transition; and 1991 the last available year) are used due to the unavailability of panel data. The CMI provides information on a varied number of firms in the same industry for different years because of either the entrance (exit) of new firms, or the under coverage by the census (a point which will be discussed later) or both. However, for the three intertemporal years, the common firms are taken for analysis (see Table 5.2). Among the common firms, firms inconsistent in terms of data and errors are omitted. For example, firms with zero value added, and firms with value added higher than total sale proceeds were dropped from the analysis. After screening the raw data, our sample size for different industries becomes, 93 for food processing, 48 for cotton textiles, 51 for jute textiles, 62 for garments and 58 for chemical industries.

Definition and Construction of Variables

Perhaps the most important consideration in productivity measurement is the measurement of inputs and output. The reliability of performance measures of economic agents hinges on accuracy of measures of output and inputs. We cannot use many variables directly from the CMI, so the following variables are constructed for empirical estimation, using information from the literature. The varying coefficient methodology used in this study facilitates taking account of quality variation in inputs used in the production process by allowing the response coefficients to vary across firms.

Output (y)

Value added figures are used in this study to represent output. Gross value added provides a measure of the contribution made by labour, materials and capital equipment in producing the output of a production unit. This has the advantage that it can be matched with the resources utilized in production (Bernolak 1980). In the literature on productivity measurement, both value added and gross output are concomitantly used to measure output. Many researchers argue that the use of value added is valid only if capital and labour are weakly separable from materials. Sudit and Finger (1981) contend that the separability assumption is economically restrictive since most production processes, probably do not exhibit independence of (core) factor inputs and other material use. Gollop and Jorgenson (1979), and Nishimizu and Robinson (1986) express similar concern. Griliches and Ringstad (1971) advance arguments in favour of using value added because it facilitates comparison of results for firms which may be heterogeneous in material consumption. Inclusion of material as an input may lead to the problem that all variation in productivity growth is captured by materials consumption, thus obscuring the role of physical and human capital.

In the literature, use of value added is considered preferable in comparing performance of firms with various degrees of vertical integration and different product mixes. It also has an advantage over the gross value of output, as it takes into account differences and changes in the quality of inputs. Solow (1957), also recommended that the best output measure for productivity measurement is net output or value added.

Value added has two measures: net value added and gross value added or census value added. Net value added is defined as gross value of output less all goods and services brought in from the outside, while census value added is equivalent to the net output, i.e. gross value of output less the value of input materials, fuel and electricity. It does not exclude such purchased services as water and other municipal services, accounting and legal services, etc. Although net value added is the most relevant measure for studying production characteristics of economic agents, it was decided to use gross value added in this study, because the CMI estimates of net value added are flawed owing to the arbitrary nature of deductions of various services from gross value of output.

Since the objective is to compare productive performances of the same production unit in three intertemporal periods, firm level data for those particular periods have been used as producers, consumers and input suppliers (households and government) all face different market prices over the periods. So it is necessary to make constant value added figures by using the proper deflation method. Double deflation method is wellknown in the literature. In this method, value of output and inputs are separately deflated, the difference between the former and the latter then giving the value added at constant prices. This method cannot be used, because of the non-availability of wholesale indices for all commodities entering as inputs or output. This study has used the 'single deflation method' - an approximation of double deflation technique assuming that the prices of outputs and intermediate inputs move together. The formula for this technique is written as

$$V_{it}^k = \frac{\left(y_i^c - m_i^c\right)}{y_i^c \Big/ y_i^{87}} \tag{5.2}$$

where y_i^c is the current gross value of output and m_i^c is the current value of inputs of the ith enterprise. $y_i^c \Big/ y_i^{87}$ is the price index of particular output of ith enterprise based 1987 prices and V_{it}^k is the constant figure of value added.

Capital (K)

Capital is one of the essential inputs in measuring productivity. Accurate measurement of the capital input is needed to explain productivity variations across firms as well as the changes in the structure of industry. Measurement of capital input is difficult, and in some ways contentious, because stock accumulates over a period of time and is valued at different stages of the life-cycle. Three items are required for measuring capital input: (i) bench-mark capital stocks, (ii) correct measurement of life of capital, and (iii) measurement of depreciation. Given these problems, various methodologies were developed in the literature to estimate capital stock, but all these measures provide estimates, which are second best type solutions and estimates have to be viewed with certain reservations.[8]

Gross fixed assets are used in this study as capital inputs. These are the aggregate book values of land, buildings, machinery, tools, transport and office equipment, etc. The CMI provides a gross book value of fixed assets net of depreciation allowances, and Balancing, Modernization, Rehabilitation & Expansion (BMRE) expenditure figures.[9] BMRE includes new machinery and equipment, building construction and development, and land improvement, etc. Taking BMRE expenditure figures as new investment and adding these figures to the year-end value of fixed assets yields the gross value of capital. This accountant's practice of measuring fixed assets net of depreciation is flawed, irrespective of which depreciation formula is applied. Accountants' depreciation rates do not necessarily accurately reflect the loss of efficiency of assets to which they pertain. However, the use of gross figures can be justified in the context of developing countries, such as Bangladesh, on the grounds that capital stocks are more often used at approximately constant levels of efficiency for a period far beyond the accounting life measured by normal depreciation until eventually discarded or sold for scrap. Thus, even though the value of the old machinery declines, it need not lead to a decline in the current services of the capital outfit. Capital figures have deflated by the wholesale price indices for non-electricity machinery and equipment to yield capital stock at the 1987 prices.

Labour (L)

In productivity analysis, the measurement of labour inputs poses both conceptual and empirical difficulties because of the heterogeneity of the labour input to production. For example, labour inputs vary according to quality; type of work; hours worked and above all, age and sex, across firms (or industry) and even within firms (or industry). However, in the CMI, the labour input is measured by the number of employees directly or indirectly engaged in production. It covers all workers, including administration, technical, clerical, sales and purchase staff, so that all production and non-production workers, except temporary daily casuals and unpaid family workers, are included in the analysis.

The number of man-hours worked is a better measure than the number of employees. Denison (1961) found better results using man-hours worked as an argument in the production function. However, it can be argued that employment is a more reliable measure than hours worked.

Hours worked is more erratic because the observations can be greatly affected by holidays, strikes, etc. occurring in the reference period. Therefore, aggregating the number of hours worked is affected by the lack of a standard unit of measurement, since one man-hour may differ from another, and aggregating all employees does not allow for differences in skill levels and experience, as well as number of hours worked. Because of all that, hours worked is subject to sampling error (Aspden 1990). Denison (1961) prefers employment data in terms of efficiency units. The United Nations (1968) acknowledges that, although the measure of labour inputs in terms of hours worked is a preferred measure, it is probably feasible to use data in respect of numbers of workers only. However, using the number of workers (including self-employees) as a measure of labour input to production, if temporary and daily-basis workers are included, would overstate labour input to production.

Labour input data, either in terms of man-hours worked or efficiency units, are not available in the CMI, the number of employees has been used for this analysis.[10] However, the varying coefficient approach followed in this study implies variations in the contribution of different inputs including labour across firms, and over time, for a firm. Employment data provide some kind of correction for any shortening of working hours. Moreover, the use of the total number employed as the measure of labour inputs implies that production and non-production workers are perfect substitutes. This is not a valid assumption.

Several other variables such as capital intensity, market structure variable (concentration ratio), effective rate of assistance, openness, etc. are constructed in Chapter 7 for the second stage analysis.

Limitations of CMI Data

There is general agreement among international agencies, academics and researchers alike that the CMI data suffer from problems such as under-coverage, under-reporting or misreporting, and measurement errors. Under-coverage is perhaps due to the complex questionnaire, non-cooperative attitudes by firms' managers or owners and the poor monitoring systems used by the BBS. However, under-coverage is not a problem in this study since it deals with sample firms of CMI reported firms of selected industries.

Under-reporting or mis-reporting of variables like gross value of output, material use, and other financial variables occurs mainly because of producers' desire for tax avoidance and their unwillingness to share information with governmental agencies because of fears that the data could be used for punitive purposes or be disclosed to competitors. Mis-reporting and measurement errors of data can clearly cause problems in empirical studies. The BBS introduced scientific devices and techniques in recent years to lessen these problems. Moreover, the BBS makes some adjustments to data for partially reported and non-reported cases. However, the data may still not be error free. In line with Griliches and Ringstad (1971) it is therefore, recognized that errors of measurement of data plague almost all empirical studies. However, compared to other methods for measuring productivity performance, the stochastic frontier production function approach used in this study makes allowance for random errors in data measurement (Barton and Caves 1990).

Results and Interpretation

Parameter Estimates

The iterated GLS estimates of Equation 5.1 for each industry group are given in Tables 5.3. to 5.5. Recalling Equation 4.3 in Chapter 4, the moments of coefficients, rather than the coefficients themselves, are fixed parameters, i.e. $\overline{\beta}_j$'s are constant across firms in an industry but β_j's are not. The approximate Aitken estimates of means of these coefficients and their asymptotic standard errors for three industry groups, textiles and ready-made garments, food processing and chemicals for three intertemporal periods (1981, 1987 and 1991) are given in column 4 of Tables 5.3. to 5.5. The year 1981 is in the pre-reform period, 1987 is in the transition period and 1991 is in the post-reform period (the most recent year for which data are available). The range of actual response coefficients and frontier coefficients are also presented in these tables. These parameters help in estimating firm-specific capacity realization and other components of output and productivity growth. Empirical estimates facilitate comparisons of enterprise productivity performance among these periods.

Table 5.3: Range of Actual Response and Mean Response Coefficients of Inputs and the Frontier Coefficients of Production Function for Textiles and Garments

Year	Input	Range of Actual Response Coefficients	Mean Response Coefficients	Coefficients of Production Frontier
		Cotton textiles		
	Constant	0.7547-0.8726	0.8642 (0.1529)	0.8726
1981	Capital	0.5516-0.6248	0.5703 (0.0224)	0.6248
	Labour	0.4220-0.4593	0.4352 (0.0226)	0.4593
	Constant	0.3513-0.3637	0.3533 (0.1353)	0.3637
1987	Capital	0.2737-0.3285	0.2911 (0.0280)	0.3285
	Labour	0.4771-0.5183	0.4939 (0.0293)	0.5183
	Constant	0.1655-0.2183	0.1805 (0.0731)	0.2183
1991	Capital	0.4237-0.4888	0.4604 (0.0138)	0.4888
	Labour	0.4258-0.5524	0.4430 (0.0145)	0.5524
		Jute Textiles		
	Constant	0.1942-0.2157	0.1987 (0.3193)	0.2157
1981	Capital	0.5421-0.5889	0.5455 (0.0496)	0.5889
	Labour	0.3399-0.3705	0.3405 (0.0468)	0.3705
	Constant	0.1043-0.2123	0.1056 (0.0402)	0.2123
1987	Capital	0.6561-0.7150	0.6628 (0.0558)	0.7150
	Labour	0.2977-0.3200	0.2978 (0.0493)	0.3200
	Constant	0.6715-0.7200	0.6783 (0.1292)	0.7200
1991	Capital	0.6997-0.7286	0.7000 (0.0197)	0.7286
	Labour	0.2777-0.3078	0.2778 (0.0163)	0.3078

Table 5.3 Continue to the next page

Continuation of Table 5.3

Ready-made Garments

Year	Input	Range of Actual Response Coefficients	Mean Response Coefficients	Coefficients of Production Frontier
	Constant	0.1121-0.1259	0.1257 (0.0274)	0.1259
1987	Capital	0.3671-0.3921	0.3709 (0.049	0.3921
	Labour	0.5578-0.5798	0.5648 (0.0414)	0.5798
	Constant	0.1289-0.1332	0.1244 (0.1571)	0.1332
1991	Capital	0.2871-0.3285	0.3024 (0.0261)	0.3285
	Labour	0.6309-0.6441	0.6339 (0.0214)	0.6441

Note: Figures in parentheses are standard errors of estimates. Note: Calculated from the Census of manufacturing Industries (CMI), BBS.

The ranges of the actual response coefficients presented in Tables 5.3 to 5.5 are quite substantial because of the large variation in the error component. This suggests the presence of randomness in the response coefficients. From this randomness among the actual response coefficients, the important information emerges that there are variations in the methods of application of production inputs across the sample firms. In other words, the combined effects of organizational and institutional factors force firms to follow different methods of application of inputs which results in contributions of inputs to output that differ from firm to firm. Consequently, firm performance measures (say, capacity realization or TFP growth) which are based on frontiers derived from firm-specific constant slope, but varying intercept production functions, necessarily lead to misleading results, because such models fail to take into account individual input responses that are created by the method of application of inputs to output while modeling firm performance.

From Tables 5.3, 5.4 and 5.5, it is evident that all mean response coefficients for the three selected industries are significant at the 5 per cent level. These estimates show that the average contribution of capital to value added has been increasing, while that of labour has been decreasing from 1981 to 1991 in jute textiles, food processing and chemicals industries. The opposite results are found in garment industries from 1987 to 1991 (Table 5.3). The recent origin, private ownership and export-oriented nature of this industry may be responsible for this outcome. In cotton textiles industry, the contribution of capital increased while that of labour remained stagnant from the pre-reform to post-reform period.

Table 5.4: Range of Actual Response and Mean Response Coefficients of Inputs and the Frontier Coefficients of Production Function for Food Processing

Year	Input	Range of Actual Response Coefficients	Mean Response Coefficients	Coefficients of Production Frontier
	Constant	0.7227-0.8447	0.8377 (0.0828)	0.8447
1981	Capital	0.5974-0.6359	0.5746 (0.0189)	0.6359
	Labour	0.4224-0.4774	0.4418 (0.0243)	0.4774
	Constant	0.8273-0.8851	0.8804 (0.0876)	0.8851
1987	Capital	0.6284-0.6635	0.6311 (0.0190)	0.6635
	Labour	0.3369-0.4003	0.3555 (0.0241)	0.4003
	Constant	0.5069-0.5815	0.5768 (0.0507)	0.5815
1991	Capital	0.7364-0.7580	0.7464 (0.0111)	0.7580
	Labour	0.1542-0.2526	0.1589 (0.0145)	0.2526

Note: Figures in parentheses are standard errors of estimates. See, note of Table 5.3.

The results also indicate that the contribution from among the best applications of capital to value added has increased while that of labour has decreased in all selected industries except in garment industry from the pre-reform to the post-reform period. The estimates of frontier coefficients, presented in the last column of Tables 5.3 to 5.5 indicate the maximum possible contribution of inputs to output when firms are following best practice method of application of inputs without the constraints imposed by the adverse effects of institutional and organizational factors. In other words, these are the production response coefficients when reform measures have been effective in eliminating the adverse effects of institutional and organizational factors on production.

The reduction in the contribution of labour to value added in the post-reform period could be due to the following reasons that are strongly afflicting the labour market in Bangladesh: (1) there has been a centralized wage setting system which is often not linked to labour productivity; (2) when industries were privatized, they were not allowed to retrench the redundant labour force immediately,

Table 5.5: Range of Actual Response and Mean Response Coefficients of Inputs and the Frontier Coefficients of Production Function for Chemicals Industries

Year	Input	Range of Actual Response Coefficients	Mean Response Coefficients	Coefficients of Production Frontier
	Constant	0.9141-0.9956	0.9150 (0.1651)	0.9956
1981	Capital	0.5948-0.6349	0.6021 (0.0325)	0.6349
	Labour	0.4354-0.4562	0.4380 (0.0377)	0.4562
	Constant	0.1156-0.1263	0.1260 (0.0788)	0.1263
1987	Capital	0.5635-0.5811	0.5687 (0.0148)	0.5811
	Labour	0.4584-0.4824	0.4674 (0.017)	0.4824
	Constant	0.1348-0.1382	0.1379 (0.0359)	0.1382
1991	Capital	0.6024-0.6385	0.6116 (0.0713)	0.6385
	Labour	0.3346-0.3641	0.3496 (0.0908)	0.3641

Note: Figures in the parentheses are standard errors of estimates. See also note of Table 5.3

which means that even if the privatized industries introduced new technologies, they would not be able to apply the best method of application of labour force required by the technology; (3) when the redundant labour force is retrenched, it involves high costs due to the existing labour regulations, and (4) the trade unions have been powerful with significant lobbying power with the government which means any reform measures involving labour will not be effective. This necessitates further research on the labour market to suggest appropriate policy measures which are needed to improve the contribution of labour to value added in industries.

Measurement of Capacity Realization

As discussed in Chapter 3, Productive Capacity Realization (PCR) is an important aspect of productivity performance that has received little attention in measuring the productivity growth of economic agents. The reason for this is that traditional theory of firm assumed away capacity underutilization, or any form of inefficiency in production. This assumption is unrealistic, because, as was shown in Chapter 3, in the absence of PCR, estimates of productivity growth are biased.

Measurement of capacity realization becomes important in analyzing the impact of policy changes on the productivity performance of firms. This is particularly important in measuring the productivity performance of manufacturing firms in a developing country such as Bangladesh, where previous policy regimes encouraged firms to hold substantial unrealized productive capacity. This sub-section empirically estimates PCR indices at the firm level for the three selected important Bangladesh manufacturing industries using the framework developed in the previous chapter.

Recalling Equation (4.18) from Chapter 4:

$$PCR_i = \frac{y_i}{exp(lny_i^*)} \tag{5.3}$$

where y_i and y_i^* represent actual realized and maximum possible output (in logarithms) of the *i*th production unit from the given set of inputs and production technology.

As mentioned in Chapter 3, accuracy of the measurement of PCR depends on how accurately the maximum possible output is estimated. This study estimates the maximum possible output by using the random coefficient production frontier as specified in Equation (5.1). This approach has three important advantages: First, it takes into account the differences in individual input responses to output, regardless of the amount of input applied in the production, unlike the conventional fixed slope and varying intercept production function. Second, it offers estimates of the maximum possible output on the basis of a non-neutral shift of production function. Third, it incorporates the combined effects of non-price factors and institutional changes in measuring the maximum possible output. Therefore, this approach provides PCR estimates which are consistent with economic theory and practice. Consequently, such estimates of productive capacity realization yield useful information about the concerned industry for both analytical purposes and for designing valid policy measures.

Following the iterated GLS procedures, the computer program *TERAN* estimates the maximum possible output, and solving Equation (5.3), gives PCR estimates. PCR indexes are estimated at the firm level for the three selected industries. Industry-wise estimates are presented in Tables 5.6 to 5.8 but firm-specific PCR indexes are not presented here due to lack of space. Interested readers can obtain from the author.

Table 5.6 shows that the average rate of PCR increased in all three sub-sectors in the textile and garment industry group from the pre-reform to post reform period. In the cotton textile industry, the rate of PCR varied from as low as 28 per cent to 91 per cent in 1981. It appears that most of the enterprises recorded low rates as the average rate of PCR was only 56 per cent. In the post reform period, the distribution of PCR rates improved, the lowest margin was 34 per cent and the highest rate achieved a maximum of 100 per cent.

However, the average rate of PCR of this industry increased by only 7 percentage points, from 56 per cent in 1981 to 63 per cent in 1991. This suggests that a large number of firms are still realizing production capacity below the industry's average rate. The low rate of capacity realization could be due to inadequate infrastructural and other operating constraints such as uncertainties of power supply, raw materials shortages, and inadequate working capital. Another reason could be the distortions due to protective policy regimes that still exist in this sector.

The mean rate of PCR for the jute textile industry showed little change from 1981 to 1991. Indeed, it declined from 47 per cent in 1981 to about 45 per cent in 1987 but improved slightly to 52 per cent in 1991 (Table 5.6). Weak domestic and international demand and the constraints of raw material supply have been partly responsible for the poor performance of enterprises in this industry. Moreover, the majority of firms of these industries are with the public sector corporations and facing unduly 'soft' financial constraints. Since firms' managers are not financially accountable, they avoid risks and have weak interest to realize full production capacity. The behaviour of enterprises has not been changed greatly, even after the economic reforms, because the authorities still control individual enterprises in various ways. Asian Development Bank (1987) showed that capacity utilization rate in most public sector firms varied from 40 to 73 per cent in 1984-85.

The average rate of PCR in the export-oriented garment industry was impressively high at around 74 per cent in 1987 and improved to around 81 per cent in 1991. The majority of units of this industry operated relatively close to the frontier as the realization rate ranged from 67 to full capacity. This could be the result of 'open market' policy and various promotional measures adopted by government, together with small size and private ownership. Although the above findings are not directly comparable to those of earlier studies, they give some indications about the past performance of enterprises.

Table 5.6: Rate of Productive Capacity Realization[1] in Textiles and Garments Industries, (selected years) (percent)

Industries	1981			1987			1991		
	Min.	Max.	Mean	Min.	Max.	Mean	Min.	Max.	Mean
Cotton Textiles (3211)	28.091	91.000	56.111	34.850	100.00	59.350	31.950	100.00	63.328
Jute Textiles (3213)	33.980	66.761	47.332	27.480	67.642	44.579	37.052	66.721	52.241
Ready Made Garments	....	....	....	53.681	100.00	73.617	67.150	100.00	80.649

Source: Calculated from CMI and BGMEA data (Master Tape, Current Production). Note: Numbers in the parentheses are industrial code from the 'Bangladesh Standard Industrial Classification' (BSIC).

[1] The computer program gives firm-specific PCR. Mean levels of PCR in different industries were calculated from firm-specific estimates of all firms in a particular industry and minimum rate is the lowest rate achieved by a firm in that industry and likewise, the maximum rate is the highest rate achieved by a firm of the industry.

Using a 'time based' approach, Afroz and Roy (1975) found average rates of capacity utilization of about 40 per cent (Sacking) and 35 per cent (Hessian) in the jute textile industry in 1972/73. In contrast, using the 'shift method', they found utilization rates of 76 per cent for Sacking and 61 per cent for Hessian in the same year.

Using capacity realization as the ratio of actual items of garments produced to capacity available, Department of Textiles (DOT) (1990) estimated utilization rates for the aggregate garment industry for the period 1977/78 to 1988/89. It showed that although utilization rates varied from 39 per cent to 61 per cent during this period, the rates steadily increased from 1977/78 to 1985/86 and then declined, swung upwards again from 1987/88 onward. It demonstrated that the decline of utilization rates in 1986/87 was due to the quota restrictions by the U.S. on garment imports from Bangladesh. On average, 46 per cent of production capacity of this sub-sector has been underutilized over the period 1977/78 to 1988/89. DOT argued that unplanned expansion of capacity in the previous years led to this underutilization.[11]

Defining capacity utilization as the ratio of actual output to installed capacity (output) at the enterprise level, Abdullah and Rahman (1989) showed that the rate of capacity utilization in textiles industries in Bangladesh has been low, ranged from an average rate of 30 per cent to 52 per cent from 1963 to 1982. They also argued that excess capacity in this sector was due to the adoption of import substitution industrial policies and overvalued currency during past decades. This put a premium on building capacity, rather than on using it efficiently. The premium was heightened by the opportunity for transferring funds through over invoicing imports.

Using a similar method and enterprise level survey data for 1992, the most recent study by Bhattachayria (1994) found average rates of capacity utilization of 69 per cent for cotton textiles, 65 per cent for jute textile and 82 per cent for the ready-made garment industry. Although all the above results conform with those presented in Table 5.6, the methodologies used in the earlier studies are weak and questionable (Appendix to Chapter 3).

Table 5.7 reveals considerable variation in capacity realization across firms in food manufacturing industries. In terms of average rate of capacity realization, hydrogenated vegetable oils was the most efficient with a 91 per cent mean and a full capacity realization for the most efficient firm in 1981. This was followed by edible oils, with a mean of about 78 per cent, tea and coffee blending at 67 per cent, and grain milling at about 62 per cent productive capacity in the same year. Fish and seafood, rice milling, bakery products, sugar factories and tea and coffee processing were relatively inefficient with mean PCR levels below the industry's average of about 51 per cent.

Table 5.7: Rate of Productive Capacity Realization[1] in Food Processing Industries, (selected years) (percent)

Industries	1981			1987			1991		
	Min.	Max.	Mean	Min.	Max.	Mean	Min.	Max.	Mean
Dairy products (3112)	48.071	86.223	61.240	51.730	88.524	61.504	62.970	83.423	72.655
Fish and sea foods (3114)	40.692	52.835	46.912	51.191	63.522	57.678	58.412	69.490	77.745
Hydrogenated veg. oils (3115)	84.069	100.00	91.075	85.078	100.00	90.929	78.729	86.055	81.411
Edible oil (3116)	57.138	88.346	78.145	52.177	90.422	76.903	61.915	100.00	82.122
Grain milling (3118)	46.257	78.969	62.186	52.415	78.833	65.705	62.574	80.579	72.293
Rice milling (3119)	44.049	75.527	59.563	35.084	85.419	56.446	46.201	81.441	62.032
Bakery products (3122)	37.582	64.105	49.747	39.895	80.797	54.569	42.079	86.260	56.429
Sugar factories (3123)	30.311	47.486	38.527	30.109	48.721	37.690	32.944	62.298	45.473
Tea and coffee processing	30.555	85.970	45.542	38.278	79.586	48.034	39.975	88.629	53.973
Tea and coffee blending	50.751	84.062	67.406	55.436	77.210	66.323	66.654	79.905	73.279
Total	30.311	100.00	51.318	30.109	100.00	53.284	32.944	100.00	58.787

Source: See Table 5.5.

[1] The computer program gives firm-specific PCR. Mean levels of PCR in different industries were calculated from firm-specific estimates of all firms in a particular industry and minimum rate is the lowest rate achieved by a firm in that industry and likewise, the maximum rate is the highest rate achieved by a firm of the industry.

Industries within the food processing industry group achieved almost similar rates of average capacity realization in the transition period (1987). The mean rate increased dramatically in the fish and sea food sector, perhaps due to its export-orientation and to the sharp increase in foreign demand for processed fish products in this period (see section 5.2 above).

In the post reform period, the edible oil industry became the most efficient, with the highest mean capacity realization of about 81 per cent. It may be argued that firms in this industry were producing closest to their production frontiers as the minimum PCR was 61 per cent. The hydrogenated vegetable oil, fish and seafood and dairy products were also well-performed. Other industries achieved moderate rates of capacity realization, but bakery products, sugar products and tea and coffee processing performed poorly by realizing PCR below the industry's mean of 58 per cent. Changes in mean capacity realization rates in the food processing industry over the three periods suggest that enterprises in different sectors within the industry gained only moderate increases in efficiency in the post reform period with increases of only 7 percentage points, from 51 per cent in 1981 to 58 per cent in 1991. Substantial unrealized productive capacity clearly still exists in most types of enterprise in the food processing industry. The lowest rate of capacity realization within this industry increased by only 2 percentage points, indicating that many enterprises of different sectors within the industry still produce far away from their frontier realizing productive capacity around the marginal rate.

On average, capacity realization increased most sharply in the fish and seafood industry by 31 percentage points, from a low mean of 47 per cent in 1981 to 78 per cent in 1991. The reason for this sharp rise may be attributed to the outward orientation of this industry and the need for competitiveness send all firms in this sector are totally export-oriented. The remaining industries showed little or no improvement and still performed poorly in post reform 1991. Of these, the sugar industry was the worst. This may be because: (i) all sugar factories belong to the public sector; and it is generally believed that managers of public enterprises are reluctant to utilize capacity full for organizational reasons, (ii) the long gestation period and the seasonality of sugar factories which prevents them from achieving full capacity realization.

These results for the food processing industry group do not conform with those of the earlier studies. A pioneering study of the food processing sector by a Bangladesh-Canada Agriculture Sector Team (B-C AST) (1991) using conventional methodology with firm level data for 1987, found mean capacity realization rates of 52 per cent for bakery products, 34 per cent for

Table 5.8: Rate of Productive Capacity Realization[1] in Chemical Industries, (selected years) (percent)

Industries	1981			1987			1991		
	Min.	Max.	Mean	Min.	Max.	Mean	Min.	Max.	Mean
Drugs & Pharmaceuticals	63.841	74.890	68.821	58.151	71.390	65.431	54.712	71.010	61.692
Fertilizers Manufacturing	46.201	75.140	66.862	56.850	81.531	71.590	59.420	73.941	67.621
Industrial Chemicals (3529)	52.570	69.381	61.330	59.520	78.872	69.382	62.470	77.440	72.042
Paints & Varnishes (3531)	58.672	87.890	73.532	56.703	73.110	64.710	54.720	88.081	70.091
Perfumes & Cosmetics	47.700	92.203	73.831	52.981	95.480	75.082	52.541	93.340	75.880
Soap and Detergent (3533)	52.013	100.00	70.920	55.620	100.00	77.650	50.700	100.00	78.460
Matches Manufacturing	39.730	96.052	60.742	54.800	84.402	68.241	52.712	86.932	66.561
Petroleum Products (3552)	46.201	83.640	67.210	56.281	82.520	72.170	55.770	82.820	69.930
Total	39.730	100.00	68.058	52.981	100.00	71.817	50.700	100.00	71.921

Source: See Table 5.6.

[1] The computer program gives firm-specific PCR. Mean levels of PCR in different industries were calculated from firm-specific estimates of all firms in a particular industry and minimum rate is the lowest rate achieved by a firm in that industry and like wise the maximum rate.

fish and seafood, 16 per cent for rice milling, 43 per cent for hydrogenated vegetables oil, and 56 per cent for sugar factories. A study conducted by the International Labour Organization (ILO) (1991) using factory level survey data for food processing industries for 1989, found that 70 per cent of its sample enterprises operated at less than 50 per cent of their production capacity, another 20 per cent operated at 51-60 per cent capacity, and only 10 per cent of the sample enterprises realized 61-80 per cent of their production capacity. It also showed many reasons, including management inefficiency, inadequate supply of raw materials, low labour productivity and political instability are responsible for low rate of capacity realization.

Using the traditional shift measure, Bhattacharya (1994) found a high average rate of 71 per cent of capacity realization in the food processing industry in 1992. The above findings do not conform with those of this study for the following reasons: (i) Bhattacharya used only firm level survey data on private sector firms for 1992; (ii) he used the conventional 'shift measure', (iii) all state-owned large firms were excluded from his analysis so a high mean capacity realization rate was more likely.

In 1981, the chemical industry group realized a mean PCR of 68 per cent (Table 5.8). There was a narrow range of mean realization rates among different industries within this group (61 to 74 per cent). However, there was considerably greater dispersion among enterprises within each industry. Broadly similar results were found in 1987 and 1991, and most strikingly, there was little improvement in the mean rates of capacity realization for the industry as a whole and among individual industries over time. The increase in mean capacity realization for the industry as a whole was only 4 percentage points, from 68 per cent in 1981 to 72 per cent in 1987. It remained unchanged in 1991, implying that economic policy reform had brought no benefits to this industry in terms of higher production capacity achievement.

The above findings highlight the substantial unrealized production capacity within industry groups in Bangladesh. The explanation may be that most of the large enterprises in different sectors are still within the public sector and enjoy a seller's market. In this market, enterprises increase productive capacity as much as possible in order to earn extra rents by obtaining scarce foreign exchange and concessionary imports but in the absence of competition huge production capacity remains unrealized. Also, there is no 'exit threat' or bankruptcy law for such enterprises. In fact, as argued by Khan and Hossain (1989) and Ahmad (1993), financial constraints of industrial enterprises' are 'soft'. The production environment encourages them to produce output by using inputs lavishly. Consequently, enterprise managers have little incentive to use inputs effectively in the production process to increase productivity and are reluctant to respond to price signals.[12] Both phenomena lead to underutilization of existing production capacity.

Another factor is the considerable and persistent variation in realization rates across enterprises within industries in each industry group. Size and age of the firms, the nature of trade orientation, and capital intensity are likely to be determinants for variation in realization rates. The next chapter will address this issue.

One of the main objectives of recent economic reform was to increase the efficiency of resource use with currently available technologies. The empirical estimates show that most firms in individual manufacturing industries have not only failed to realize maximum production capacity after the implementation of economic reform, but are still producing well inside the frontier. In the light of these findings and in the context of chosen reform policy and further reform measures, the proportion of enterprise TFP or output growth that is contributed by increases in capacity realization rate is a vital issue that needs to be addressed. The following chapter will address this issue.

Conclusion

This chapter presented structure and performance of three main industry groups of Bangladesh, namely, textiles and garments, food processing and chemicals. These are the three largest industry groups in terms of contribution to output, value added, employment and foreign exchange earnings. It also discussed data sources and construction of variables used in empirical estimation of productive capacity realization of manufacturing firms of these selected industries. There are a number of sources of manufacturing data in Bangladesh. Since data from the most of the sources cannot be used for comprehensive analysis this study found CMI data are useful for empirical measurement. Several variables are constructed using the most up to date concept and formulae from the literature for empirical calculation. It has also highlighted that the nobility of the developed framework is to make allowance for random errors in data measurement.

Using the principle of random varying coefficient model developed by Hildreth-Houck and popularized by Swamy, firm-specific productive capacity realization indexes have been estimated for both pre-reform and post-reform periods. The results suggest, though improvement occurred in realization of productive capacities after the implementation of economic reforms, there is, however, sufficient room for further improvement in increasing output by realizing the unrealized capacity through appropriate reform measures.

Appendix

Table A5.1: LM Test for Parameter Variation

Industries	1981 $\chi^2_{(k-1)}$ value	1987 $\chi^2_{(k-1)}$ value	1991 $\chi^2_{(k-1)}$ value
Cotton textiles	18.03	23.18	22.01
Jute textiles	17.95	27.05	19.12
Ready-made garment	43.65	32.82	36.70
Food processing	46.06	63.24	38.75
Chemicals	24.38	21.28	32.09

Source: Author's calculation.

Notes

[1] Not only has the ready-made garment industry been the engine of Bangladesh's export earnings, but it has also provided a solid underpinning and carried on its shoulders the rest of the manufacturing sector in recent years. Recently, Bakht and Bhattacharya (1995) performed some counter-factual simulations with the Bangladesh Bureau of Statistics' Quantum index of industrial production and found that sub-sectoral index of manufacturing output decreased by 23 per cent when the ready-made garment industry was excluded from the calculations.

[2] Wage levels in labour abundant developing countries like Bangladesh, Pakistan, Sri Lanka, India, Hong Kong, and Korea are respectively 2 per cent, 5 per cent, 5 per cent, 9 per cent, 19 per cent, and 21 per cent of the US wage level in recent years (ILO-ARTEP 1986).

[3] Food processing industries are classified into 19 product groups as outlined in the Industrial Investment Schedule (IIS) published by the government of Bangladesh. Under each product group different types of products are produced. See, for detail list of products ILO (1990, p: 23).

[4] *TERAN* was developed in the Division of Economics, Research School of Pacific and Asian Studies, The Australian National University. The program, written in Fortran 77, can be compiled and run on UNIX and VAX based mainframe computers and on IBM PC/AT with 640K memory using Microsoft FORTRAN V.5 and LAHEY FORTRAN V.5.

[5] The data set (except for garments' industries) for this study is taken from the CMI computer tape. This differs from the published data in that the BBS publishes CMI data at aggregate industry level.

[6] According to a World Bank study (1992), chemical industries are the most capital intensive industry group. Capital intensity measured as the asset-employment ratio is Taka 40 million for chemical industry group compared to Taka 3.9 million for the average in manufacturing sector of Bangladesh. The second most capital intensive industry group is food-beverage-tobacco, with an average asset value Taka 11 million per employee. Capital intensity is low in non-metallic products, textiles, garments and leather industry.

[7] The use of aggregate data in the estimation of TFP growth requires some strong assumptions regarding the homogeneity of production processes within industries and regions. Luger and Evans (1988) demonstrate the bias that the use of those assumptions creates. Therefore, aggregate analyses may be misleading in the policy context.

[8] For example, a perpetual inventory method is widely used to census data including depreciation series, at book value, to estimate capital stock. Since depreciation at book value grossly over estimates the true capital consumption, it produces bias estimates of capital stock.

[9] BMRE figures are given for government firms and such expenditures for the private firms are known as addition and alteration costs.

[10] This is also justified as Kibria and Tisdell (1985) rightly mentioned that the conventional approach of measuring labour services in terms of man-hours is not exactly appropriate in the Bangladesh situation. Since the industrial practice in Bangladesh industries is that, once reporting for duty, a worker is supposed to work the full hours of a shift (8 hours) the possibility of varying hours of a daily work of a labourer being thus eliminated.

[11] The investment approval system (as discussed in Chapter 2) failed to clear guide to potential investors. Moreover, many projects were gotten approved through side payments to the officials without proper scrutiny with regard to their economic viability. As a result, there has been mashroom growth of garment factories in 1980s and thereby unbalanced over capacity was built.

[12] For example, a World Bank study (1995) showed that there are 8000 surplus employees in 16 state owned sugar milling enterprises. Likewise, all other public enterprises are also plagued with over employment. This finding is consistent with Kornai's assertion that the system of 'soft budget constraint' created a permanent excess demand for labour by state owned enterprises because of the underlying incentive structure (Kornai 1979).

6 Sources of Output Growth: Empirical Estimation and Interpretation of Results

Introduction

Common perceptions about the sources of output growth are of increases in inputs, improvements in TFP growth (technological progress), or both. The first is associated with movements along the frontier, and the second with shifts of the production frontier.[1] Actual production usually takes place at the point where marginal cost starts to rise. In such a circumstance, where output growth has to be achieved by inducing firms to apply more inputs, either output prices must rise, or input prices must fall. Thus, increasing inputs as a source of output growth generally requires an increase in relative input-output prices. Such an input-driven growth in output, as discussed in Krugman (1994), has awful implications for the long-run growth of the country. The point is that 'input-driven growth is bound to be limited by diminishing returns'. In other words, an input-driven growth must slow down eventually. Therefore, it cannot be relied upon as an effective method to increase output. This means, increasing TFP growth (innovation-driven) is the most effective way of output growth. TFP growth comprises two components: technological progress and productive capacity realization. Technological progress is often embodied in the improved quality of human and physical capital and returns to innovation of new technology, so that more output becomes available from the same amount of inputs. As discussed in Chapter 3, the importance of productive capacity realization to output growth has been often ignored by the researchers. If some of the constraints on existing capacity realization are eliminated through policy changes, more output will be available with the same amount of inputs from the same technology. Therefore, output growth can be decomposed into components stemming from changes in capacity realization, technological progress and increase in inputs.

The identification of sources of output growth has important policy implications. For a given technology, it may be significant whether the gap between 'best practice' techniques and realized production function is diminishing or widening over time. Changes in productive capacity realization (PCR) can be substantial and may outweigh gains from technological progress. It is, therefore, important to know how far away a production unit is from the frontier at any point in time, and how quickly a production unit can 'catch up' to reach the frontier. It is also important to know how much a firm's frontier shifts, at its observed input mix, for policy formulation. For instance, for a developing country like Bangladesh which borrows technology from abroad, any failure to acquire and adapt new technology will be reflected by the lack of a frontier shift over time. Consequently, the movement of the frontier over time reflects the success of explicit policies to facilitate the acquisition of foreign technology. Similarly, changes in PCR over time, and across individual firms, indicate the level of success of a number of important dimensions of industrial policies.

This chapter empirically investigates the sources of output growth of some selected industries in Bangladesh. These industries are textiles and ready-made garments, food processing and chemicals. The framework developed in Chapter 4 following, the arguments of Callan (1986) and Kalirajan *et al* (1996), output growth is decomposed into changes in capacity realization, technological progress and increases in inputs. Section 6.2 of this chapter presents empirical estimation of sources of growth and interpretation of results. Comparisons of these estimates with those of other developing countries are given in section 6.3, followed by decomposition of TFP growth of selected industries. Biases of technological progress are analyzed in section 6.4, followed by summary and conclusion of the chapter.

Sources of Growth Analysis

As discussed above, output growth in any production unit depends not only on factor accumulation and their allocation among various production units but also on total factor productivity growth. In production economics literature, TFP growth is considered to be the significant driving force in output growth of production units. In this section, the analysis focuses on measurement of sources of output growth in the three largest industry groups (textiles and ready-made garments, food processing and chemicals industries) to determine the contribution of each source to output growth.

Recalling Equation (4.22) from Chapter 4:

$$y_{2i,t} - y_{1i,t-1} = \Delta\text{TFP} + \dot{y}_x \qquad (6.1)$$

where $\Delta\text{TFP}= \left[\left\{\left(y_{1i,t-1}^{*}-y_{1i,t-1}\right)-\left(y_{2i,t}^{*}-y_{2i,t}\right)\right\}+\left(y_{1i,t}^{*}-y_{1i,t-1}^{*}\right)\right]$ and $\dot{y}_{x}$ represents input growth estimated residually. $y_{2i,t}$ and $y_{1i,t-1}$ represent realized output (in logarithm, value added in this study) of ith production units for tth and t-$1st$ periods, and $y_{2i,t}^{*}$ and $y_{1i,t-1}^{*}$ are maximum possible outputs obtained from given inputs by the same production agents in the tth and t-$1st$ periods. y_{1}^{*} and y_{2}^{*} are estimated by using the specified random coefficient model 5.1 of the previous chapter applying the iterated GLS procedures. Using these estimated maximum possible outputs, TFP growth is computed by using the above equation, and input growth is then computed as a residual, unlike the conventional approach where TFP growth is not estimated but is obtained as the residual. The main advantage of obtaining the input growth component as a residual is the avoidance of problems usually encountered such as the omission of important inputs and adjustments for input quality changes.

Following Equation (6.1), the sources of output growth were computed at the firm level for the selected industry groups. Industry wise average estimates are presented in Tables 6.1 to 6.3 while firm-specific results are given here due to space limitation but can be obtained from the author upon request.

Table 6.1 shows the pattern and sources of output growth in textiles and garment industries during 1981-87 and 1987-91 periods. Two conventional sources of output growth are included corresponding to Equation (6.1). Jute textiles experienced relatively faster output (value added) growth than cotton textiles during both periods. Value added growth declined for jute textiles, from 1981-87 to 1987-91. TFP growth increased marginally in this sector but input growth was substantially lower in this period. In cotton textiles, output growth was substantial in both periods. Input growth was dominant during 1981-1987 but TFP growth was substantial during 1987-1991. In the earlier period, jute goods were the country's leading export item. It could be argued that jute industries had to face international competition which induced TFP growth in these industries but this may not be a strong argument, since Bangladesh is the single largest jute exporter in the international market. Competition was not as high as in the case of other manufacturing items. Consequently, TFP growth in jute textiles was marginally higher than in cotton textiles during 1981-87 (Table 6.1). The other reason, as argued by Mondal and Ahmad (1984), is that the technology used in the cotton textiles industry was much older than that of the jute textile industry.

Table 6.1 also reveals that output growth in both the cotton and jute textile industries occurred mainly due to input growth. In the latter period, although input growth declined in both industries due to reforms, it still contributed a greater proportion to output growth. These two industries were, and still are, dominated by public sector enterprises, so that they faced unduly 'soft budget' constraints (Khan and Hossain 1989). According to Kornai (1986) and Goldfled and Quandt (1988, 1990), firms under 'soft budget' constraints use more productive resources than they otherwise would. In such cases, incentives are lacking to improve productivity.[2] Industries in centrally planned economies, as well as industries with public sector corporations in developing countries (such as these industries in Bangladesh), commonly face this problem.

Table 6.1: Annual Average Output Growth Rates of Textiles and Garments Industries by Sources, 1981-91 (percentage)

Industries	1981-87			1987-91		
	Output Growth	TFP Growth	Input Growth	Output Growth	TFP Growth	Input Growth
Cotton Textiles	2.600	0.458	2.142	2.761	1.016	1.745
Jute Textiles	3.790	0.748	3.042	2.859	0.880	1.979
Ready M. Garments	....	....	....	2.708	0.916	1.791

Source: Calculated from CMI and BGMEA data (Master Tape, Current Production).

Note: Industrial codes and numbers of firms used here are the same as in the previous chapter. Figures represent industry wise annual average growth rates.

The annual average growth rate of output (value added) in the ready-made garment industry was 2.7 per cent during 1987-91. Despite being Bangladesh's highest export earner, this industry experienced lower output and TFP growth than the other sub-sectors in the textile and ready-made garment industry group. As discussed earlier, the ready-made garment industry relies heavily on the use of imported fabrics, with about 95 per cent of demand for textile items met by imports (Islam *et al* 1993). As a result of the high import content, the scope for increasing the growth of value added and TFP are limited. One very recent study, conducted by Centre for Policy Dialogue (1995), showed that net earnings, or value added, is only 30 per cent or less, in this industry.

Detailed estimates of sources of output growth for ten sectors of the food processing industry group for the periods 1981-87 and 1987-91 are presented in Table 6.2. There were considerable variations of performance among the sectors within this industry group. Dairy products, fish and sea foods, and tea and coffee processing and blending were well-performed sectors, in terms of output and TFP growth, in both periods.

Table 6.2: Annual Average Output Growth Rates of Food Processing Industries by Sources, 1981-91 (percentage)

Industries	1981-87			1987-91		
	Output Growth	TFP Growth	Input Growth	Output Growth	TFP Growth	Input Growth
Dairy products	3.300	1.374	1.926	4.701	1.357	3.004
Fish and sea foods	5.480	3.027	2.453	4.695	2.573	2.122
Hydrogenated veg. oils	2.822	1.073	1.750	3.858	1.084	2.774
Edible oils	2.767	0.688	2.079	0.698	-0.358	1.056
Grain milling	2.485	0.841	1.643	0.783	-0.951	1.734
Rice milling	3.873	1.382	2.491	2.096	0.397	1.698
Bakery products	2.802	1.127	1.675	2.990	0.658	2.332
Sugar factories	2.719	0.127	2.592	2.776	-0.911	3.687
Tea & coffee processing	3.227	1.096	2.131	3.897	1.407	2.489
Tea & coffee blending	4.194	1.618	2.576	4.768	1.689	2.917

Source: Calculated from CMI data (Master Tape, Current Production).

Note: See the note of Table 6.1.

Fish and sea foods experienced the highest rate of growth, of about 5.5 per cent and 4.7 per cent per annum during 1981-87 and 1987-91 periods respectively. This sector is typically composed of small units, with little capital and abundant natural resources supporting the growth of this industry. As mentioned earlier, the production of this sector is geared mainly towards export markets and the opening up of the economy during the 1980s further stimulated its growth. As a result, it recorded the highest total factor productivity growth of 3 per cent per annum during 1981-87 and about 2.5 per cent per annum during 1987-91. Also, this is the only sector where TFP grew faster than input growth in both periods.

Sugar factories are the so-called large-scale industry within this industry group and in the manufacturing sector as well. All enterprises in this industry are publicly owned and are run by the Bangladesh Sugar and Food Industries Corporation (BSFIC). Since these enterprises enjoyed a seller's market (i.e. no competitors in the market), managers or producers have been reluctant to improve productivity. Consequently, sugar factories were the worst performers with TFP growth of only 0.12 per cent per annum during 1981-87 and a negative rate of 0.91 per cent per annum during 1987-91. Other industries that experienced declining TFP growth were edible oils, grain milling, rice milling and bakery products, all of which are domestically oriented traditional industries.

Table 6.3: Annual Average Output Growth Rate of Chemical Industries by Sources, 1981-91 (percentage)

Industries	1981-87			1987-91		
	Output Growth	TFP Growth	Input Growth	Output Growth	TFP Growth	Input Growth
Drugs & Pharmaceuticals	1.745	0.981	0.764	2.938	1.040	1.898
Fertilizer Manufacturing	3.641	1.624	2.016	4.703	2.469	2.234
Industrial Chemicals	3.241	1.831	1.410	3.009	1.653	1.356
Paints & Varnishes	3.013	1.320	1.693	3.050	1.157	1.893
Perfumes & Cosmetics	2.538	1.623	0.916	3.530	1.686	1.844
Soap and Detergent	2.179	0.124	2.055	2.341	0.796	1.546
Matches Manufacturing	2.240	0.395	1.844	2.625	1.159	1.466
Petroleum Products	1.200	0.098	1.102	1.476	0.797	0.679

Source: Calculated from CMI data (Master Tape, Current Production).

Note: See the note of Table 6.1.

Empirical estimates of sources of output growth of eight industries within the chemical industry group are presented in Table 6.3. In terms of output growth, fertilizers, industrial chemicals and paints and varnishes were expanded rapidly within the group during both the 1981-87 and 1987-91 periods. Fertilizer was the highest performer, with an average rate of output growth of 3.6 per cent during 1981-87 and 4.7 per cent during 1987-91. TFP growth increased from 1.6 per cent per annum to 2.5 per cent per annum in the same periods. There are at least three reasons for the rapid growth of this industry: First, as already mentioned, Bangladesh is rich in natural gas, the principal raw material of the fertilizer industry. Second, Bangladesh is an overwhelmingly agricultural country and the demand for fertilizers has been increasing in recent years with government emphasis on food self-sufficiency. Third, foreign collaboration, particularly from Japan in supplying machinery and equipment, and technical personnel has also contributed to the rapid growth of this industry.

Table 6.3 also reveals that, with the exception of industrial chemicals, all industries within this industry group experienced increased output and TFP growth, though marginal in some industries, from early to late 1980s. The reasons include foreign participation, the production of necessary goods (except perfumes and cosmetics), which have heavy domestic demand, and enhanced competition due to liberalization and open-market policies, particularly in trade and industry.

The empirical estimates, presented in Tables 6.1 to 6.3 show that there were considerable variations of performance both in terms of output and TFP growth rates among industries. Output growth varied from 1 to 5 per cent per annum during 1981 to 1987 and from less than 0.7 to 4.7 per cent per annum during 1987 to 1991. Output growth rates declined in five out of twenty-one industries and stagnated in many others from the early to the late 1980s. TFP growth varied from 0.12 to 3 per cent per annum, during the earlier period, and from -0.95 to 2.5 per cent per annum during the latter period. The highest range of TFP growth dropping by 0.5 per cent, and the lowest rate turned negative. These findings imply that there was no dramatic improvement in TFP growth among industries in the selected industry groups.

The above decomposition of output growth into its two major components provide valuable perspectives concerning productivity. Although most industries experienced accelerated output growth from the early to late 1980s, growth rates were not high. Moreover, growth of inputs contributed significantly to output growth in almost all industries, and in many industries input use increased at approximately the same rates as output growth. This occurred because firms were encouraged to inject more resources as a consequence of the incentive structure provided by the government in the 1970s and 1980s, particularly in the trade sectors. TFP growth did contribute substantially to output growth in some industries such as fish and seafoods, drugs and pharmaceuticals, industrial chemicals, and perfumes and cosmetics industries from 1981 to 1987 and fish and seafoods, fertilizer, industrial chemicals and petroleum products during 1987 to 1991. In some other industries, although TFP growth improved from early to late eighties, nonetheless, growth of inputs still remained the major contributor to output growth.

Some Comparative Analysis

In the last three decades or so, numerous studies have measured the relative contributions of factor inputs and factor productivity growth to output growth in the empirical literature on economic growth. International comparison may shed light on the relative performance of Bangladesh industries. In explaining sources of economy wide growth, Chenery *et al* (1986), found that, while for a group of developed countries TFP growth accounted on average for more than 50 per cent of total growth, for developing countries the contribution of TFP growth was only about 31 per cent. Pack (1988), however, has drawn attention to the fact that this was to a large extent due to a much faster (4.3 per cent per annum) growth of factor inputs in the developing economies than in the developed economies (2.7 per cent per annum). Some micro level studies of developing countries' manufacturing sectors have reached similar conclusions. The picture that emerges here for Bangladesh manufacturing is not much different.

Kim and Kwon (1977) showed that, for a considerable part of the period studied (1962-1971), increasing capacity utilization was a major source of TFP growth in Korean manufacturing. Similar results were found by Hondoussa *et al* (1986) for Egyptian manufacturing industries. They argued that a considerable amount of TFP growth was due to the movement of inefficient firms towards the best practice frontier as a result of increasing capacity realization. This was made possible by the greater availability of foreign exchange after the implementation of economic reforms. In contrast to the Egyptian results, Nishimizu and Page (1982) found that, in half of the Yugoslavian socialist state industries they analyzed, there was no change in the best practice frontier over thirteen years (1965-1978), and that in many sectors there was a decline in efficiency relative to best practice. Using data from the 1970s, Tsao (1985) also found similar findings for Singapore manufacturing industries. So, international findings are mixed. Comparisons of findings of this study with those of other studies on similar industries for some developing countries, below provide closer perspectives on comparative performance of Bangladesh.

Because of differences in industrial growth, industrial composition, and policy regimes, precise inter-country comparisons of sources of growth are not possible. A review of findings is nevertheless of some interest. Table 6.4 shows patterns of output growth and percentage shares (contributions) of TFP and input growth to output growth in selected industries of six developing countries including Bangladesh.[3]

Table 6.4 shows considerable variation in output growth for selected industries across countries. In food processing, Sri Lanka was the highest performer with 34 per cent output growth per annum, followed by South Korea with about 19 per cent growth per annum.[4] India was the weakest performer with about 2.7 per cent output growth per annum from 1961 to 1986. Bangladesh recorded marginally higher (0.3 percentage points) growth than India.

Table 6.4: Contributions[a] of TFP Growth and Input Growth to Output Growth (average percentage change per annum) for Selected Countries

Countries

Industries	Bangladesh[b,c] (1981-91)			India[e] (1961-1986)		
	Output Growth	TFP Growth	Input Growth	Output Growth	TFP Growth	Input Growth
Food Processing	3.00	10.70	89.30	2.70	-70.37	170.37
Cotton Textiles	2.62	11.38	88.62	2.00	10.00	90.00
Jute Textiles	2.75	14.18	85.83	0.60	16.67	83.33
Garments[c]	1.86	33.83	66.17	n.a	n.a.	n.a.
Chemicals	3.41	12.48	87.52	8.90	-19.10	119.10

Industries	South Korea[e] (1963-1979)			Sri Lanka[d]* (1981-1988)		
	Output Growth	TFP Growth	Input Growth	Output Growth	TFP Growth	Input Growth
Food Processing	19.00	37.89	62.11	33.92	13.86	86.14
Cotton Textiles	19.20	23.44	76.56	16.97	67.71	32.29
Garments[c]	26.90	34.57	65.43	18.31	56.14	43.86
Chemicals	23.40	5.13	94.87	9.94	95.47	4.53

Industries	Taiwan[d] (1977-1991)			Turkey[d] (1963-1976)		
	Output Growth	TFP Growth	Input Growth	Output Growth	TFP Growth	Input Growth
Food Processing	7.81	14.05	81.95	7.10	-1.27	101.27
Cotton Textiles	7.49	36.85	63.15	10.00	11.40	88.60
Garments[c]	9.77	22.42	77.58	18.70	13.37	86.63
Chemicals	14.15	14.77	85.23	15.20	10.99	89.01

[a] Contribution of each component to output growth is calculated as the rate of growth of each component divided by output growth (e.g. percentage shares). [b] Estimates are averaged over firm level estimates. [c] Wearing apparel, garments and clothing are used here synonymously. This sector includes wearing apparel and footwear in some of these countries. Calculation for garments industries in Bangladesh is for the period of 1987-91. [d] Estimates based on gross output. [e]Estimates based on value added. *Estimates are only for private sector industries.

Sources: Bangladesh: author's calculations; India: Ahluwalia (1991); Sri Lanka: Athukorala (1994) South Korea: Dollar and Sokoloff (1990); Taiwan: Wang (1996); Turkey: Krueger and Tuncer (1982).

Taiwan and Turkey achieved moderate rates of growth of 7.8 and 7.1 per cent per annum respectively. In cotton textiles, South Korea achieved the highest rate of output growth of 19 per cent per annum followed by Sri Lanka with 17 per cent, Turkey with 10 per cent and Taiwan with 7 per cent growth per annum. India and Bangladesh attained only 2 per cent and 2.6 per cent growth per annum respectively. Similar patterns of growth were revealed for other industries.

It is apparent from Table 6.4 that the contributions of TFP and factor inputs differed greatly, but contributions of factor inputs were more important in explaining the variation in output growth in these countries. The contribution of TFP growth to output growth was less than 50 per cent for all industries except for the Sri Lankan textile, garments and chemical industries. India showed a negative contribution of TFP growth to output growth in food processing and chemical industries and Turkey in food processing industries.

Patterns of output growth across industries in Bangladesh are similar to those of other developing countries, such as India, but are lower than countries such as Sri Lanka, South Korea, Taiwan and Turkey. Compared to these faster growing countries, industries in Bangladesh achieve lower TFP growth, which reduced Bangladesh's competitiveness in the international market for manufactures. Also, its low relative contribution to output growth makes a high pace of industrial growth difficult.

Decomposition of TFP Growth

As discussed, TFP growth has two components, technological progress and change in productive capacity realization (PCR). Technological progress involves innovation while capacity realization involves the 'catching up' of performance of given technology which provides a significant driving force for output growth of production agents. Could it be the sluggish industrial growth in most of the industrial sectors in Bangladesh manufacturing industries was due to little or no technological progress, or to 'catching up' problems.

Quantitative analysis of sources of TFP growth in a particular industry, or in the manufacturing sector as a whole in Bangladesh has been virtually nil. This study attempts to fill this gap. The analytical model developed in the previous chapter has been used to separate the contribution of each component (change in capacity realization and technological progress) to output growth in selected manufacturing industries.

TFP growth is usually defined as the growth in output not explained by input growth, i.e. rewriting Equation (6.1):

$$\Delta\text{TFP} = \underbrace{\left(y_{2it} - y_{1it} \right)}_{output\ growth} - \underbrace{\overset{*}{y}}_{Input\ Growth}$$

From Equation 6.1, ΔTFP equals

$$\left\{ \left(\overset{*}{y}_{1i,t-1} - y_{1i,t-1} \right) - \left(\overset{*}{y}_{2i,t} - y_{2i,t} \right) \right\} + \left(\overset{*}{y}_{1i,t} - \overset{*}{y}_{1i,t-1} \right) \tag{6.2}$$

Equation (6.2) can be rewritten as

$$\Delta\text{TFP} = \left[\underbrace{\left(y_{2i,t} / \overset{*}{y}_{2i,t} \right)}_{PCR_2} - \underbrace{\left(y_{1i,t-1} / \overset{*}{y}_{1i,t-1} \right)}_{PCR_1} \right] + \underbrace{\left(\overset{*}{y}_{1i,t} - \overset{*}{y}_{1i,t-1} \right)}_{TP} \tag{6.3}$$

y_1, y_2, $\overset{*}{y}_1$, and $\overset{*}{y}_2$ defined earlier while PCR_1 and PCR_2 stand for productive capacity realization in periods 1 and 2 and TP stands for technological progress. Productivity growth of firms is thus regarded as a consequence of two different factors: (i) the adoption of technological innovations in processes and in products, pushing the potential production frontier upward, which is measured by technological progress; (ii) changes in capacity realization which reflect the efficiency of firms in improving production with a given set of inputs and technology. These two TFP components are analytically distinct, and their measurement provides an added dimension in terms of deriving policy implications, particularly for developing countries. Co-existence of a high rate of technological progress with declining capacity realization, in certain production units is possible as is coexistence of low technological progress with rising productive capacity realization. Consequently, policy actions need to be tailored to address the different combinations of sources of productivity growth.

Following Equation (6.3), components of TFP growth are calculated using firm level data for the selected industry groups. Industry wise empirical estimates of average rate of changes in capacity realization and technological progress are presented in Tables 6.5 to 6.7 while firm level results are not presented here due to space limitation but can be obtained from the author upon request.

Table 6.5 reveals that TFP growth rates in the cotton textiles and jute textiles industries were very low during the early 80s. The reason for this poor performance might be the large share of public sector enterprises in these industries. Allocation of imported inputs and the pricing of inputs and output were exercised by the government. Growth of sources of TFP growth was rather sluggish. Greater capacity realization in cotton textile industries was negligible, and was negative for jute textile industries from 1981 to 1987, so technological progress accounted for virtually all TFP growth. TFP growth increased for cotton textiles but not significantly for jute industries, during the late 80s, after implementation of economic policy reforms. Capacity realization showed little growth so again technological progress was responsible for virtually all TFP growth during this period. This was also true for ready-made garments.

Table 6.5: Decomposition of Annual Average TFP Growth Rates of Textiles and Garments Industries 1981-91 (percentage)

Industries	1981-87			1987-91		
	TFP Growth	Changes in PCR	Tech. Prog.	TFP Growth	Changes in PCR	Tech. Prog.
Cotton Textiles	0.458	0.032	0.426	1.016	0.040	0.976
Jute Textiles	0.748	-0.028	0.776	0.880	0.077	0.803
Ready-made Garments				0.916	0.070	0.846

Source: Calculated from CMI and BGMEA data (Master Tape, Current Production).

Note: Industrial codes and numbers of firms used here are the same as in the previous chapter.

Because of differences in methodology, data and time periods studied, the above findings cannot be directly compared to those of the earlier studies, but they do provide some intuitive explanations of the patterns of productivity growth of these industries. A study conducted by the World Peace Academy of Bangladesh (WPAB) (1985) examined two aspects of operating efficiency: machine productivity and capacity utilization. It found that productivity growth of cotton textile industries (in terms of output per running spindle) declined from 0.019 per cent per annum during 1970-74 to 0.017 per cent per annum during 1979-83. However, using an index number approach, Mondal and Ahmad (1984) found that capital productivity in the cotton textiles industries increased at an annual compound rate of 0.008, labour productivity fell at -0.014 while total factor productivity increased at 0.002 over the period 1962-63 to 1977-78. They also found that capital productivity in the jute manufacturing sector fell at an annual compound rate of -0.002 per cent, labour productivity at -0.003 per cent and total factor productivity at -0.006

per cent over the period 1962-63 to 1977-78. Thus, their findings show almost an unchanged growth in partial and total factor productivity in these industries throughout the period studied.

The most recent study, conducted by the Harvard Institute of Development (HIID) under the Employment and Small Enterprise Policy Planning (ESEPP) project for the Bangladesh Planning Commission, used establishment level data for the 1975/76 to 1983/84 period. Using the conventional growth accounting approach, HIID (1990a) found that the TFP growth of cotton and jute textiles industries fluctuated over the period studied. TFP growth in the cotton textile industry varied from about 0.93 per cent to 2 per cent annually, and that of the jute textile industry varied from 0.29 per cent to 1.35 per cent in the same period. However, TFP growth in the garment industry increased steadily from 0.24 per cent in 1981/82 to about 1.31 per cent in 1983/84. None of the above results conform with the findings of the present study, perhaps because of differences in methodology, data and time period studied.

Table 6.6: Decomposition of Annual Average TFP Growth Rates of Food Processing Industries 1981-91 (percentage)

Industries	1981-87			1987-91		
	TFP Growth	Changes in PCR	Tech. Prog.	TFP Growth	Changes in PCR	Tech. Prog.
Dairy products	1.374	0.004	1.370	1.357	0.088	1.269
Fish and sea foods	3.027	0.100	2.927	2.573	0.044	2.529
Hydrogenated veg. oil	1.073	-0.003	1.075	1.084	-0.094	1.178
Edible oils	0.688	-0.010	0.698	-0.358	0.050	-0.407
Grain milling	0.841	0.036	0.805	-0.951	0.065	-1.016
Rice milling	1.382	-0.029	1.410	0.397	0.053	0.344
Bakery products	1.127	0.051	1.075	0.658	0.016	0.642
Sugar factories	0.127	-0.009	0.137	-0.911	0.079	-0.990
Tea & coffee processing	1.096	0.022	1.074	1.407	0.062	1.346
Tea & coffee blending	1.618	-0.010	1.628	1.689	0.069	1.783

Source: Calculated from CMI data (Master Tape, Current Production).

Note: Industrial codes and numbers of firms used here are the same as in the previous chapter.

Table 6.6 shows that the TFP growth rates in the food processing industry group were disappointingly low, ranging from 0.13 per cent per annum to 3.03 per cent per annum during 1981 to 1987, but only one industry (fish and seafood) exceeded 1.6 per cent. The changes in capacity realization rates for various sectors of this industry group were not significant showing that these industries failed to improve performance with the existing production technology, and some even declined marginally during this period. The maximum rate was only 0.10 per cent in the fish and seafood sector. This industry also achieved the highest rate of technological progress, at nearly 3 per cent per annum. The recent origin of this industry, and steeply rising external demand probably led to this growth. The above results conform with those of HIID (1990) and Sahota *et al* (1991), although they used traditional growth accounting method and TFP was measured as the residual.

The average rates of TFP growth of different sectors of the food processing industry group did not increase much during the post reform period (1987-1991). Edible oils, grain milling, and sugar factories experienced negative TFP growth rates. Average rates of capacity realization among these sectors improved from the previous period but did not grow fast enough to outweigh the negative rates of technological progress.

Although some industries experienced declining rates of technological progress from the early eighties to late eighties, technological progress still accounted for most of TFP growth. In the production process, technological progress originates from many sources: through improved methods of utilizing existing resources so that a higher output per unit of input is obtained, often referred to as *disembodied* technological change; through changes in input quality, often referred to as *embodied* technological change; or through the introduction of (imported) new process and inputs. In Bangladesh, technological progress stemmed from the latter source, due to the opening of the domestic economy to the world market. A study conducted by the Asian Development Bank (1987) demonstrated that there was a policy bias in favour of relatively large capital-intensive production over small labour intensive production. This study also reported that industrial policies in Bangladesh favoured imported over local technology. It can also be argued that slow growing industries cannot incorporate improved *embodied* technology as it occurred (Abdullah and Rahman 1989). Nevertheless, a study conducted by the International Labour Organisation (ILO) (1991) showed that there had been assimilation of indigenous technology and innovations in various sectors, particularly in fish and seafood, rice milling and bakery products of this industry group in a few cases recorded in the 80s. For example, the Bangladesh Council of Scientific and Industrial Research (BCSIR) developed several processes and registered a few patents in food processing. Even then, Bangladesh is still dependent on foreign hardware technology.

It is apparent from Table 6.7 that average rates of TFP growth for various industries in the chemical industry group were slow. The contribution of average changes in capacity realization to TFP growth in all industries was negligible, and were even marginally negative in drugs and pharmaceuticals, and paints and varnishes' industries from 1981 to 1987. During this period, technological progress was effectively the only source of TFP growth in almost all industries except for soap and detergent, matches manufacturing and petroleum products industries where technological progress itself was negative. Consequently, there was no appreciable rate of TFP growth for any industry in this group. Similar results were found by HIID (1990) for the earlier periods, although methodology and data used were different.

Table 6.7: Decomposition of Annual Average TFP Growth Rates of Chemical Industries of Bangladesh 1981-91 (percentage)

Industries	1981-87			1987-91		
	TFP Growth	Changes in PCR	Tech. Prog.	TFP Growth	Changes in PCR	Tech. Prog.
Drugs & Pharmaceuticals	0.981	-0.034	1.015	1.040	-0.037	1.077
Fertilizers Manufacturing	1.624	0.047	1.577	2.469	-0.040	2.509
Industrial Chemicals	1.831	0.081	1.751	1.653	0.027	1.627
Paints & Varnishes	1.320	-0.088	1.408	0.157	0.054	0.104
Perfumes & Cosmetics	1.623	0.013	1.610	1.686	0.008	1.678
Soap and Detergent	0.124	0.067	0.057	0.796	0.009	0.787
Matches Manufacturing	0.395	0.075	0.321	1.159	-0.017	1.176
Petroleum Products	0.098	0.050	0.049	0.797	-0.022	0.819

Source: Calculated from CMI data (Master Tape, Current Production).

Note: Industrial codes and numbers of firms used here are the same as in the previous chapter.

All industries, except industrial chemicals, and paints and varnishes' industries, within the chemical industry group gained higher TFP growth during 1987 to 1991. However, the relative shares of rates of change of capacity realization and technological progress to TFP growth in different industries remained almost unchanged. Among the various industries in the chemical industry group, fertilizer manufacturing gained the highest rate of technological progress, attributable to the opening up of the economy. But the contribution of changes in capacity realization to TFP growth of this sector declined from the pre-reform period, attributed mainly to high market concentration (see Appendix to Chapter 7) and entry barriers. The next well-performed sector was perfumes and cosmetics with approximately 1.69 per cent TFP growth per annum. The contribution of both changes in PCR and technological progress increased in this sector from the pre-reform to post reform period. This has been one of the vibrant industries since the beginning of the 1980s with the promulgation of the New Industrial Policy (NIP) which encouraged private (domestic and foreign) participation in industrialization. Consequently, a large number of multinational subsidiary companies participated in this industry. As with the findings of Chen and Tang (1987), Blomström (1986) and Wang (1996) in other developing countries, it may be argued that foreign participation enhanced competition and improved productivity of this sector in chemical industries.

Although the contributions of technological progress to TFP growth increased significantly in drugs & pharmaceuticals, matches and petroleum products sectors from the pre-reform to post-reform period the contributions of changes in PCR to TFP growth declined in this period. These industries have been largely dominated by foreign subsidiary companies. Since foreign firms facilitate access to the latest and best practice technology, improvement in technological progress is not unexpected, particularly after the implementation of economic reforms in these industries. But firms in these industries failed to realize maximum possible production capacity perhaps because of high concentration and various structural problems such as frequent power failure, inadequate raw material supply, and a dearth of a trained and skilled work-force (ADB 1987).

In the light of the empirical evidence, conclusions regarding productivity growth for selected industries are dismal. The contribution of the changes in capacity realization to TFP growth of industries was negligible. In addition, whatever level of TFP growth was experienced by enterprises in these selected industries was mainly attributable to technological progress, particularly from 1987 to 1991. Technological progress in this period could have been induced by government adoption of market oriented policies, which withdrew import licences and import bans.[5] But, in spite of the adoption of new technology over several years, manufacturing performance has remained sluggish. As reported in an ADB study (1987), firms simply import foreign equipment but use it according to the prevailing norm. No individual efforts were undertaken to improve the utilization of existing resources, particularly in large firms, thus no really effective change took place in the production method, since industrial enterprises do not have their own in-house R&D activities. Again, they do not have effective linkages with government sponsored R&D organizations. So modification or improvement of imported technology and the rate of innovation has been very low in recent years. New technology combined with old methods of application of inputs, failed to provide any significant 'technological break-through' through innovation (ILO 1991, World Bank 1992b).

The poor performance of the manufacturing sector indicates that a general hypothesis that firms would exploit the technology fully, once made available to them, is not valid. The whole issue of appropriate balance in emphasis between efficient choice of technology and efficient use of chosen technology has, in recent years, received too little attention. It has been erroneously assumed, that, while firms can operate technology efficiently, they can not select alternatives efficiently. The results demonstrate that firms in manufacturing industries failed to achieve dynamism of productivity growth through higher capacity realization, even after the implementation of market oriented reforms.

Attention is required for this unexpected situation of technological advancement with no appreciable improvement in production and productivity growth for manufacturing industries. It may, for example, be attributable to inappropriate choice of technology. Biases in technological progress in this respect, are now examined.

Biases in Technological Progress

Technological progress embodies increased efficiency of factors in production. Generally, this improvement in efficiency is biased towards certain factors; technological progress during a certain period can, therefore, be described as labour-bias or labour-saving and capital-biasor capital-saving. Labour-saving technological progress generates an increase in efficiency of labour, so that a given quantity of output can be produced with less labour input, i.e. output per unit of labour increases. The impact of labour-bias technological progress is therefore a decline in the cost of labour per unit of production. Likewise, capital-saving technological progress increases the efficiency of capital so that less is required per unit of production.

In the previous section, empirical estimates showed that technological progress took place in some sectors of selected manufacturing industries. This section examines the direction in which technological progress took place (labour-saving or capital-saving) and its consistency with the country's resource and factor endowment.

Biases of technological change can be measured through the simple ratios (i.e. output-labour and output-capital ratios) [6] and through the use of various sophisticated functional forms, cost function analyses, in particular. Unavailability of cost and price data precluded the application of functional form analysis in this study. However, biases of technological progress cannot be measured precisely, so whatever method used can only show a broad picture. To get some indication of the direction of biases of technological progress, simple ratios were estimated. These estimates for the three selected industry groups are presented in Tables 6.8 to 6.10.

Table 6.8: Biases in Technological Progress in Textiles and Garments Industries (selected years)

Industries	1981 Output /Lab.	1981 Output /K	1987 Output /Lab.	1987 Output /K	1991 Output /Lab.	1991 Output /K
Cotton Textiles	35.4	0.54	38.7	0.58	39.9	0.53
Jute Textiles	27.4	0.73	28.9	0.68	31.0	0.56
Ready Made Garments	....	....	15.8	0.37	16.6	0.48

Source: Calculated from CMI and BGMEA data (Master Tape, Current Production).

Note: Industrial codes and numbers of firms used here are the same as in the previous chapter.

Table 6.8 shows that output per unit of labour increased in cotton textile and jute textile industries from the pre-reform period to the post-reform period, while output per unit of capital declined during the same period. Similar findings were also obtained by Khan and Chowdhury (1986). Their estimates showed that between 1974/75 and 1981/82, overall labour productivity in manufacturing industries increased at a rate of about 8 per cent per annum. It may be argued that technological progress led to increased labour productivity and not capital productivity. In a relatively labour abundant economy like Bangladesh, it is generally expected that technological progress embodies higher labour productivity so that this domestic abundant factor can be utilized in order to increase output. However, when these economies are also capital scarce (like Bangladesh) technological progress that embodies capital productivity is desirable. Protected trade regimes in the 1950s and 1960s made capital cheap relative to labour and encouraged manufacturing firms in the developing countries to employ more capital.[7] So capital-saving technological progress due to market-oriented reforms is fruitful, in the sense that these countries are able to utilize this already employed capital, thereby allowing saved foreign exchange to be used for Research and Development (R&D). Empirical estimates show that technological progress in jute and cotton textiles industries are labour-saving which is inconsistent with the labour abundant economy. Both output per unit of labour and output per unit of capital increased in garment industries and provides no clear-cut evidence as to the nature of the technological progress.

Table 6.9: Biases in Technological Progress in Food Processing Industries (selected years)

Industries	1981		1987		1991	
	Output /Lab.	Output /K	Output /Lab.	Output /K	Output /Lab.	Output /K
Dairy products	41.0	0.47	40.4	0.45	45.3	0.47
Fish and sea foods	26.1	0.37	31.5	0.43	26.4	0.38
Hydrogenated veg. oil	66.6	0.80	59.4	0.73	52.4	0.57
Edible oils	42.5	0.61	42.3	0.60	42.9	0.56
Grain milling	30.0	0.57	33.2	0.57	33.7	0.52
Rice milling	28.2	0.47	28.7	0.41	29.8	0.43
Bakery products	34.4	0.33	40.7	0.35	38.5	0.34
Sugar factories	34.3	0.35	29.1	0.30	29.7	0.29
Tea & coffee processing	33.8	0.35	34.3	0.35	35.9	0.34
Tea & coffee blending	47.9	0.51	43.0	0.53	48.2	0.50

Source: Calculated from CMI data (Master Tape, Current Production).

Note: Industrial codes and numbers of firms used here are the same as in the previous chapter.

Fish and sea foods and bakery products industries experienced increased capital and labour productivity from 1981 to 1991 (Table 6.9), and provides no indication of the direction of technological progress. However, labour productivity increased while capital productivity declined, in all other industries except hydrogenated vegetable oils during the same period, suggesting that there was labour-saving technological progress in these industries. Both labour and capital productivity declined in hydrogenated vegetables oil industry and provide no direction of biases of technological progress.

Table 6.10 shows that drugs and pharmaceuticals achieved capital-saving technological progress while fertilizer manufacturing experienced labour-saving technological progress during 1981 to 1991. However, empirical estimates of output-labour and output-capital ratios for all other industries in the chemical industry group, give no indication as to the direction of technological progress. The above findings do not conform with those of Bhattacharya (1994) who found labour-saving technological progress in chemical industries. He used firm level survey data only on private sector industries applying the same methodology as this study. Using the same methodology as for this study, but classifying their samples into 'moribund' (firms that operated early in the studied period but exited later), 'old' and 'new', Sahota *et al* (1991) concluded that there was no clear evidence of labour-saving technological progress in small as against large firms in the 'old' and 'moribund' subsamples. However, there was labour-saving technological progress, both in small and large firms in the 'new' sub-sample.

Table 6.10: Biases in Technological Progress in Chemical Industries (selected years)

Industries	1981		1987		1991	
	Output /Lab.	Output /K	Output /Lab.	Output /K	Output /Lab.	Output /K
Drugs & Pharmaceuticals	77.5	0.34	73.2	0.31	59.3	0.47
Fertilizers Manufacturing	119.1	0.40	118.4	0.35	129.9	0.31
Industrial Chemicals	61.7	0.32	70.0	0.34	104.9	0.39
Paints & Varnishes	70.3	0.42	64.9	0.34	72.0	0.46
Perfumes & Cosmetics	56.2	0.53	56.6	0.51	67.9	0.54
Soap and Detergent	42.5	0.56	48.2	0.59	52.9	0.65
Matches Manufacturing	59.8	0.40	63.6	0.44	61.5	0.48
Petroleum Products	50.8	0.41	54.6	0.43	59.2	0.52

Source: Calculated from CMI data (Master Tape, Current Production).

Note: Industrial codes and numbers of firms used here are the same as in the previous chapter.

Capital-saving technological progress is desirable in a capital shortage and labour surplus economy, but the empirical estimates presented in Tables 6.8 to 6.10 indicate that, instead, labour-saving technological progress occurred in many industries from 1981 to 1991, but the estimates are not based on rigorous and sophisticated methodology, conclusions that emerge from the above analysis are tentative. The way the labour productivity is measured above could indicate improvement for any of the following reasons: (1) the labour force declined due to the displacement of labour by imported technology but output remained constant, or (2) output increased but labour force remained constant, or (3) both output and labour force increased but the rate of increase of output was faster than that of labour.

As mentioned earlier, industrial policies in Bangladesh favour imported over local technology. This policy bias could create severe consequences on labour employment. For example, the growth of mechanized rice milling sector, which has been favoured by policy measures, is estimated to have displaced 5 million man-days per year (ADB 1987). This points to the first possibility. Looking at the PCR rates it can be deduced that output could have increased though not significantly due to improvement in capacity realization whereas the utilization of labour declined. This points to second possibility. Third possibility is ruled out here, because output growth in manufacturing has been sluggish (or stagnant) for many years.

Summary and Conclusions

This chapter empirically estimated the sources of output growth in selected manufacturing industries in Bangladesh. The two main sources of output growth, viz., TFP growth and input growth were estimated using firm level data for 1981, 1987 and 1991. TFP growth was decomposed into changes in capacity realization and techno-logical progress. The random coefficient frontier production function approach was used for measuring the TFP growth and input growth was obtained as a residual, unlike the conventional approach where TFP growth is not estimated but is obtained as a residual after accounting for growth of inputs. The chief advantage of the current approach is that individual input response to output in the production process is taken into account in measuring the TFP growth. Moreover, obtaining input growth as a residual avoids the adjustment problems of quality variations in inputs.

Empirical estimates showed that output growth across firms in selected industries was caused mainly by input growth. TFP growth was sluggish in all industries from 1981-1987 and increased only marginally in a few sub-sectors within these industries during 1987-1991. These results provided support for the view that restrictive trade regimes may produce lower rates of output growth per unit of input than more liberalized regimes. Indeed, these findings differ little from findings for developed and other developing countries in earlier studies (Corden 1974, Chen 1977, Kelly and Williamson 1979, and Nishimizu and Page 1982). Decomposition of TFP growth into changes in capacity realization and technological progress, showed that technological progress was the major force in TFP growth in these industries.

A substantial part of technological progress was probably due to economic reforms which facilitated the withdrawal of import licensing and bans. It is paradoxical that output growth was not significant in individual enterprises even though there was considerable technological progress. However, this outcome is not entirely surprising, given that technological progress did not come through improvements in the skill and knowledge of the labour force, or through improvements in management and organization practices. There might be difficulties in adapting Western technology implying that imports had little impact on productive capacity realization. Moreover, the majority of firms of selected industries have remained with the public sector corporations. It is likely that their financial constraints have remained soft, which have encouraged extensive and inefficient use of inputs and discouraged industrial innovation and full utilization of chosen technology. Therefore, throughout the periods studied, contributions of changes in capacity realization to TFP growth were insignificant.

There might be an additional reason for this paradoxical situation, i.e. biases of technological progress. In relatively labour abundant and capital scarce economies like Bangladesh, technological progress that improves labour productivity would be appropriate. However, increased labour productivity reduces the volume of employment, unless additional employment opportunities are created through expanding existing manufacturing enterprises. As the consequences of a reduction in employment in these economies is severe, it is desirable that technological progress should embody both labour and capital productivity. This paves the way to full utilization of overemployed scarce capital, since earlier policy regimes encouraged manufacturing firms to extensive factors employment, particularly capital. Empirical estimates showed that technological progress was labour-saving in almost all industries suggesting a reduction in labour employment. Such type of technological progress alone might not be fruitful to increasing output in Bangladesh.

Empirical findings suggest that there is a possibility of large productivity gains within firms of Bangladesh manufacturing industries without introducing new technologies but simply by utilizing existing inputs more efficiently. The policy implications for the above findings are that importation of foreign technology in isolation does not improve productivity growth. Utilization of existing technology must be improved through learning by doing, innovation and human capital development. In this context, labour market reform is mandatory to remove all sorts of rigidities and to link wages to productivity.[8] In view of the country's huge population, there is a clear need to rationalize policy measures and encourage local technology development. In order to attain a competitive advantage in production, trade and investment policies should be directed towards a market-oriented approach.

There are some limitations in the empirical estimates: First, while the estimates of PCR and TFP growth in textile and garment industry group have been calculated using firm level data from each sector separately, the estimates for the food processing and the chemicals industry groups were made using firm level data from all sectors together because of insufficient and inconsistent firm level data at the sectoral level, i.e. there may be aggregation problems. The results would have been more robust, had sufficient firm level data been available for each sector separately.

Second, this study uses value added as output in empirical estimation. Some authors, Norsworthy and Jang (1992), and Oulton and O'Mahony (1994), for example, argued that the use of value added as a measure of output distorts technology in estimating TFP growth because all raw and semifinished materials, subassemblies, energy, and purchased services, as well as imports, are omitted from measured inputs. Their combined influence is consequently missing from the price and cost of production, and the description of technology, so such a framework is inadequate for explaining the performance of industrial units in reforming economies such as Bangladesh.

Third, as mentioned previously, estimates of labour and capital inputs used in this study are not as refined as would be desirable. Therefore, the productivity measures in this study should be considered as indicative rather than precise, since any errors in constructing inputs or output may overshadow the actual productivity change or variation. Fourth, intertemporal comparisons among enterprises' performance are made by using empirical estimates from cross-section data. It is argued by some authors (Hsiao 1974, Swamy and Mehta 1977, Harvey 1978) that cross-section estimates cannot incorporate some information, e.g. different levels of output may be obtained from the same amount of input for a particular production unit over different years in view of technological progress and improvement in capacity realization. In this case, panel data model could be appropriate.

However, it may be argued that these problems are frequently encountered in empirical studies. The problem of unavailability of relevant data is unavoidable. The use of value added in empirical analysis is justified when labour and capital inputs are separable from material inputs. Moreover, while panel data may have some advantages, they have some serious drawbacks. For example, the homogeneity assumption of a firm's performance over time is not valid and there is a likelihood of problems both of autocorrelation and heteroscedasticity, while cross-section data are prone only to heteroscedasticity. These problems together create severe problems in estimating parameters with panel data.

Notes

[1] This explanation is due to Solow (1957) and is known as Solow's dichotomy in the literature.

[2] Jobs and income of enterprises' managers are secured against poor performance as a result of soft-budget constraint.

[3] Countries were not selected by following any specific criterion. However, studies analyzed similar industries of certain countries, as this study does, are taken from contemporary literature. These studies are neither conclusive nor exhaustive.

[4] Sri Lanka's output, TFP and input growths are only for private sector industries, which explain why the figures are so robust.

[5] Recent economic reforms in Bangladesh also include removal of quantitative restrictions, rationalisation of tariff structure, uniform the multiple exchange rates, various incentives on imports for export oriented firms, etc. to encourage production and productivity (Chapter 2).

[6] Harrod (1956) classified technological progress to be capital-using, neutral, and labour-using where output-capital ratio increases, remains unchanged, and diminishes at a given rate of interest.

[7] Protected trade regime kept the rental price of capital artificially low through various incentives such as cash licenses to import capital goods at 30 to 40 per cent lower than official exchange rate, duty draw back, tax holidays, income tax rebate, etc.

[8] Public wage policies and minimum wage regulations have allowed real wages to increase faster than productivity, and the spillover effects of this on private sector wages have resulted in a loss of international competitiveness.

7 Determinants of Capacity Realization: An Empirical Analysis

Introduction

Even if firms use an equal set of inputs and production technology, variations in their capacity realization are observed. Although the traditional theory of firm does not attach significance to such differences, empirical studies of production must take differences in the utilization of productive resources into account, since, in the real world, producers are not all equally efficient. In Chapter 5, empirical measurement has shown that most firms in the selected industry groups failed to produce on the best practice frontier by realizing full production capacity. Considerable variations in capacity realization rates have been found across firms both within industries, and between industries (Table 7.1). Some earlier studies also found substantial variations in capacity realization across firms and industries in the Bangladesh manufacturing sector. Using industry level data for 1973/74, Afroz and Roy (1977) found that capacity realization varied from 22 per cent to 75 per cent in selected manufacturing industries. While using enterprise level survey data for 1970, Habibullah (1974) found the efficiency of the best performing firm was seven times higher than that of the worst performing firm. However, little research has been done to identify factors influencing inter-firm variation in capacity realization in Bangladesh.

The identification of these factors is critical for industrial policy formulation and industrial growth. Their identification is more critical to a developing rather than to a developed economy, because, as argued by many authors, the opportunity cost of holding unrealized productive capacity is higher in developing economies than in developed countries. Phillips rightly pointed out that '....it is far more important for the less developed countries to find out why scarce resources are underutilized than to determine the precise degree of under-utilization' (1970 p:21). One way of finding out these factors would be to identify the causes of sluggish performance of firms, and differences in PCR across firms. The significance of the causal variables and their role in the improvement in

PCR would provide a valuable guide to the formulation and evaluation of industry policies designed to increase efficiency. The main objective of this chapter is to pinpoint the major determinants of production capacity realization in Bangladesh manufacturing industries.

Table 7.1: Inter-firm Dispersion in PCR Rates in Selected Industries

Industries	Estimated standard deviation of capacity realization (%)		
	1981	1987	1991
Cotton textiles	12.97	12.84	12.70
Jute textiles	6.75	7.36	7.21
Ready-made garment	....	9.23	9.16
Food processing	17.12	16.26	15.72
Chemicals	13.80	13.11	12.42

Source: Author's calculation from estimated firm-specific PCR in the previous
    Chapter. Note: The symbol .... denotes not available.

The remainder of this chapter is organized as follows. Section 7.2 presents theoretical underpinnings and empirical evidence of determinants of capacity realization. In section 7.3, an analytical model is developed which draws heavily on theoretical and empirical studies in the Industrial Organization literature. This is followed by estimation of the specified model and interpretation of results in section 7.4. Summary and conclusions are given in the final section.

Determinants of Capacity Realization: Theory and Evidence

Theoretical Underpinning

As mentioned earlier, all producers are not equally efficient in production, because access to information, structural rigidities (for example, pattern of ownership), time lags to learn technology, differential incentive systems, and organizational factors (such as X-efficiency and human capital related variables) all affect firms' ability in production. Mueller rightly pointed out that '.....the role of non-physical inputs, especially information and knowledge, which influence the firm's ability to use its available technology set fully' (1974 p:731). Given these factors, few firms achieve maximum feasible output from their available inputs and existing technology. This is represented by the potential output frontier Q_p, which lies above the actual output function Q_a in figure 7.1. The PCR indices reported in this study have been measured as the ratios of actual output to maximum potential output. But, maximum possible output is not equivalent to technically feasible output. While the former output reflects the existing production environment faced by firms, the latter output comes from an ideal production environment without any constraints on the application of technology, i.e. a laboratory environment. Technically feasible output is represented here by the frontier Q_T, which lies far above the potential frontier in figure 7.1. Firms cannot produce on the technically feasible frontier because of various constraints, such as government regulatory policies, demand conditions, and market structure, etc. The potential frontier could coincide with the technically feasible output frontier if and only if all constraints were removed, leading to an ideal environment for the operation of the given technology.

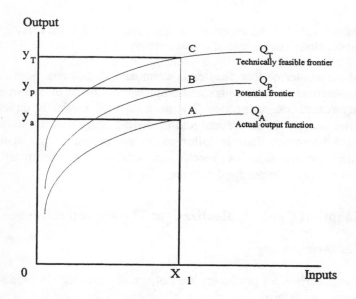

Figure 7.1: Actual Output, Potential and Technically Feasible Frontier Functions

Thus, there are two types of factors which cause divergences between actual to potential output and potential to technically feasible output of firms. However, these two types of factors can not be distinguished sharply. Some factors may be overlapping. This means, one factor may affect both best practice and technically feasible outputs of firms, for example government policies. So, in this section, a theoretical framework is developed in the light of this argument.

There are two classic views on the explanation of productive capacity under-realization of production agents. One of these purports capacity under-realization as a long-run problem in which the patterns of productive capacity realization depend on non-price factors affecting managerial decisions such as economies of scale, oligopolitistic market structure, cyclical demand for output and insufficient supply of complementary inputs. Marris (1964), Winston (1971) and Baily (1974) developed their models of capacity realization in line with this argument. The other view is that capacity under-utilization is a short-run phenomenon and its analysis is concerned with the determinants of the profitability of increasing capacity realization of production units. It claims that increases in profitability lead to higher capacity realization. However, this analysis does not include non-price elements (such as the market structure and the size of the market) as explanatory variables of capacity realization. Schydlowsky (1973), Winston and McCoy (1974) and Betancourt and Clague (1976) developed the theory of capacity realization based on this view. The underlying assumption is that firms choose their capacity realization rate to maximize profit. However, testing these models empirically has proven to be quite difficult. Lecraw (1978) concluded, while studying the determinants of capacity utilization in Thai manufacturing sector, that the available data at best show that the level of capacity realization moves in the direction predicted by the profit-maximization analysis.

Winston (1974) offers two other explanations for under-realization of productive capacity. These are intended or *ex ante* decisions by rational entrepreneurs anticipating future events, and unintended or stochastic factors which prevent entrepreneurs from realizing full production capacity. Intended excess capacity arises from some form of non-profit maximizing managerial behaviour, such as lack of information, risk aversion and government control, while unintended unrealized productive capacity exists due to demand fluctuations, input shortages, technological failure or managerial errors.

Recent theoretical works in Industrial Organization literature offer two other views on the differences in observed capacity realization of firms. Firms may build excess capacity for both strategic and non-strategic reasons. Profit-maximizing firms may hold non-strategic excess capacity in markets where demand is cyclical or stochastic, where plants are inherently lumpy or subject to economies of scale, or where imported inputs are allotted on the basis of built-in production capacity (Lieberman 1987). The last reason was and still is more common in developing countries, particularly countries which adopted, or still follow an import substituting industrial strategy. Strategic excess capacity may be built to deter entry or to pre-empt existing rivals. This entry deterrence hypothesis was provided by Wenders (1971) and Spence (1977). Later, Eaton and Lypsey (1979), and Dixit (1981) also provided arguments in favour of this hypothesis.

Empirical evidence for the above explanations is quite sparse. Some earlier studies addressed the issue differently, attempting to explain what determines capacity realization of production units. Leibenstein (1976) emphasized the importance of organizational factors, while Lecraw (1978) and Førsund and Hjalmarsson (1979) indicated the importance of technology related factors, such as capital intensity and scale of operation, as being responsible for differential performance of firms. On the other hand, Forest (1979) identified both organizational and technological reasons for variations in capacity realization. These are: demand fluctuations, periodic fluctuations in input supplies, replacement without scrappage, inter-industry, or inter-product demand shifts, lumpiness and non-transferable capital, imperfections in market structure, economies of scale and related effects, interindustry imbalances and bottlenecks in supplies of strategic factors. While Schydlowsky (1973, 1976) offered six possible reasons why capacity realization of production units varies substantially: factor intensities, relative factor prices and, particularly, the cost differential between labour shifts (i.e. the shift premium), economies of scale, the elasticity of substitution between inputs, the elasticity of demand and the availability of working capital. Goldar and Renganathan (1989) argued that differential performance of firms in terms of realization of productive capacity could be analyzed through the well-known structure-conduct-performance (S-C-P) theory of industrial economics. Porter (1979), Oster (1982) and Caves and Barton (1990) also maintain that inter-industry differences in efficiency and capacity realization result from inter-industry differences in stable elements of market structure.

The recently developed 'endogenous' growth theory (Romer 1986, 1987 and Lucas 1988, 1990) emphasizes the role of human capital on firm's productivity performance. The crucial role of human capital in the production process is two-fold: first, management skills strongly influence the firm's ability to produce the maximum possible output by realizing existing production capacity. The realization rate increases through the implementation of many specific activities, such as maintenance, design and modification, and quality control. Second, there is an important feedback effect to the firm's endowments of human capital from efforts to improve productivity in response to external stimuli. For example, successful implementation of a worker training program may, by increasing human capital endowment, augment the ability of a firm to undertake further improvement.

Leibenstein type analysis is related to firm-specific (organizational) characteristics, such as size, age, proportion of non-production (white collar) workers to total workers, and managerial efficiency. Neoclassical S-C-P is related to the dimension of market structure, such as the degree of seller concentration, growth of demand and so on. On the other hand, endogenous growth models, suggest expenditures on research and development (R&D) in order to improve human capital. In a closed economy, these variables would be theoretically sufficient to analyze inter-firm variation in capacity realization. However, in a relatively open economy like Bangladesh, a more complete specification of the model would have to allow for analyzing the influence of international trade policies on a firm's capacity realization.

Recent studies investigating the variability in inter-firm (industry) capacity realization in Bangladesh, and elsewhere, largely ignore trade and domestic regulatory and incentive policy issues, while these policies play a critical role in determining capacity realization of manufacturing firms. Therefore, this study is concerned with assessing the role of these policies on determining firm's productive capacity realization. In studying the impact of trade and industrial policies on India's industrial sector, Bhagwati and Srinivasan (1975), advanced a number of hypotheses linking excess capacity and these policies. They argue that firms are often provided import licences in proportion to installed capacity, which in turn lead them to build excess capacity to be qualified for low priced imported inputs. Moreover, domestic industrial licensing along with import restrictions has created a situation in which a licensed firm can make high profits even at low rates of capacity realization. As a result, new firms find it profitable to commence production and extend the overall industry's production capacity of which substantial portion remains underutilized. Finally, they also argue that this licensing system creates bottlenecks by preventing speedy availability of inputs for the production process and by holding up the import of necessary spare parts and critical equipment, which affect firms' capacity realization. This analysis is also applicable to the Bangladesh economy since Bangladesh and India pursued the similar interventionist and protectionist policy regimes focussing on the leading role of the public sector during the 1970s. However, since the early 1980s, investment, industry and trade policies have become substantially open and outward looking in Bangladesh, which have influenced the production environment of firms. In view of the importance of international trade as well as domestic subsidy and other promotional policies for the Bangladesh manufacturing sector, this study has taken these issues into consideration by adding three policy variables, the effective rate of assistance (ERA), openness (OPN), and ownership pattern to the analysis.

Earlier Empirical Studies

Empirical studies identifying factors influencing capacity realization are few. The impact of firm-specific characteristics, such as age and size of firms, market structure and policy related variables, such as concentration and effective rate of protection (ERP) on a firm's (industry's) performance in terms of profitability have been widely tested in industrial organization literature.[1] However, relatively few studies have been carried out to test these hypotheses taking capacity realization as firms' (industries') performance. This sub-section reviews these and the following features should be noted when interpreting their findings. First, all these studies have attempted to explain the gap (Q_T–Q_A) without distinguishing Q_P from Q_T (distinction among Q_A, Q_P, and Q_T are made in Figure 7.1). Further, in the majority of studies, capacity realization measures are not reliable, since these measures are *ad hoc* and are not adequately based on economic theory. For example, some studies used electricity based measures, some engineering capacity (installed capacity), some shift measures, and some capital utilization. Few studies used estimated realization rates through the traditional production (or cost) functions. As discussed in Chapter 3, all these capacity realization measures are subject to limitations. Second, to explain variations in capacity realization, the majority of studies included only a few variables, such as firm size, age, and market structure, etc. Domestic and international trade policies (such as subsidies and tariffs) play an important role in firms' capacity realization. Some earlier studies included the effective rate of protection (ERP) to analyze the impact of these policy issues on capacity realization. However, ERP is a narrow measure as it only takes account of trade policy issues. As noted by Bhagwati and Srinivasan (1980), the repercussions of a change in trade policy on different activities cannot be forecast from a simple examination of the relative ERPs measures. The ERA (effective rate of assistance) is a better measure than the ERP, as it incorporates both domestic and trade policy issues, and indicates the potential gains from resource re-allocation due to policy changes.

Third, the majority of these studies are now dated. Many changes took place in the production environment of developing countries due to market-oriented policy reforms in the 1980s, but few of these studies were done after these changes took place. Other problems are encountered in measuring the independent variables included in these studies, increasing the need to interpret these results cautiously. A summary description of the earlier studies, listed in chronological order, is contained in Table 7.2.

The principal finding that emerges from these studies is that, in most cases, capital intensity, market structure, openness, import content in production, and scale of operation are important variables in determining capacity realization. Most studies found statistically significant positive association between technology related variables, such as capital intensity and productive capacity realization. The authors argue that a capital intensive firm has an incentive to utilize production capacity at a higher rate, in order to economize on the high cost of scarce capital, because, modern technology involves high capital intensity. Two studies, one on Bangladesh, and one on Israel manufacturing industries found a negative association between these two variables, but these results were not statistically significant.

Most studies found a significant positive association between the scale of operation (size of firm) and capacity realization (Table 7.2). Capacity realization was viewed as a measure of efficiency, so a positive relationship between these two variables could be expected, because a more efficient firm (industry) expands faster than a less efficient one. They also argued that large firms could enjoy both technological and managerial economies of scale, and it could generally be expected that they would operate at higher levels of realization than for small firms. Pasha and Qureshi (1984) found a negative association between size of firm and realization in a study on Pakistan. Since Pakistan had followed an import substitution strategy for several decades, capacity realization depends on the availability of imported inputs and machinery. Large firms enjoyed undue advantage through political power in terms of easier access to loans and import licenses and were able to accumulate more productive resources than small firms. However, they were less obliged to realize maximum possible production capacity (White 1974). Under these circumstances, a negative association between firm size and capacity realization was not unexpected.

All studies presented in Table 7.2, except Goldar and Renganathan's (1989) study for India, found a negative relationship between market structure and capacity realization. The inverse relationship between these two variables is not unexpected according to the theory of industrial organization. In a highly concentrated market, firms would generally be in a position to make super-normal profits, even when the rate of capacity

Table 7.2: Determinants of Productive Capacity Utilization (PCU): Selected Studies

Variables

Studies	Countries	AG	PNWT	SO	CI	MS	GD	IS	OPN	IC	ERP	DPVT	DFRN	R^2
Winston (1971)	Pakistan			+*	+*	+**		-	+*					0.90
Paul (1974)	India			+		-**	+	-		-				0.72
Diokno (1974)	Philippines			+*	+*	-**			+**		-			0.28
Islam (1978)	Bangladesh			+*	-	-		+**	+				-	0.70
Lecraw (1978)	Thailand	+		+**	+**									0.85
Bautista (1981)	Philippines				+**	-			+					0.51
Thoumi (1981)	Colombia			+**	+**	-**			+**	-*				0.36
Morawetz (1981)	Israel	+		+**	-	-**			+	-			-	0.57
Lim (1981)	Malaysia			+**	+**				+**	-				0.29

Pasha and Qureshi (1984)	Pakistan	-	-	-*	+**		+*		+*	0.48
Goldar and Renganathan (1989)	India				+	+**		-		0.34
Srinivasan (1992)	India			-*	-.*	+				0.41

Note: Definition of Variables: AG = Age of firm (industry), PNWT= Proportion of non-production workers to total workers, SO = Scale of Operation (usually proxied by the size of firm in terms of fixed assets, or employment, or real output, or value added), CI = Capital Intensity, MS = Market Structure (usually proxied by CR4), GD = Growth of Demand (usually measured by growth of real output of firm or industry), IS = Import Substitution (usually defined import as a percentage of total supply), OPN = Openness or Export-orientation (usually defined export as a percentage of total firm's or industry's output), IC = Import Content of Production (usually proxied by raw material allocation to firm or industry), ERP = Effective rate of protection, DPVT = Dummy variable equals 1, if the firm is foreign or joint venture and zero otherwise, and DFRN = Dummy variable equals 1, if the firm is privately owned and zero otherwise. The symbols + and - indicate positive or negative association between PCR and independent variables and * denotes significant at the 1 per cent level and ** denote significant at the 5 per cent level. If there is no such signs indicating variables are not significant.

realization is low, and would, therefore, have less incentive to improve capacity realization. Exceptionally, in the Indian study, capacity realization appears to increase with levels of market concentration; a feature that may reflect the outcome of the anti-monopoly policies of that country (Sawhney and Sawhney 1973 and Katrak 1980). Goldar and Renganathan (1989), however, argued that restrictions on the entry of new firms helped existing firms to realize a higher level of production capacity.

In some studies, the use of an 'openness' variable expressed in terms of the ratio of exports to total output plays an important role in explaining variation in capacity realization. Five studies found a significant positive relationship between openness and capacity realization. According to these studies, openness influences capacity realization from both demand and supply standpoints. Exports increase demand for a product, stimulates firms to increase output through increased realization of production capacity, in order to take advantage of the greater demand. On the supply side, exports enhance competition and international competition, leading to increased efficiency.

Some studies investigated the influence of import content of raw materials in production on capacity realization and found a negative relationship. The authors pointed out that foreign exchange crises are most common in developing countries and supply of imported inputs are subject to rationing. Either the supply of inputs is delayed, or sometimes it is inadequate, so that capacity realization is adversely affected by the erratic supply of imported inputs along with variable quality.

Earlier studies also identified some other explanatory variables, such as age of firm (industry), proportion of non-production workers to total workers of firm (industry), growth of demand, import substitution, effective rate of protection and ownership dummy variables. However, no single variable was uniquely determined (statistically significant in all studies). Most variables were determined ambiguously (different signs) and provided contradictory interpretations. The weak results of these studies may be due to the poor quality of data, or to the omission of information in estimating independent variables, or the dependent variable or both. This study uses firm level data and relatively reliable techniques from those available in the literature to estimate these variables.

Analytical Model

Variables Construction

The following variables are constructed for the second stage analysis.

Firm Size (SZ): Firm size can be measured by taking one of the attributes of firms: value added, value of shipments, sale proceeds, employment, or fixed assets. However, the measurement of firm size by using value added, value of shipments, and sale proceeds is not reliable, since these variables are susceptible to price fluctuations. Price inflation or deflation alters firm size measurement. Again, the employment measure can be compromised by technological change, which alters capital to labour ratios in production (Koch 1980). None of these alternatives is particularly suitable as a unit of measurement of firm size. Hence, the fixed asset measure, while not optimal, is used in this study.

Capital Intensity (CI): There are a number of alternative measures of capital intensity. The most common measure is the capital-labour ratio (K/L) where K is fixed assets and L is the total number of workers employed. The main limitation of this approach is that it ignores the quality of labour in the production process. An alternative measure of capital intensity in the literature uses a value added criterion i.e value added per employee (Lary 1968). An increase in the value added per employee is assumed to reflect, on average, an increase in the use of physical capital relative to labour, or a higher proportion of skilled employees, or both. According to Lary, if the value added per employee of a firm (or industry) is less than the average of all firms (industries), then that firm (industry) is labour intensive, while if the value added exceeds the average of all firms (industries), it is capital intensive. The main advantage of Lary's method is that relative capital intensity for a particular firm or industry can be estimated without having capital data. Moreover, it takes account of quality, and variation of inputs (and the human capital issue), in measuring capital intensity since value added reflects the contribution of both skilled and unskilled factor inputs.

There are some severe limitations of Lary's method of measuring capital intensity. First, it confuses labour productivity with capital intensity. Second, it cannot capture the quality variations or human capital issue in the presence of widespread market imperfections and excessive government intervention in an economy's factor and product markets, particularly in developing countries. Third, economies of scale of firms (or industries) are not reflected in this measure. For example, a firm (industry) enjoying economies of scale would yield a larger value added per employee than another, even though the latter used more skilled labour and capital per employee (Islam 1970). Therefore, it was not considered appropriate to use Lary's method in this empirical analysis.

Another method of measuring capital intensity was suggested by Morawetz (1974) in which the various categories of capital and labour are weighed with accounting prices. As the available data do not permit such a disaggregation of labour and capital, this method could not be undertaken. This study uses the capital-labour ratio, as a measure of capital intensity, which is less controversial and computationally simpler.

Market Structure: The best known and most frequently used measure for market structure is concentration. There are a wide variety of possible measures of concentration.[2] The simplest, and most widely used is the *concentration ratio*. The X-firm (where X is number of firms) concentration ratio, CR_x, is defined as the share of the largest X firms in the industry concentrated (using whatever measure of size is thought to be appropriate and available). This is formally written as

$$CR_x = \sum_{i=1}^{x} P_i \qquad (7.1)$$

where CR_x is the measure of X-firm concentration ratio and P_i is the share of firm i in sales, value added, employment, or whatever measures of economic activity are chosen. Now, a value of CR_x close to zero would indicate that the largest X firms supply only a small share of the market while 100 per cent would indicate a single or monopoly supplier. The chief problem with this measure is the selection of X, the number of firms. Unfortunately, economic theory suggests nothing in this regard. In USA, 8-firm, 20-firm and even 50-firm concentration ratios are available. However, a value of X in the range of three to five firms has been frequently used at the industry level in empirical studies. This study constructs a four-firm concentration ratio using gross value of output of four-digit level selected manufacturing industries of Bangladesh, ranking by the size of fixed assets (Table 7.3).

The measurement of size in terms of assets may overstate the level of concentration if the larger factories use more capital intensive techniques than the smaller ones. Again, the share of the four largest firms may give a rather unsatisfactory picture of the market structure, as it ignores the size distribution of the remaining units in the industry. Cowling and Waterson (1976) have built a model, which suggests that the appropriate measure of concentration is the *Herfindahl* index. Vanlommel *et al* (1977) also come up with a similar conclusion. However, unavailability of data for constructing this index precludes its use in this study.

Effective Rate of Assistance (ERA): Effective Rate of Protection (ERP) is the conventional measure for analyzing the impact of policies on production units. Another measure recently developed in the literature is known as the Effective Rate of Assistance (ERA). The ERP accounts only for trade policies while the ERA incorporates both trade and domestic assistance policies.

Table 7.3: Four-firm Concentration Ratios for Selected Manufacturing Industries of Bangladesh (selected years)

	Concentration Ratios		
	1981	1987	1991
Dairy products	0.815	0.762	0.623
Fish and sea foods	0.529	0.315	0.201
Hydrogenated veg. oil	0.573	0.551	0.428
Edible oil	0.452	0.214	0.138
Grain milling	0.258	0.221	0.086
Rice milling	0.321	0.172	0.153
Bakery products	0.272	0.354	0.214
Sugar factories	0.427	0.518	0.372
Tea and coffee processing	0.221	0.147	0.590
Tea and coffee blending	0.729	0.815	0.724
Cotton textiles	0.122	0.120	0.078
Jute textiles	0.315	0.307	0.286
Readymade garments	....	0.126	0.069
Drugs & pharmaceuticals	0.715	0.672	0.525
Fertilizer manufacturing	0.905	0.879	0.715
Industrial chemicals	0.697	0.612	0.637
Paints & varnishes	0.516	0.437	0.465
Perfumes & cosmetics	0.425	0.534	0.390
Soap and detergent	0.152	0.129	0.182
Matches manufacturing	0.385	0.479	0.482
Petroleum products	0.815	0.804	0.762

Source: Author's calculation using CMI (current production) data.

To elaborate, ERA measures the degree of assistance afforded to a production process, and represents the net results of policies affecting the costs of all inputs plus policies which increase the value of the final product. In other words, ERA measures the value added to the final product as a result of all forms of assistance, whether these be external measures such as customs duties (tariffs and sales tax) and exchange rate adjustments or internal measures like the provision of subsidized credit and preferential tariff rates.

Calculation of the ERA allows analysis of how trade policies protect domestic industries and how domestic assistance policies help particular firms (or industries) survive. Since economic reform in Bangladesh commenced in the 1980s, various concessions were given to domestic industries, coupled with removal of various protection measures (Chapter 2). The ERA is the relevant measure for this study. A study conducted by the Harvard Institute of International Development (HIID) (1990) for the Planning Commission of Bangladesh estimated the ERA for about 60 four-digit industries for the period 1973 to 1988,[3] and these estimates of ERAs were used in this analysis.

Other Variables: Several other variables used in this study are constructed using simple calculations:

The proportion of non-production workers to total work force (NPWT) is non-production workers over the total work force of the firm. The age of a firm (AG) is computed as the difference between the year of the census and the year of operation for production. Openness (OPN) is calculated as the ratio of exports of a particular firm over total output at the three-digit industry level. Finally, two dummy variables (DUMPVT, DUMJNT), reflecting the type of ownership are used.

Key Variables and Hypotheses

Studies discussed above, demonstrated that variations in capacity realization across firms could be caused by a number of factors. Drawing on theoretical and empirical studies, this sub-section attempts to identify these factors and outlines a range of hypotheses that pertain to inter-firm (inter-industry) differences in capacity realization. These variables are grouped in four main categories: (i) firm-specific characteristics, such as size and age of firm, (ii) technology conditions, such as scale of production, capital intensity, quality of management, research and development (R&D) and energy intensity, (iii) market structure characteristics, such as industry concentration, accessibility of markets, foreign ownership in terms of foreign capital, and (iv) government policy related factors, such as effective rate of protection (or assistance), and openness.

Other variables also influence a firm's productive capacity realization, such as fluctuations in output demand, periodic fluctuations in input supplies; organisational capacity of managers or entrepreneurs; the proportion of unskilled or skilled labour in the total work force; unionization or political affiliation of the work force;[4] imported raw material dependence; servicing of capital equipment; electricity and power supplies; economies of scale and related effects; inter-product demand shifts and the non-transferability of capital. Some of these factors may help and some may hinder firms in realizing maximum production capacity. Not all these factors which can change capacity realization could be defined here for quantitative analysis due to data limitations and possible measurement problems.

The following variables were selected for empirical analysis, based on the availability of data. The maintained hypotheses that reflect the possible relationships between PCR and these independent variables are discussed below.

Age of Firm: In the literature, it is hypothesized that there is a negative relationship between age and productive capacity realization, because equipment and machinery used by older firms does not embody the most recent technological advances, whereas younger firms are able to adopt the most efficient technologies available at the time of their establishment (Pitt and Lee 1981). However, there is a contrary hypothesis, that AG captures the learning by doing phenomenon in a firm. The longer a firm is in production, the greater is the management experience and the fewer are labour bottlenecks (Lecraw 1978) and thus, older firms may have higher capacity utilization. Empirical findings in earlier studies are mixed. Kopp and Smith (1980) found a positive relationship between these two variables in their empirical findings in steam-generating electric plants in the United states. Lecraw (1978) and Morawetz (1981) also came up with the same conclusion in their studies on Thailand and Israel. However, Pasha and Qureshi (1984) failed to replicate these results in their joint study on Pakistan, while Chen and Tang (1987) also found firms' efficiency levels decreased significantly with their ages.

As mentioned several times earlier, the industrial sector in Bangladesh is at an early stage of development. Only jute textiles and a few cotton textile industries were established during 1950s and 1960s when Bangladesh was a peripheral province of Pakistan. Industrialization in Bangladesh virtually started with independence in 1971. Except for jute and cotton textile industries, all other industries have recent origins. Most firms in these industries are less than 20 years old and some firms are still expanding production capacity with modern technology. So, age of firm in most industries, except for jute and cotton textile industries, may positively influence capacity realization in Bangladesh.

Size of Firm: Economists argue that firm size reflects the existence of scale economies. Larger firms have better access to foreign technology, a greater ability to bear risk and greater advantages from R&D. The larger the firm size, the lower the unit cost (because of scale economies and externalities in production) and the higher is the demand for output. As a result, capacity realization increases with firm size, so a positive relation is expected between these two variables. Other explanations for this positive correlation were suggested by Winston, '....if high rates of utilization indicate efficiency, then efficient firms would probably have grown larger than the inefficient firms; or, if political power is greater for larger firms - influencing political-economic decisions such as licensing of imports, then larger firms would operate at higher rates of utilization' (1971:44). Pitt and Lee (1981) also hold the similar views, suggesting that large firms may be more efficient than small firms due to economies with respect to organisation and technical knowledge, and perhaps to firms' growth resulting from past efficiency. Their empirical results, and those of Tyler (1979), are consistent with this hypothesis. Similar results were reported by Meeusen and van den Broeck (1977b).

Pilat (1995) argued that firm size can give little information about the effect of scale economies on capacity realization, even if firm size does give an indication that it would be biased towards low capacity realization, because it could profitable to have a large firm operating for a few hours per day. Millan (1975), and Betancourt and Clague (1977) hypothesised a negative relationship between firm size and capacity realization. They argued that small firms adopt more appropriate technology, are more flexible in responding to changes in technology, product lines and markets, and foster more competitive factor and product markets, and thus, are able to realize a higher rate of productive capacity. Empirical findings of Pasha and Qureshi (1984) supported this hypothesis.

In Bangladesh, previous industrial policies encouraged firms to increase output to fulfil the planned targets without emphasizing efficiency and higher capacity realization in production. By influencing government administration large firms were able to accumulate subsidised imported inputs and machinery and to disregard full utilization of plant capacity. A negative relationship may, therefore, be possible between firm size and capacity realization.

Proportion of Non-production Workers to Total Workers (PNWT): In the production process, the proportion of non-production workers to total employment includes managerial administration, labour relations, R&D

and engineering personnel who contribute to effective acquisition and combination of productive resources. Klotz, Madoo and Hanson (1980) found this variable to be positive and statistically significant. Campbell (1984) suggested that PNWT reflected average education levels in the industry. He argued that those industries with a higher proportion of highly educated labour would also be more receptive to new approaches to production and management, leading to a positive association between the share of non-production employees and the rate of PCR.

However, this view is opposed by an OECD study in 1986 which argues that an increase in the proportion of 'white collar' or managerial staff imposes a certain rigidity in the production process, thereby retarding rapid adjustment to variations in demand. There is also a view that increasing bureaucratization of the production process may reflect 'feather bedding' and the development of X-inefficiencies within the context of protected and regulated industries. Economic theory is indeterminate in postulating the relationship between this variable and the rate of PCR.

In Bangladesh, a large proportion of industrial enterprises are in public sector, with excessive employment and excessive wage and fringe benefits for employees. Bangladesh does not have a social security system, so employment in clerical and administrative activities has been used as one way of helping people to improve their quality of living. An ADB study (1987) showed that much of the Bangladesh industrial sector is plagued with substantial over-manning and a large proportion of non-production workers, which suggests a negative relationship between PNWT and PCR. In Pakistan, Pasha and Qureshi (1984) found a negative but non-significant association between PNWT and capacity realization.

Capital Intensity: Capital intensity has been shown to be an important variable in determining capacity realization. It is hypothesized that firms with higher capital intensity are likely to operate at higher realization rates, because they cannot afford the rental cost of unused capital. In other words, more capital intensive plants have a greater incentive to economize on cost of capital through a high rate of capacity realization. Some empirical studies support this contention (Winston 1971, Lecraw 1978, Lim 1981). However, if the cost of capital becomes relatively cheap due to subsidised credit or low interest rates, then firms may accumulate more capital than is required for production and are likely to operate at a lower rate of capacity realization, so a negative relationship could be expected between these two variables. Empirical findings of Islam (1978), Morawetz (1981) and Srinivasan (1992) support this hypothesis although only Srinivasan's finding was statistically significant.

During the 1970s and 1980s, industries in Bangladesh enjoyed various types of concessions and incentives such as tax holidays, accelerated depreciation allowances and exemption of reinvested income from both corporation and personal income taxes. Heavy protection was also given to industries in the form of subsidised inputs and machinery through import licensing, making capital relatively cheap. Thus, distorted factor prices and import licensing rules encouraged capital intensive techniques and over-expansion of industrial capacity. Capacity realization remained low in most of the large industries, particularly in import substituting capital intensive industries, so a negative relationship is hypothesised between capital intensity and rate of realization.

Market Structure(MS): Market structure is generally seen as a potentially important variable in determining the level of capacity realization. The usual practice is to employ a proxy for market structure using a firms' concentration ratio. In the standard industrial organization paradigm, a high concentration ratio is expected to diminish competitive rivalry among firms with the likelihood of under-utilization of production capacity.

Chamberlin (1938) pioneered the analysis of the relationship between market structure and capacity realization. His well-known explanations for the existence of excess capacity in industries is based on monopolistic competition. Due to the absence of competition among sellers, few firms undertake independent experiments to seek better ways of carrying out production activities (Caves and Barton 1990). Scherer (1986) contended that concentration does not lead to greater R&D intensity, and so leads to a decrease in capacity realization. Again, concentration may inhibit the information flow across firms within an industry and thus permit inefficient production units to survive (McCain 1975). Parry remarked that 'Under-utilization of capacity is perpetuated where the rate of growth of the market is insufficient to cover optimum output runs within the life of the plant' (1978:222). All these arguments suggest that, *ceteris paribus*, rates of capacity realization decrease with a greater concentration of producers. Empirical studies which support this argument include Esposito and Esposito (1974), Thoumi (1981), and Srinivasan (1992), among others (Table 7.2).

However, another line of argument suggests that high concentration brings about greater innovation and technological change, which may be sufficient to offset the adverse monopoly effects of high concentration (Goldschmid, Mann and Weston 1974). Merhav (1970) also argues that concentrated industries suffer from less uncertainty of demand than other firms and can plan better for high utilization of production capacity. These arguments suggest a positive relationship between industry concentration and the rate of PCR. Empirical studies such as Winston (1971) and Goldar and Renganathan (1989) support this hypothesis.

Bangladesh possesses an oligopolistic market structure in the industrial sector, created by the policy regimes pursued during the seventies to early eighties (Ahmad 1993). Foreign competition was eliminated through trade restrictions, and domestic competition was hindered through a system of industrial licensing and various fiscal and financial privileges directed to specific groups of entrepreneurs. The usual proxy of market structure, the 4-firm concentration ratio is estimated for the selected industries and presented in Appendix Table 4.1. This table reveals that the concentration ratio declined in some industries, such as jute, garments, fish and seafood industries, perhaps due to the removal of the investment ceiling and import licenses as part of economic reforms. But still the market structure in Bangladesh manufacturing remains concentrated. Given the oligopolistic market structure, our *a priori* expectation is a negative relationship between market structure and capacity realization. However, it is true that market oriented reforms facilitate firms compete in the world market and as such they do not have market power. Even if they do have market power, their cost functions remain unchanged. So, there is no reason to expect low PCRs. Thus, the relationship between market structure and PCRs remains an empirical issue.

Openness (OPN): This variable has been used mostly in aggregate analysis. Many earlier studies have documented a positive association between exports and growth at an aggregate (national) level in many developing countries (Michaeley 1977, 1979, Balassa 1978, 1985, Feder 1982, Jung and Marshall 1985). Some industry (firm) level studies (Table 6.2) also lend support to a positive relationship between openness and performance. However, Findlay (1985) demonstrated that export-orientation *per se* is not 'necessarily growth-inducing'; the missing link is found in such real determinants of growth as capital formation, capacity utilization and technological progress which are so vital for the dynamic internal economic transformation of these economies. This study tests the openness variable to explain the variation in firm level capacity realization and hypothesises a positive relation between openness and capacity realization. Export-oriented firms (industries) are expected to realize higher production capacity than non-exporting firms for two reasons: first, firms with high export proportions are likely to be subject to more external competition than firms producing mainly for local consumption. This competition may cause a 'cold-shower' effect on domestic managers. To stay in business, a firm competing in the world market might be forced to realize a higher production capacity than one selling only in a sheltered domestic market. "There is an implicit 'challenge-response' mechanism induced by competition, forcing domestic industries to adopt new technologies, to reduce 'X-inefficiency', and generally to reduce costs whatever possible" (Nishimizu and Robinson 1984: 179). The findings of Caves (1984), and Hill and Kalirajan (1993) point in this direction. Second, a firm selling in more than one market has an advantage over a firm selling in a single market, particularly when it comes to coping with unexpected demand problems. Diokno (1974) and Pasha and Qureshi (1984) have also argued in this direction and their empirical findings support this contention. Other than these two reasons, the exposure of manufacturing firms to the international market may act as an important conduit for the inflow of foreign technology, and thus enhance productive capacity and improve firm's productivity through higher capacity realization.

However, neoclassical theory suggests that capacity realization is exogenous and therefore is unaffected by trade openness. It may be argued, in line with 'new' growth theories, that trade policies affect capacity realization and technological progress which, in turn, lead to long-run growth. In these models, openness to trade provides access to imported inputs, which embody new technology and increase the effective size of the market facing producers, raising the demand for output and leading to higher utilization of technology (Grossman and Helpman 1990).

High export intensity may signal the achievement of economies of scale. Caves (1984) and Kaldor (1966) have rightly pointed out that export markets allow firms and industries to reap the benefits of economies of scale. Khalizadeh-Shirazi (1974) argued that exporting may involve relatively greater risks and consequently firms may attempt to export only if the return is higher than on domestic sales. This suggests that firms will exploit avenues to reduce costs and this is possible by realizing a higher rate of production capacity.

Most industries in Bangladesh are import substituting except jute, leather and tea. However, following the economic reforms in the early eighties, some export oriented sub-sectors within various industries were developed such as ready-made garments, fish and sea food and electronics. Manufacturing exports as a percentage of total exports of the country steadily increased since 1982 (Chapter 2). From all the above arguments, *a priori*, a positive relationship between export-orientation and the capacity realization of firm is presumed.

Effective Rate of Assistance: Trade and industrial policies have an important influence on PCR. Traditionally, economists quantify these policies by estimating an effective rate of protection (ERP). However, the

ERP is mainly concerned with trade policies. Other than these trade policies and explicit fiscal and financial incentives, the estimated ERAs take into account domestic policies which directly affect the prices of factors, material inputs, products, the assistance in the form of price and quantity controls, import bans, and similar policies were also translated through appropriate methodologies into quasi-taxes and quasi-subsidies including debt default (which was assumed as a subsidy) (Sahota 1990). Thus, the ERAs have the advantages over the traditional ERP measures as they are more informative and serve as summary variables to gauge the impact of policy reforms. The estimates of ERA measures are taken from Sahota and Huq (1991) which provide only consistent estimates from 1975 to 1988. The estimated ERAs used in this study are for the years 1981, 1987 and 1988.

In general, tariff protection and other industry regulatory or assistance measures are thought to lessen the competitiveness of industry, because all of these assistance measures protect domestic industries from foreign competition. These policies also create price distortions and have indirect costs which increase exponentially with the magnitude of price distortions. By limiting competition with foreign products, all sorts of protection become counter-productive. Therefore, protection is expected to have an adverse impact on firm-specific capacity realization. However, in line with the so called 'infant industry argument', it can be argued that protection helps to realize higher production capacity. Caves (1984) maintained that low rates of protection may promote best practice techniques and thereby improve capacity realization due to the reduction of risk provided by protective barriers. This is similar to the argument of Schumpeter (1942) that a reduction in competitive pressures, or an increase in market power may reduce the risk and stimulate the rate of PCR of a firm. Parry (1978) points out that tariff protection tends to promote the existence of plants in industry that are sub-optimal, in the sense that they fail to exploit available economies of scale. The above arguments for and against protection lead to the conclusion that economic theory is indeterminate concerning the nature of the relationship between the ERA and PCR of firm (industry).

Protection and regulation have historically been an important feature of Bangladesh industry, but in recent years subsidies, import quotas and licensing have been substantially reduced. Sahota (1990) argued that domestic industries in Bangladesh have failed to grow because of the excessive assistance provided to them in recent years and that therefore ERA is a crucial determinant of low capacity realization of Bangladesh industries.

Ownership (OWN): Many authors argue that ownership of firm is also an important factor in determining capacity realization. In addition to public and private firms, there are joint ventures between private and public firms or foreign participation with either public and private firms. In the literature, it is hypothesized that public sector firms have greater access to import licences, credit and technology, and so operate at a high level of capacity realization. The 'property right school', however, argues that managers within public firms tend to look after their self-interest rather than profit maximization. Since property rights are non-transferable in the case of public enterprises, the 'owners' (that is the public at large) have no incentive to pressure the managers of these enterprises to realize high levels of production capacity, so public enterprises perform less efficiently than private enterprises. However, 'the empirical evidence actually provides weak support for this hypothesis' (Boadman and Vining 1989). Bardhan (1992) argued that whether a firm is public or privately owned is less important. As long as its financial constraint is 'hard', there is no reason that this firm performs poorly.

Joint venture firms are assumed to realize high production capacity for at least two reasons. First, they have good management experience and good organizational structure (Pitt and Lee 1981); second, they encourage research and development. Garnicott (1984) demonstrates that foreign participation facilitates access to the latest and best practice technology and offers a positive impact on research and development. However, because of structural rigidities, joint venture firms may fail to cope simultaneously with domestic and foreign markets and so firms cannot operate at a high level of capacity realization. Economic theory, therefore, gives little guidance about the relationship between ownership and capacity realization of firm. This is therefore, an empirical question.

Two dummy variables are used to examine the above hypotheses, one is DUMPVT which takes the value of unity if the firm is privately owned, or zero if otherwise; the other is DUMJNT which takes the value of one if the firm is a joint venture, or zero otherwise.

The Equation

Drawing on earlier theoretical and empirical studies the following equation is specified. Accordingly, this model facilitates comparison of the results with those reported in previous studies.

$$PCR_i = f(\alpha_i, \overset{?}{AG_i}, \overset{?}{PNWT_i}, \overset{?}{SZ_i}, \overset{?}{CI_i}, \overset{?}{MS_i}, \overset{?}{ERA_i}, \overset{+}{OPN_i},$$

$$\overset{+}{DUMPVT}, \overset{+}{DUMJNT}) + u \qquad i = 1,2,3,........n \qquad (7.2)$$

Where:

PCR = Productive Capacity Realization; following on from Chapter 4, firm-specific *PCR*, estimated from observed inputs and output, is used as the dependent variable

α =   Constant term

AG =   Age of firm

$PNWT$ =   Proportion of non-production (such as administrative staff) workers to total workers

SZ =   Size of firm

CI =   Capital intensity

MR =   Market structure (defines here as four firm concentration ratio, CR4)

ERA = Effective rate of protection

OPN = Openness

$DUMPVT$ = Dummy variable for a private firm (takes value 1 when the firm is private or zero otherwise)

$DUMJNT$ = Dummy variable for a joint venture firm (takes value 1 for a joint venture firm or zero otherwise)

and u = Stochastic disturbance term respectively.

Empirical Results and Interpretation

To identify the variables which determine realization rates, multiple regression analysis was carried out separately for each industry group,[5] using ordinary least square (OLS) method. The hypotheses discussed in the previous section were tested in each case (industry) wherever data were available. Cross-section research in industrial organization usually encounters multicollinearity, and the nature of regressors used in this study indicates its presence. Therefore, before carrying out the regression analysis, multiple correlation matrices among the independent variables were estimated for each industry in order to detect the degree of multicollinearity among variables. These matrices are presented in Appendix Tables A7.1 to A7.5. These results showed no perfect multicollinearity between any two independent variables. However, there were some cases where two independent variables were seen to be fairly strongly associated which undermine regression results. These cases will be explained later when interpreting results.

Heteroscedasticity is a common problem of cross-section data, so a test was also carried out. Evidence of heteroscdasticity was found in some cases. This problem is taken care of by using White's (1980) remedial procedures. Heteroscedasticity adjusted regression results for the selected industries are presented in Tables 7.4 to 7.8. In each case, three equations were estimated for three intertemporal periods (i.e. 1981, 1987 and 1991). Since the dependent variables (PCR indices) vary from 0 to 1, after estimating the regressions, the predicted values have been checked to see whether any these values exceed this range. None was observed in any industry group.

Table 7.4: Determinants of Productive Capacity Realization in the Cotton Textile Industry

Coefficient	1981	1987	1991
Constant	0.7401	0.6765	0.6702
	(.0318)	(.1166)	(.0658)
AG	-0.0115*	-0.0078*	-0.0370**
	(.0013)	(.0017)	(.0094)
PNWT	-0.2631*	-0.2503**	-0.4866
	(.0289)	(.0733)	(.7996)
SZ	0.0012***	-0.07216	0.0053
	(.0005)	(.05865)	(.0065)
CI	-0.0952	-0.0629***	-0.1382***
	(.0498)	(.0115)	(.0314)
DUMPVT	0.0532	0.0762	0.1070**
	(.0221)	(.0348)	(.0217)
R^2	0.54	0.43	0.48
F-statistics	25.77	15.05	7.63

Note: The results are heteroscedasticity adjusted. Figures in the parentheses under the regression coefficients are standard errors. The symbol *, **, and *** indicates that the slope coefficient is significantly different from zero at the 1 per cent, 5 per cent, or 10 per cent level, respectively.

Table 7.4 displays the regression results for the cotton textile industry. Depending on availability of data five explanatory variables are included in each regression. Age of firm (AG) is the only variable found to be statistically significant throughout. This variable, as hypothesized, produces significant and negative effects on PCR, implying that, when a firm's machinery and equipment become old, there is less likelihood of achieving full capacity realization. Cotton textile is one of the oldest industries in Bangladesh, so this finding is in accordance with expectations. The high replacement cost of capital in the textile industry along with small savings in the economy may result in the retention of spindles and looms that fail to embody more advanced technologies and lead to the reduction in capacity realization. In evaluating the performance of cotton textile industry, Abdullah and Rahman (1989) argued that old and outdated technology was the main cause of poor performance.

The variable PNWT (proportion of non-production workers to total work force) is also negatively related with PCR, suggesting that the higher the proportion of non-production workers in the total work force, *ceteris paribus*, the lower the rate of PCR. This variable is statistically significant at one and five per cent levels of significance for 1981 and 1987 respectively, but was not significant for 1991, although it has the correct sign. While economic theory is indeterminate about the relationship between PNWT and PCR, the negative relationship is in accordance with expectations in the case of the cotton textile industry, which as mentioned earlier, is plagued with over-manning and particularly with clerical and administrative staff (ADB 1987). Due to the legal systems and the socio-economic structure of the country, labour market issues have remained untouched in recent economic reforms, so over-manning continues to retard firms in realizing maximum production capacity.

Results in Table 7.4 show an ambiguous relationship between size of firm (SZ) and PCR. Although economic theory gives little guidance about the relationship between these two variables, the industrial structure and institutional systems in Bangladesh (Chapter 2) provide some expectations of a negative relationship for cotton textile industries. The coefficient of SZ is positive and significant for 1981, negative and statistically insignificant for 1987 and positive but insignificant for 1991. These results except for 1987 are not consistent with *a priori* expected hypothesis. Until 1981, the economy of Bangladesh was *autarkic*, so it may be argued that large firms took advantage of licensing and other protective measures by influencing policy regimes which might help to acquire scale economies which may explain the 1981 result. The 1991 result may be attributed to economic reforms, particularly to privatization of firms which is a significant aspect of Bangladesh's economic reforms and may have induced to exploit underutilized production capacity.

Capital intensity, as expected, influences PCR negatively. This variable is not significant for 1981 and is weakly significant at 10 per cent level both for 1987 and 1991. These results appear to be consistent with the country's trade and industrial policy regimes. Enterprises were supplied with foreign equipment and machinery at subsidized rates, on the basis of installed capacity, which encouraged firms to build excess capacity without regard for its utilization. Islam (1978) and Roy (1988) also found a negative relationship which they attributed to the same reasoning.

The dummy variable DUMPVT is not statistically significant for 1981 and 1987 but is significant for 1991, which means privatization of firm failed to influence firm's capacity realization until 1987. This does not conform with the expected hypothesis discussed in the previous section. The explanation is that although government launched a privatization program since the late 1980s, the private sector remained shaky owing to various structural and institutional teething problems. The 1991 result is consistent with the expected hypothesis that privatization induced firms to realize higher productive capacity. However, this result is not certain because DUMPVT may capture some other changes in the economy (or industrial sector) over the years.

Overall results are not robust. The F-statistic for each period is significant which implies that all explanatory variables are jointly significant, even though not all explanatory variables are individually significant. R^2 values for all these regressions are low. Variables included in these regressions explain substantial proportions (54, 43 and 48 per cent) of inter-firm variations of capacity realization for selected periods respectively, but may be limited by the omission of other important variables from the analysis due to data limitations on variables, such as market structure, R&D expenditures, effective rate of assistance (ERA), and export-orientation.

The most influential variable in determining capacity realization in the jute textile industry is export-orientation or openness (Table 7.5). This variable is positively related to PCR and is statistically significant throughout at the one per cent level. This finding is consistent with economic theory (correct sign), i.e. export orientation enhances competition which in turn induces firms to maximize capacity realization for greater efficiency. For Bangladesh in particular these results are not unexpected since jute goods used to be the single largest export item until 1988.

The other variable PNWT (proportion of non-production workers to total work force) is also consistently significant at a high level of significance throughout, with negative coefficients, indicating that PNWT adversely affected capacity realization of firms. Again, these results are expected because of over-manning, as in the case of the cotton textile industry. Amongst other explanatory variables, age of firm (AG) and DUMPVT have consistent signs but showed little or no significance. Most of the enterprises of the jute industry are old, which causes under-utilization of production capacity. But, recent privatization of public enterprises has led to increase production capacity realization, so the negative signs for AG and positive signs for DUMPVT are according to expectations. Other variables such as SZ and CI had ambiguous signs and were not consistently significant.

Table 7.5: Determinants of Productive Capacity Realization in the Jute Industry

Coefficient	1981	1987	1991
Constant	0.4974	0.304	0.2466
	(.0223)	(.0399)	(.0332)
AG	-0.0032*	-0.0003	-0.0004
	(.0007)	(.0009)	(.0006)
PNWT	-0.2002*	-0.1944**	-0.2108**
	(.2124)	(.0230)	(.0694)
SZ	0.0001	-0.0062**	0.0088
	(.00005)	(.0005)	(.0694)
CI	-0.3601**	0.0012	0.6257*
	(.0442)	(.0007)	(.1667)
OPN	0.5207*	0.3027*	0.3498*
	(.0553)	(.0406)	(.0283)
DUMPVT	.0049	0.0228	0.0141
	(.0137)	(.0153)	(.0093)
R^2	0.83	0.65	0.86
F-statistics	37.02	16.74	44.12

Note: The results are heteroscedasticity adjusted. Figures in the parentheses under the regression coefficients are standard errors. The symbol *, **, and *** indicates that the slope coefficient is significantly different from zero at the 1 per cent, 5 per cent, or 10 per cent level, respectively.

Overall, the inclusion of all these explanatory variables in regression is valid, since all F-statistics are statistically significant. In all cases, R^2 values are quite high, indicating that the variables included in these models can explain inter-firm variations in capacity realization fairly well in each year. Had it been possible to include other excluded variables, such as market structure, ERA, and human capital variables, these results would have been more robust.

Table 7.6: Determinants of Productive Capacity Realization in the Garment Industry

Coefficient	1987	1991
Constant	0.2822	0.6135
	(.0900)	(.1046)
AG	0.0559*	0.0105*
	(.0073)	(.0081)
PNWT	0.0154	0.5946**
	(.6552)	(.1293)
SZ	-0.0025*	0.0022
	(.0006)	(.0015)
CI	0.1597	0.0697
	(0.0942)	(.0056)
DUMJNT	0.0854**	0.1178*
	(.0192)	(.0276)
R^2	0.64	0.36
F-statistics	22.12	7.60

Note: The results are heteroscedasticity adjusted. Figures in the parentheses under the regression coefficients are standard errors. The symbol *, **, and *** indicates that the slope coefficient is significantly different from zero at the 1 per cent, 5 per cent, or 10 per cent level, respectively.

Age of firm (AG) and DUMJNT are two important variables in determining capacity realization in the garment industry (Table 7.6) with positive and highly significant coefficients. Age has a positive influence on capacity realization, because firms in this industry are of very recent origin. Most firms are less than 10 years old and embody most recent technological advances. These firms are almost 100 per cent export-oriented so that a competitive environment and high external demand pressure induce them to employ and utilize recent technology. Foreign participation in collaboration with domestic firms, is one of the catalysts of success for Bangladesh's garment industry. Since the Multi-Fibre Arrangement (MFA) imposed restrictions on the established exporters of clothing from developing countries, exporters sought entrepreneurs for joint venture arrangements in other developing countries, such as Bangladesh which were unaffected by the MFA. As foreign partners are well-established exporters, joint venture firms are better managed, which has enabled them to realize high levels production capacity in joint ventures garment industries.

Among the other explanatory variables, PNWT (proportion of non-production workers to total work force) and CI (capital intensity) have expected signs, i.e. these variables positively influence capacity realization of firms. But the coefficients of CI are statistically insignificant in both periods while those of PNWT are statistically significant only for 1991. From regression results, the relationship between size and capacity realization in this industry is not clear, because the sign of SZ is negative and significant for 1987, but positive and not significant for 1991.

The F-statistics for regressions are statistically significant indicating validity of inclusion of all explanatory variables. R^2 values vary from 0.36 for 1987 and 0.64 for 1991 respectively which implies that a large proportion of inter firm variation in capacity realization remains unexplained, but less so in 1991 after reforms.

Regressions were carried out by taking all sectors together within the food processing industries, so were able to include some industry-wise variables, such as market structure (four-firms' concentration ratio), effective rate of assistance (ERA), etc. Therefore, there are nine independent variables in each regression. Table 7.7 demonstrates that there is no single variable which strongly determines capacity realization of firms in the food processing industry. In other words, no variable is consistent and statistically significant throughout.[6]

The coefficients of AG are negative for all years and statistically significant in pre-reform years (1981, 1987) but it was not significant in the post-reform period (1991). The negative coefficient supports the argument that older firms have lower capacity realization rates. However, after the opening up of the economy, incumbent firms had to restructure their technology to face the prospect of competition from abroad. As mentioned in Chapter 2, policy reform in Bangladesh is still half-hearted, so it may be that competition and the learning by doing effects were not enough to offset the 'old age' effect. The sign of the coefficients of AG remained negative but became insignificant after the reforms.

PNWT (proportion of non-production workers to total work force) is positively related with PCR throughout and statistically significant at 5 and 10 per cent levels of significance for the transition and post-reform years respectively. One explanation of this positive association of PNWT with

PCR may be that all sub-sectors of food processing industries, except for sugar products, are at an early stage of development, so that increases in non-production workers in these industries are due to expansion and demand pressure from home and abroad following the policy reforms and were needed to obtain higher PCR, with modern technology.

Table 7.7: Determinants of Productive Capacity Realization in the Food Processing Industry

Coefficient	1981	1987	1991
Constant	0.7189	0.4782	0.5618
	(.0614)	(.0725)	(.0637)
AG	-0.0102*	-0.0245*	-0.0026
	(.0012)	(.0021)	(.0020)
PNWT	0.3248	0.4056**	0.5432***
	(.2962)	(.0373)	(.0281)
SZ	0.0002	0.0373**	0.0034*
	(.0008)	(.0095)	(.0007)
CI	0.1450	0.2944	0.3618
	(.2884)	(.2612)	(.2734)
CR4	-0.4704*	-0.0852	-0.0863**
	(.1630)	(.1273)	(.01242)
OPN	0.0217	0.2053**	0.2572*
	(.0612)	(.0584)	(.0482)
ERA	0.0761*	-0.1044	-0.0998
	(.0148)	(.0776)	(.3103)
DUMPVT	0.0053	0.443	0.0548
	(.0347)	(.0363)	(.0353)
DUMJNT	0.0797	0.0439	0.1067
	(.0422)	(.0595)	(.0571)
R^2	0.59	0.42	0.45
F-statistics	13.12	6.56	7.76

Note: The results are heteroscedasticity adjusted. Figures in the parentheses under the regression coefficients are standard errors. The symbol *, **, and *** indicates that the slope coefficient is significantly different from zero at the 1 per cent, 5 per cent, or 10 per cent level, respectively.

This explanation is supported by the positive association of SZ (size of firm), OPN (openness) and the technology variable CI (capital intensity) with PCR. Since increases in non-production workers imply development of human capital, a positive impact of PNWT on capacity realization is expected.

The negative signs of the market structure (CR4) variable supports the hypothesis that the higher the concentration ratio or degree of monopoly in an industry the lower is capacity realization. This variable is statistically significant in both pre- and post-reform years, which suggests that the (monopolistic and oligopolistic) market structure did not change after the implementation of economic policy reforms. This is supported by the views of many policy-makers and international donor agencies who believe that economic policy reforms in Bangladesh are incomplete (World Bank 1992, Reza and Mahmood 1995, and Ahammad 1995).

The influence of ERA on capacity realization is not clear. It seems to have exerted a significant positive influence before reforms, a negative nonsignificant influence in the transition period, and a significant negative influence on capacity realization after the reforms. Before the reforms, most of the enterprises in the food processing sector, except for sugar products were new, and ERA provided insulation for these firms from external influences and thus helped to realize higher production capacity, at least in the short run. But, when ERA is continued over a longer period, it has the potential to produce a negative effect on PCR which is found in this study.

As discussed in Chapter 2, the reforms have included removal of measures which allow uncompetitive firms to survive such as quantitative restrictions, reduction of tariffs and increasing assistance (subsidies, tax holidays, tax exemptions). Some firms survive only because of such protection and assistance and not through the efficient utilization of their capacity. Therefore, the negative correlation between ERA and PCR is not unexpected. The two ownership dummies exerted an insignificant influence, although their coefficients have the expected positive signs in all years. Since these variables are not statistically significant, it may be concluded that rate of capacity realization is independent of the locus of ownership. Such an outcome might be the result of the failure of liberalization to promote competition because of the replacement of the public sector monopoly by private sector monopolies. In fact, the privatization process in Bangladesh has been judged as grossly mismanaged (Sobhan 1990).

There are nine explanatory variables in each regression in the chemical industry group as in the case of the food processing. The regressions' results for the chemical industry group show that two variables AG and CR4 are consistently significant throughout with expected signs (Table 7.8).

Table 7.8: Determinants of Productive Capacity Realization in the Chemical Industry

Coefficient	1981	1987	1991
Constant	0.8306	0.8494	0.9075
	(.0557)	(.0974)	(.0905)
AG	-0.0126*	-0.0687***	-0.0522***
	(.0016)	(.0222)	(.0192)
PNWT	0.3306	0.1918	0.0886
	(.2897)	(.3687)	(.0358)
SZ	-0.1592*	0.1478	0.1604**
	(.0127)	(.3639)	(.0321)
CI	-0.0351	-0.1560***	-0.1715***
	(2498)	(.0244)	(.0199)
CR4	-0.6261*	-0.1918***	-0.2185**
	(.0546)	(.0476)	(.0171)
OPN	0.2276	0.2697	0.2208
	(.1235)	(.1616)	(.3207)
ERA	-0.3093***	-0.1209	-0.0021
	(.0854)	(.0734)	(.0763)
DUMPVT	0.0041	0.0191	0.0103
	(.0248)	(.0429)	(.0488)
DUMJNT	0.0321	0.1076**	0.0434
	(.0302)	(.0326)	(.0653)
R^2	0.49	0.35	0.37
F-statistics	12.00	15.22	14.59

Note: The results are heteroscedasticity adjusted. Figures in the parentheses under the regression coefficients are standard errors. The symbol *, **, and *** indicates that the slope coefficient is significantly different from zero at the 1 per cent, 5 per cent, or 10 per cent level, respectively.

The consistently negative sign of the age variable indicates that capacity realization has declined due to the obsolescence and high maintenance costs of capital associated with old and aging machinery of firms. It is interesting that, in the pre-reform period, the age of firm (AG) is significant at 1 per cent level of significance, while in the post-reform period, it is significant only at 10 per cent level of significance.

The explanatory power of the regressions are quite limited as shown by the coefficients of determination (R^2). Only 59, 42 and 45 per cent of variations in realization rates are explained by the independent variables in these models for 1981, 1987 and 1991 respectively. These results are not robust perhaps because of high multicollinearity among the independent variables (Appendix Table 7.4) and exclusion of variables owing to data limitations. However, results of F-statistics show that all independent variables are jointly significantly different from zero implying that their inclusion is valid.This may be because of improvements in capital stock within the firm owing to economic reforms. The industry concentration ratio is negative and significant at 1, 10 and 5 per cent levels in the pre-reform, transition and post-reform years respectively. Various sub-sectors of chemical industries (such as fertilizer, pharmaceuticals, matches and petroleum products) are known as concentrated industries (Ahmad 1993). After the reform period, perhaps concentration decreased owing to the growth of foreign subsidiary companies in these industries. If so, the results are not unexpected.

The coefficients of PNWT and OPN have consistently positive signs but none is statistically significant. PNWT is not correlated with other independent variables so it can be concluded that it has no influence on PCR. However, OPN is highly correlated with CR4 for 1987 and 1991 (Appendix Table 7.5) so it is not possible to reach a conclusion regarding its influence on PCR. The variable SZ (size of firm) exerts a negative and significant influence before reform but a positive and significant influence on PCR in the post reform year. Small enterprises generally have less influence over the high powered bureaucrats in acquiring necessary inputs and appropriate technology, which may explain their low rate of capacity realization. The coefficients of the technology variable CI (capital intensity) is consistently negative throughout but is not significant in the pre-reform period. This result supports the hypothesis that highly capital intensive firms utilize less of their production capacity, though high multicollinearity between SZ and CI suggests that the above conclusions are only tentative.

The variable ERA, as expected, exerts a negative influence on PCR. This is, however, significant at 10 per cent level of significance only for the pre-reform period. This is attributable to the survival of uncompetitive enterprises with the numerous protective measures (tariff, quotas, bans) and availability of assistance policies (subsidies, tax exemption). Thus government policies have encouraged the creation of excess capacity rather than its utilization. This variable becomes insignificant in the transition and post-reform years but continues to exert a negative influence on PCR. Since this variable is highly correlated with industry's concentration (CR4) in these periods (Appendix Table 7.5), it is difficult to reach a fair conclusion.

Ownership dummies are positively related with PCR, but DUMJNT is significantly different from zero only for the transition period, which means that joint venture enterprises realize higher production capacity in chemical industries. But except for this period, it can generally be concluded that ownership does not influence capacity realization of firms. In this context, it may be argued that efficiency gains hinge on the structure of the manufacturing sector and overall economic environment of the economy rather than just on the change of ownership. This is in agreement with Hemming and Monsoor who concluded that '...... if privatization involves no more than a transfer of activities from the public to the private sector, it may yield only limited gains' (1988:15).

The overall fit of regressions is restricted. Variables included in these regressions could explain only 49, 35 and 37 per cent of inter-firm variations of capacity realization. This implies that other important variables, which may have an important influence on PCR, are omitted from these regressions. However, significant F-statistics validate the inclusion of the independent variables.

Summary and Conclusions

This chapter analyzed the influence of a number of variables on PCR across firms within and between years. The objective was to identify influential variables which might be manipulated by government policy to improve the rate of PCR. While there was no single variable which was consistently significant across all industries, there were some important indicators for policy purposes. One is that initiatives are required to be industry specific to target accurately those influential variables which can improve productivity performance in terms of capacity realization. For example, age of firm (AG) was one of the influential variables which negatively affect capacity realization of firms in all industries except the (recent) garment industry. The policy implication is obviously that modernization in terms of plant and equipment in all the other industries will tend to improve the rate of capacity realization.

A striking finding was the insignificance of the current trade and industrial policy reforms related variables (such as OPN and ERA). This implies that policy reform to remove impediments to the competitive process may have had little impact to date on productive capacity realization. This might be because they are incomplete. This study used three selected years (1981, 1987 and 1991) based on the availability of data, but these years could be transitional periods. Further reform was initiated in 1991 but unavailability of data precluded more recent analysis. Many policy-makers believe policy reforms remain half-hearted and further reforms, with judicious dismantling of the existing tariff structure, are suggested to promote a more competitive market. Greater emphasis on export promotion would accelerate improved resource allocation performance and increase realization of production capacity in the industrial sector.

Given the limitations of cross-section data, the estimated equations displayed reasonably high explanatory power for inter-firm variations of PCR across industries but are probably limited by omission of some important variables. Variables that were omitted from the regressions, largely because of difficulties of quantitative measurement, such as management variables, input quality, and unavailability of data for some measurable variables, such as R&D expenditures, energy intensity, growth of demand, managers' education and training, proportion of skilled and unskilled labour, and unionization or political affiliation of work force.

Two more caveats on findings reported in this chapter should be noted. First, the measurement of market competition proxied by a four-firm concentration ratio is not satisfactory according to the modern theory of industrial organization. This measure is extremely susceptible to misrepresentation, partly because it essentially captures only some of the myriad of forces that combine together to influence the level of competition in any particular sector. In particular, it frequently fails to capture the impact on the contestability of markets of the potential, as opposed to the actual threat of entry and competition. Second, there are relatively high degrees of association among some independent variables (for example ERA and SZ, SZ and PNWT, CI and SZ) which have contributed to the insignificance of some estimates reported in this study (Appendix Tables A7.1 to A7.5). Therefore, the findings of this chapter should be treated with caution and subjected to further detailed analysis.

Appendix

Table A7.1: Estimated Correlation Matrix of Independent Variables in the Cotton Textile Industries

1981

Variables	AG	PNWT	SZ	CI	OPN
AG	1.000				
PNWT	-0.101	1.000			
SZ	0.190	-0.309	1.000		
CI	0.240	-0.010	0.3833	1.000	

1987

Variables	AG	PNWT	SZ	CI	OPN
AG	1.000				
PNWT	-0.383	1.000			
SZ	0.393	-0.620	1.000		
CI	0.295	-0.162	0.352	1.000	

1991

Variables	AG	PNWT	SZ	CI	OPN
AG	1.000				
PNWT	-0.372	1.000			
SZ	0.364	-0.606	1.000		
CI	0.254	0.087	0.345	1.000	

Table A7.2: Estimated Correlation Matrix of Independent Variables in the Jute Industry

1981

Variables	AG	PNWT	SZ	CI	OPN
AG	1.000				
PNWT	0.026	1.000			
SZ	0.086	0.710	1.000		
CI	-0.034	-0.357	-0.001	1.000	
OPN	-0.390	-0.077	-0.018	0.165	1.000

1987

Variables	AG	PNWT	SZ	CI	OPN
AG	1.000				
PNWT	0.125	1.000			
SZ	0.084	0.635	1.000		
CI	-0.094	-0.042	0.007	1.000	
OPN	-0.248	-0.104	-0.165	-0.100	1.000

1991

Variables	AG	PNWT	SZ	CI	OPN
AG	1.000				
PNWT	-0.190	1.000			
SZ	0.024	-0.022	1.000		
CI	-0.213	-0.124	-0.105	1.000	
OPN	-0.072	-0.055	-0.174	-0.115	1.000

Table A7.3: Estimated Correlation Matrix of Independent Variables in the Garment Industry

1987

Variables	AG	PNWT	SZ	CI
AG	1.000			
PNWT	-0.072	1.000		
SZ	-0.087	-0.427	1.000	
CI	0.060	-0.013	0.163	1.000

1991

Variables	AG	PNWT	SZ	CI
AG	1.000			
PNWT	0.209	1.000		
SZ	-0.082	-0.446	1.000	
CI	-0.040	-0.061	0.380	1.000

Table A7.4: Estimated Correlation Matrix of Independent Variables in the Food Processing Industries

1981

Variables	AG	PNWT	SZ	CI	CR4	OPN	ERA
AG	1.000						
PNWT	-0.396	1.000					
SZ	0.519	-0.189	1.000				
CI	0.136	-0.073	0.429	1.000			
CR4	-0.073	0.503	0.223	-0.073	1.000		
OPN	-0.252	0.045	-0.204	-0.089	0.093	1.000	
ERA	-0.118	0.545	0.693	-0.100	0.085	-0.138	1.000

1987

Variables	AG	PNWT	SZ	CI	CR4	OPN	ERA
AG	1.000						
PNWT	-0.031	1.000					
SZ	0.314	-0.113	1.000				
CI	0.044	0.004	0.425	1.000			
CR4	0.084	0.237	0.397	-0.036	1.000		
OPN	-0.122	0.151	-0.176	-0.060	0.040	1.000	
ERA	0.336	0.0572	0.651	-0.048	0.689	-0.184	1.000

1991

Variables	AG	PNWT	SZ	CI	CR4	OPN	ERA
AG	1.000						
PNWT	-0.011	1.000					
SZ	0.324	-0.048	1.000				
CI	0.046	0.053	0.466	1.000			
CR4	0.056	0.247	0.363	-0.029	1.000		
OPN	-0.028	0.127	-0.110	0.077	0.062	1.000	
ERA	0.333	0.104	0.649	-0.033	0.672	-0.170	1.000

Table A7.5: Estimated Correlation Matrix of Independent Variables in the Chemical Industries

1981

variables	AG	PNWT	SZ	CI	CR4	OPN	ERA
AG	1.000						
PNWT	0.212	1.000					
SZ	0.222	0.351	1.000				
CI	0.204	0.130	0.672	1.000			
CR4	0.131	0.073	0.317	0.643	1.000		
OPN	-0.396	-0.159	-0.121	0.027	0.253	1.000	
ERA	0.248	-0.217	-0.158	0.173	0.262	-0.080	1.000

1987

Variables	AG	PNWT	SZ	CI	CR4	OPN	ERA
AG	1.000						
PNWT	0.337	1.000					
SZ	0.267	0.296	1.000				
CI	0.235	0.220	0.651	1.000			
CR4	0.152	-0.005	0.378	0.595	1.000		
OPN	-0.049	-0.062	-0.057	0.052	0.407	1.000	
ERA	0.263	0.020	-0.007	0.287	0.415	-0.137	1.000

1991

Variables	AG	PNWT	SZ	CI	CR4	OPN	ERA
AG	1.000						
PNWT	0.249	1.000					
SZ	0.262	0.281	1.000				
CI	0.285	0.253	0.728	1.000			
CR4	0.237	0.055	0.335	0.533	1.000		
OPN	-0.103	-0.139	0.124	0.164	0.485	1.000	
ERA	0.263	-0.012	-0.019	0.188	0.638	-0.055	1.000

Notes

[1] For recent reviews, see Chapter 3 in Kirkpatrick et al 1985, Geroski 1988 and Schmalensee 1989.

[2] Aaronovitch and Sawyer (1975) provide an extensive list of measures of concentration. Curry and George (1983) give further analysis on industrial concentration.

[3] About the calculation procedures of the ERA see Harvard Institute of Development (HIID) (1990), An assessment of the impact of industrial policies in Bangladesh, Working paper no. 16, Planning Commission, Dhaka.

[4] Bangladesh's work force in manufacturing sector is highly politicized. So, unionization or political affiliation of work force is one of the crucial variables which inhibit capacity realization of firm. However, unavailability of relevant data precluded the inclusion of this variable in the analysis.

[5] Regression analysis was carried out separately for each of the industries within the textiles and garment industry group because each of these industries has sufficient observations (number of firms). Therefore, we could not include some industry-specific variables such as market structure and ERA.

[6] The correlation coefficients are 0.52 between AG and SZ, 0.50 between PNWT and CR4, 0.54 between PNWT and ERA, and 0.69 between ERA and SZ respectively for 1981 and 0.65 between ERA and SZ and 0.69 between ERA and CR4 respectively for 1987. Again, the correlation coefficients are 0.65 between ERA and SZ and 0.67 between ERA and CR4 respectively for 1991 (Appendix Table 6.4). Having these fairly strong correlations among the explanatory variables, it may be argued in line with Klein (1962) that multicollenearity is quite damaging for undermining regression results. Keeping this in mind, regression results are explained.

8   Conclusions and Policy
Implications

In the 1980s, many developing countries including Bangladesh embarked on trade and industrial policy reforms, following the structural adjustment policies advocated by the World Bank and the IMF. These policy reforms have been widely discussed in the development economics literature but their impact on the productive performance of an economy is still inconclusive. The theoretical literature does not provide solid foundation for examining such an association. It, thus, remains an empirical issue. This thesis developed a framework to examine whether recent economic reforms improved productivity growth of Bangladesh manufacturing firms. By focussing on the principal sources of productivity growth, namely, change in capacity realization and technological progress in selected manufacturing industries, this study sought to illuminate the issues which policy reform now needs to be addressed on the basis of empirical findings.

Total factor productivity (TFP) growth as a source of sustained economic growth has become major issue on the analysis of economic performances in developing countries in the context of market-oriented economic reforms and globalization. TFP growth comprises two components: change in capacity realization (catching up) and technological progress. Several earlier studies were conducted at an aggregate level (either industry, sector or national level), using the traditional growth accounting method in which capacity realization was ignored, and thus identified TFP growth solely with technological progress and therefore, provided flawed results. Further, none of the earlier studies paid attention to the determinants of productive capacity realization (PCR) and, in particular, to the effect of the 1980s' trade and industrial policy reforms on PCR in Bangladesh and elsewhere.

This thesis makes theoretical and empirical contributions to economic analysis and economic modelling in order to address these neglected issues. The major contributions can be summarised as follows:

(1) it develops an appropriate methodology using the varying coefficient frontier production function model to estimate capacity realization indices of manufacturing firms; (2) it develops a framework by following Kalirajan *et al* arguments to measure TFP growth in terms of its components (change in capacity realization and technological progress) which provided a theoretically sound basis for analysing productivity growth; (3) it applied these methodologies to firm level data of selected manufacturing sectors for empirical measurements; (4) it estimated and identified determinants of capacity realization including the recent trade and industrial policy reforms.

Major Findings

This study provides an empirical analysis of the productive performance of manufacturing firms of three key industry groups before, during and after economic reforms in Bangladesh. The three selected industry groups are textile and garments, food processing and chemical industries. The overall picture that emerges in terms of productive capacity realization and total factor productivity growth is not as illuminating as anticipated. However, the rate of capacity realization and TFP growth in most sectors within these industry groups showed little improvement. In a few, however, such as ready-made garments, fish and sea food, and industrial chemicals were found to be rising. Thus, manufacturing industries have so far achieved mixed results after the economic reforms.

Empirical results indicated substantial unrealized productive capacity across firms. A large number of firms within the selected industry groups produced below their potential output frontier. During the pre-reform year (1981), the average rates of enterprise capacity realization were 56 per cent in cotton textiles, 47 per cent in jute textiles, 73 per cent in garment, 51 per cent in food processing and 68 per cent in the chemical industry groups. There were wide variations in capacity realization across industries as well as across firms within industries. Manufacturing industries responded a little to the implementation of economic reforms. In the post reform year (1991), average rates of enterprise capacity realization improved marginally in some sub-sectors but declined in others (hydrogenated vegetables oil, drugs & pharmaceuticals, paints & varnishes) within industry groups, indicating that firms are still producing below their potential. These differentials in capacity realization across firms pose severe constraints on industrial growth of the country.

This study also shows that TFP growth in Bangladesh manufacturing industries has been sluggish. The share of output growth accounted for by input growth is, as expected, high in nearly all industries and periods (both before and after reform). In some industries the estimated rate of TFP growth was negligible or even negative. It is interesting to note that similar estimates for other developing and fast growing East Asian countries' industries range from 2 to 11 per cent per annum (Chapter 5). Thus, with respect of TFP growth in the industrial sector, Bangladesh compares unfavourably not only with fast growing East Asian countries, but also with other developing countries. The low rate of TFP growth diminishes Bangladesh's competitiveness in the international market for manufactures. The low relative contribution of TFP to output growth makes the achievement of a high pace of industrial growth difficult.

The most significant positive feature of the productivity experience of Bangladesh manufacturing industries to emerge from this study is that technological progress plays a significant role in TFP growth across firms within a number of sub-sectors in the selected industries. However, the sustenance of industrial growth also depends crucially on the efficient utilization of productive resources, and the empirical results show that the relative contribution of capacity realization to TFP growth was not substantial even after the implementation of economic reform. In other words, changes in PCR were not equal or outweigh gains from technological progress in most sub-sectors of these industry groups. Indeed, some sectors experienced negative changes in PCR over the period 1981 to 1991. A further striking result is that the technological progress that did occur in these sectors failed to produce spectacular growth in output because of labour saving technological progress.

This study identified a number of firm-specific and policy related factors which influenced capacity realization and contributed to differentials in realization rates across firms. Age of firm was found to influence capacity realization negatively in all industries except for garment industry, which is of very recent origin. The older the firm, the less likely it is to utilize its full production capacity because of obsolescence of equipment and machinery.

Other firm-specific and technology related variables, such as the proportion of non-production workers to total work force (PNWT), size of firm (SZ), and capital intensity (CI) had mixed signs across industries and periods. However, these findings are broadly consistent with the structure and performance of industries in Bangladesh. The market structure related variable four-firm concentration ratio (CR4) had consistently negative signs in the food processing and chemical industries, indicating that the more concentrated industries had a likelihood of high under-utilization of production capacity.

The three policy related variables, trade orientation or openness (OPN), the effective rate of assistance (ERA), and privatization had consistent signs. The analysis shows that greater openness of a firm or industry, led to higher capacity realization and higher assistance in terms of protection or subsidies received by a firm or industry, reduced its capacity realization. Privatization had positive signs indicating that it can lead to higher capacity realization. However, none of these variables was consistently significant across industries and throughout the periods. The most striking finding was that the privatization dummy was not significant for any industry or in any period. Since the list of included variables was not comprehensive, the regression results would have been more robust had it possible to include variables, like R&D expenditure, licensing or supply of imported raw materials and entrepreneurs' level of education and training.

Policy Implications

Several policy implications can be drawn from the empirical findings of this study:

The results support the view that the growth in capacity realization rate as a component of TFP growth is too significant to be ignored in developing economies such as Bangladesh. Resource scarcity, particularly of capital, is considered to be the chief handicap to rapid growth of the country. The best possible use of available resources is mandatory, because gains from factor allocation are bound to be eliminated, and in the long run, factor accumulation cannot supplant productivity growth as the engine of growth. The findings confirm that there is considerable scope for improving industrial performance at the firm level by improving utilization of existing technology. In other words, it is possible to increase manufacturing output greatly without employing additional inputs. It would appear that the problem faced by manufacturing industries in Bangladesh is more one of utilizing existing technologies rather than the acquisition of new technologies. There is evidence of improvements of capacity realization due to market-oriented policy reforms and suggest the need for further reform of economic policies. Also, the large variations in the rates of firm-level capacity realization suggest that this might be reduced by adoption of proper policy measures to ensure better dissemination of information among firms in similar activities.

Although opportunities have been created through economic reforms to import new technology from abroad, the country does not currently have the capacity to adapt and modify this technology for effective use in the local production environment. Imported technology failed to produce high growth in the domestic industries during the period under review. The policy implication is that there is a clear need to develop the country's internal capability to adapt scientific and technological knowledge for industrial use and to develop local technology by encouraging the private sector to undertake research and development activities. Successful absorption of imported technology could also be possible through the establishment of appropriate institutions for the transfer and adaptation of technology to local conditions.

Empirical evidence on the impact of privatization on productive performance was inconclusive. The benefits from privatization have been limited, perhaps because of imperfections that exist in the labour, capital and financial markets. Also, excessive government expenditure on rehabilitation (through direct and indirect subsidies) and modernization of state-owned enterprises gave the wrong signals to the private sector investors as these have been contrary to the market oriented adjustment strategy. This analysis suggests that changing ownership in isolation does not improve the performance of firms, and the policy implication is that future reforms which address imperfections in various markets and, above all, 'harden' budget constraints of firms (public or private) through liberalization and deregulation may lead to an increase in productivity of manufacturing firms.

There is a vital need for the creation of employment opportunities in a country where unemployment is a staggering problem. But such employment creation is not desirable at the cost of efficiency in terms of capacity under-utilization and low productivity growth in manufacturing industries. The empirical results suggest an urgency for implementing labour market reform at least in linking wages to productivity to enhance the benefits of the country's export oriented growth strategy. In view of serious unemployment and under-employment retrenchment of the redundant labour force is very difficult, particularly in the context of organized resistance from highly politicised labour unions in Bangladesh. Under these circumstances, reform measures such as re-training and on-the-job training, among others, are urgently needed to improve the efficiency of the labour force without affecting the livelihood of workers.

The insignificant influence of export orientation (openness) and the effective rate of assistance (ERA) on the productive performance of manufacturing firms may be attributed to piecemeal and partial nature of policy reforms. While it is true that the economy is more open and the trade regime more liberal than two decades ago, progress in reform has been slower than anticipated owing to bureaucrats' vested interests and a lack of commitment by political regimes, reflected in 'rent-seeking' activities and massive corruption. The evidence suggests the need for further reform of trade policies, in particular, focusing on reducing nominal and effective protection levels and steeper tariff reductions in order to enhance competition and competitiveness. Greater attention needs to be given to complementary policies for investment and institutional changes. Simultaneously, transparency in policies must be ensured, and macroeconomic stability must be maintained as a basis for the success of all other policies. On the whole, a coherent set of policies has to be more vigorously pursued so that an efficient pattern of production can take firmer root in the industrial sector of the economy.

Limitations and the Focus of Further Study

The empirical findings of this study facilitate understanding concerning the impact of policy reforms on productive performances of manufacturing industries in Bangladesh. However, there are some limitations which need to be taken into account in interpreting results as well as in carrying out further empirical studies.

Data used in this study are subject to certain weaknesses because of conceptual problems in the measurement of inputs and output, which are difficult to overcome. In addition, the measures of output by value added, and other inputs used in this study may not be entirely accurate. The use of value added in the production function does not represent the true technology. Since all raw and semifinished materials, sub-assemblies, energy, and purchased services as well as imports are omitted while measuring inputs and consequently, their influences are missing from the price and cost of production, and the description of technology. Moreover, price variation across firms within a specific industry could be a source of value added variation as is productivity growth. Thus, the reported results could be biased and inter-industry comparisons might be distorted.

Policy reforms adopted in Bangladesh are partial or half-hearted, and remain at the implementation stage. These reforms are only a few years old and have been implemented after years of active government intervention, so it is not reasonable to attribute the changes in industrial performance solely to these reforms. The results reported in this study may coincide with the transition stage. The incorporation of more recent policy changes and use of longer time period data to examine the effects of reforms would be fruitful in future research.

Finally, the coverage of this study is inadequate for assessment of industrial performance since this study considers only the common firms throughout the period 1981 to 1991. New and 'moribund' [firms existing in the earlier period that subsequently withered during the period studied] firms were left out of the analysis. Omitting 'moribund' firms possibly does not create problems, but omitting new firms may omit some important information. For example, all new firms are private sector firms (since the government has not undertaken any new investment, taking care only of the old nationalized industries over the last few years), so it would be interesting to examine the performance of these newly established private firms and their response to the government policy shift. This study also omits small and cottage industries and handloom industries, which have been more successful in achieving high growth and have contributed substantially to total manufacturing value added. Thus, this study neither includes firms which have become important during the 1980s and 1990s, nor small and cottage industries and handlooms and thus has limited coverage.

Despite these limitations, this study has made an important contribution in theoretical and empirical analysis of productivity measurement. This is one of the first studies which has examined the influence of economic reforms on the performance of manufacturing enterprises with sophisticated econometric techniques. The empirical findings of this study should be important guides for future policy making in Bangladesh. Additionally, it develops a new methodology for measuring firm level capacity realization and total factor productivity growth. The major feature of this approach is that, unlike most conventional methodologies it explicitly considers productive capacity realization in measuring productivity growth. As this approach is consistent with economic theory, it would be useful for future research in order to measure the impact of reforms on the production units. Otherwise, the influence of policy reforms on productive performance of manufacturing firms, and therefore the benefits of liberalization through productivity growth would be under-measured. A natural sequel to this study would be the application of this approach to other developing countries which have undergone liberalization reforms.

Bibliography

Aaronovitch, S., and M. Sawyer, 1975, *Big Business: Theoretical and Empirical Aspects of Concentration and Mergers in the United Kingdom*, Macmillan, London.

Abdullah, A. A., and A. Rahman, 1989, 'Bangladesh: A Case of Technological Stagnation', Research Report No. 110, Bangladesh Institute of Development Studies (BIDS), Dhaka.

Abramovitz, M., 1956, 'Resource and Output Trends in the United States Since 1870', *American Economic Review*, 46, pp: 5-23.

Afroz, G., and D. K. Roy, 1976, 'Capacity Utilization in Selected Manufacturing Industries in Bangladesh', *Bangladesh Development Studies*, 4, pp: 275-88.

Agarwala, R., 1983, 'Price Distortions and Growth in Developing Countries', World Bank Staff Working Paper No 575, Washington D. C.

Ahammad, H., 1995, *Foreign Exchange and Trade Policy Issues in a Developing Economy: The Case of Bangladesh*, Avebury, Aldershot, Hong Kong and Singapore.

Ahluawalia, I. J., 1991, *Productivity and Growth in Indian Manufacturing*, Oxford University Press, New Delhi.

Ahmad, A. K. M. M., 1987, 'Factor Intensity, Trade Policies and Exports of Manufacturers: A Case Study of Bangladesh', Ph. D. Thesis, Sydney University, Australia.

Ahmad, A., 1993, 'Economic Reforms Under an Import-Substitution Regime: The Bangladesh Experience', in Hansson, G., (ed.), *Trade, Growth, and Development: The Role of Politics and Institutions*, Routledge, London and New York.

Ahmad, Q. K., 1973, 'A Note on Capacity Utilization in the Jute Manufacturing Industry of Bangladesh', *Bangladesh Economic Review*; 1, pp: 103-14.

Aigner, D. J., Lovell, C. A. K., and P. Schmidt, 1977, 'Formulation and Estimation of Stochastic Frontier Production Function Models', *Journal of Econometrics*, 6, pp: 21-37.

Alauddin, M., 1995, 'The Readymade Garment Industry of Bangladesh and Changing Structure of Foreign Trade', Paper presented at *The Third International Conference on Development and Future Studies*, jointly organised by The International Institute for Development Studies and The Swedish School of Economics and Business Administration, Helsinki, Finland, July 31-August 2.

Alauddin, M., Squares, D., and C. Tisdell, 1993, 'Divergency Between Average and Frontier Production Technologies: An Empirical Investigation for Bangladesh', *Applied Economics*, 25, pp: 379-88.

Artus, J., 1977, 'Measures of Potential Output in Manufacturing for Eight Industrial Countries 1955-1978', *International Monetary Fund Staff Papers*, 28, pp: 1-35.

Asian Development Bank (ADB), 1987, 'Industrial Development in Bangladesh: Performance and Prospects', Dhaka, (mimeo).

Aspden, C., 1990, 'Estimates of Multifactor Productivity, Australia', Occasional paper, Australian Bureau of Statistics, Canberra.

Athukorala, P., 1994, 'Economic Liberalization and Industrial Adjustment in Sri Lanka', Paper Presented in the Conference on *Economic Liberalisation in South Asia*, The Australian National University, 30 November 2 December.

Aw, B. Y., and A. R. Hwang, 1995, 'Productivity and the Export Market: A Firm Level Analysis', *Journal of Development Economics*, 47, pp: 313-32.

Baily, M. D., 1974, Capital Utilization in Kenya Manufacturing Industry, unpublished Ph. D. dissertation, Department of Economics, MIT, Cambridge.

Bakht, Z., and D. Bhattacharya, 1991, 'Investment, Employment and Value Added in Bangladesh Manufacturing Sector in 1980s: Evidence and Estimate', *Bangladesh Development Studies*, 19, pp: 1-50.

Bakht, Z., and D. Bhattacharya, 1995, Independent Review of Bangladesh: IV industry, Centre for Policy Dialogue, Dhaka.

Balassa, B. *et al*, 1971, *The Structure of Protection in the Developing Countries*, Johns Hopkins University Press, Baltimore.

Balassa, B., 1978, 'Exports and Economic Growth: Further Evidence' *Journal of Development Economics*, 5, pp: 181-89.

Balassa, B., 1985, 'Exports, Policy Choices and Economic Growth', *Journal of Development Economics*, 18, pp: 23-35.

Balassa, B., and Associates, 1982, *Development Strategies in Semi-Industrial Economies*, Baltimore: John Hopkins University Press.

Bangladesh Bank, 1994, 'Economic Trends', 20, April.

Bangladesh Bureau of Statistics (BBS), 'Report on Census of Manufacturing Industries of Bangladesh', (various issues), Statistics Division, Bangladesh Secretariat, Government of Bangladesh.

BBS, 1985-86, 1989, Labour Force Survey, Statistics Division, Bangladesh Secretariat, Government of Bangladesh.

BBS, 1993, Twenty Years of National Accounting of Bangladesh (1972-73 to 1991-92), Statistics Division, Ministry of Planning, Government of Bangladesh.

BBS, 1995, 1992, 1989, 1984, 1982, *Statistical Yearbook of Bangladesh* (various issues), Statistics Division, Ministry of Planning, Government of Bangladesh.

BBS, Census of Manufacturing Industries (CMI) of Bangladesh (various years, unpublished tapes), Statistics Division, Bangladesh Secretariat, Government of Bangladesh.

Bangladesh-Canada Agriculture Sector Team (B-C-AST), 1991, Proposal for Stimulating the Development of Agro-Processing in Bangladesh, Ministry of Agriculture, Government of Bangladesh, May, (mimeo).

Bardhan, P., 1992, 'Economics of Market Socialism and the Issue of Public Enterprise Reform in Developing Countries', *Pakistan Development Review*, 30, pp: 565-79.

Battese, G. E., 1992, 'Frontier Production Functions and Technical efficiency: A survey of Empirical Applications in Agricultural Economics', *Agricultural Economics*, 7, pp: 185-208.

Bauer, P. W., 1990a, 'Recent Developments in Econometric Estimation of Frontiers', *Journal of Econometrics*, 46, pp: 39-56.

Bauer, P. W., 1990b, 'Decomposing TFP Growth in the Presence of Cost Inefficiency, Non-constant Returns to Scale, and Technological Progress', *Journal of Productivity Analysis*, 1, pp: 287-99.

Bautista, R. M. *et al*, 1981, *Capital Utilization in Manufacturing*, A World Bank research publication, Oxford University Press.

Bautista, R. M., 1974, 'The Electricity Based Measure of Capital Utilisation in Philippine Manufacturing Industries', *Philippine Review of Business and Economics*, 11, pp: 13-33.

Bautista, R. M., 1981, 'Philippines: country study' in Bautista, R. *et al* (eds), *Capital Utilization in Manufacturing*, Oxford University Press.

Belsley, D. A., 1973a, 'On the Determination of Systematic Parameter Variation in the Linear Regression Model', *Annals of Economic and Social Measurement*, 2, pp: 487-94.

Belsley, D. A., 1973b, 'A Test for Systematic Parameter Variation in Regression Coefficients', *Annals of Economic and Social Measurement*, 2, pp: 495-500.

Berndt, E. R., and C. J. Morrison, 1981, 'Capacity Utilization: Underlying Economic Theory and an Alternative Approach', *American Economic Review*, 71, pp: 48-52.

Berndt, E., and M. Fuss, 1986, 'Productivity Measurement with Adjustment for Variations in Capacity Utilization and Other forms of Temporary Equilibrium', *Journal of Econometrics*, 33, pp: 7-29.

Berndt, E. R., and D. M. Hesse, 1986, 'Measuring and Assessing Capacity Utilization in the Manufacturing Sectors of Nine OECD Countries', *European Economic Review*, 30, pp: 961-80.

Bernolak, I., 1980, 'The Measurement of Output and Capital Inputs', in Bailey, D., and T. Hubert (eds), *Productivity Measurement*, Gower Publishing Co. London.

Bernolak, I., 1982, (ed.) *Productivity Measurement and Analysis: New Issues and Solutions*, Asian Productivity Organization, Tokyo, Japan.

Betancourt, R. R., and C. K. Clague, 1975, 'An Economic Analysis of Capital Utilization', *Southern Economic Journal*, 42, pp: 69-78.

Betancourt, R., and C. Clague, 1981, *Capital Utilization: A Theoretical and Empirical Analysis*, New York, Cambridge University Press.

Bhagwati, J. N. 1978, *Foreign Trade Regimes and Economic Development: Anatomy and Consequences of Exchange Control Regimes*, Cambridge: Ballinger, Lexington, MA.

Bhagwati, J. N. 1988, 'Export-Promoting Trade Strategy: Issues and Evidence', World Bank Research Observer, 1, pp: 27-58.

Bhagwati, J. N., and T. N. Srinivasan, 1975, *Foreign Trade Regime and Economic Development:* India, Columbia University Press, New York.

Bhagwati, J. N., and T. N. Srinivasan, 1980, 'Domestic Resource Costs, Effective Rate of Protection, and Project Analysis in Tariff-Distorted Economies', *Quarterly Journal of Economics*, 94, pp: 205-209.

Bhattachayria, D., 1994, 'An Aggregate Level Analysis of the Manufacturing Sector', in Data International Limited (ed.), *The Structure and Performance of Bangladesh Manufacturing, 1992* Data International Limited, Dhaka.

Bhuyan, A. R., and M. A. Rashid, 1993, *Trade Regimes and Industrial Growth: A Case Study of Bangladesh*, International Center for Economic Growth, San Francisco, U. S. A.

Blomström, M., 1986, 'Foreign Investment and Productive Efficiency: The Case of Mexico', Journal of Industrial Economics, 15, pp: 97-110.

Boardman, A., and A. Vining, 1989, 'Ownership and Performance in Competitive Environments: A Comparison of the Performance of Private, Mixed and SOEs', *Journal of Law and Economics*, 32, pp: 1-33.

Bonelli, R., 1992, 'Growth and Productivity in Brazilian Industries: Impacts of Trade Orientation', *Journal of Development Economics*, 39, pp: 85-109.

Bosworth, D., 1985, 'Fuel Based Measures of Capital Utilization', *Scottish Journal of Political Economy*, 32, pp: 20-38.

Bravo-Ureta, B. E., and A. E. Pinheiro, 1993, 'Efficiency Analysis of Developing Country Agriculture: A Review of the Frontier Function Liturature', *Agricultural and Resource Economics Review*, 22, pp: 88-101.

Breusch, T. S., and A. R. Pagan, 1979, 'A Simple Test for Heteroscedasticity and Random Coefficient Variation', *Econometrica*, 47, pp: 1287-94.

Brown, R. L. *et al*, 1975, 'Techniques for Testing the Constancy of Regression Relationships Over Time', *Journal of the Royal Statistical Society*, B-37, pp: 149-92.

Callan, S., J., 1986, 'Decomposition of Total Factor Productivity Growth, Additional Evidence: The Case of the U.S. Electric Utility Industry, 1951-1978' *Quarterly Journal of Business and Economics*, 25, pp: 55-71.

Campbell, C., 1984, 'Correlates of Residual Growth in New Zeland Manufacturing Industries, 1952-73', Paper presented to the Economics Section ANZAAS, Canberra.

Capalbo, S. M., and Trang T. V., 1988, 'A Review of the Evidence on Agricultural Productivity and Aggregate Technology', Resources for the Future (RFF), Washington D.C. (mimeo).

Cassel, J. M., 1937, 'Excess Capacity and Monopolistic Competition', *Quarterly Journal Economics*, 51, pp: 426-43.

Caves, D. W., Christensen, L. R., and W. E. Diewert, 1982, 'The Economic Theory of Index Numbers and the Measurement of Input, Output and Productivity', *Econometrica*, 50, pp: 1393-414.

Caves, R. E., 1984, 'Scale, Openness, and Productivity in Australian Industries', Paper presented at the Brookings Survey of the Australian Economy Conference, Canberra.

Caves, R. E., and D. R. Barton, 1990, *Efficiency in U. S. Manufacturing Industries*, Cambdrige, Mass: The MIT Press.

Centre for Policy Dialogue, 1995, *Independent Review of Bangladesh*, University Press Limited, Dhaka.

Chamberlin, E. H., 1938, *The Theory of Monopolistic Competition: A Reorientation of the Theory of Value*, Cambridge, Mass: Harvard University Press.

Chambers, R. G., 1988, *Applied Production Analysis: A Dual Approach*, Cambridge University Press, New York, Sydney.

Chandler, C., 1962, 'The Relative Contribution of Capital Intensity and Productivity to Change in Output and Income', *Journal of Farm Economics*, 44, pp: 335-48.

Chen, T., and D. Tang, 1987, 'Comparing Technical Efficiency Between Import-Substitution Oriented and Export Oriented Foreign Firms in a Developing Economy', *Journal of Development Economics*, 26, pp: 277-89.

Chen, T., and D. Tang, 1990, 'Export Performance and Productivity Growth: The Case of Taiwan', *Economic Development and Cultural Change*, 38, pp: 577-85.

Chenery, H. B., 1952, 'Overcapacity and Acceleration Principle', *Econometrica*, 20, pp: 1-28.

Chenery, H., *et al*, 1986, *Industrialization and Growth: A Comparative Studies*, Oxford University Press.

Chow, G. C., 1984, 'Random and Changing Coefficient Models', in Z. Griliches and M. D. Intriligator (eds), *Handbook of Econometrics*, Volume 2, North-Holland, Amsterdam.

Christensen, L. R. and D. W. Jorgenson, 1970, 'U.S. Real Product and Real Factor Input, 129-1967', *Review of Income and Wealth*, 16, pp: 19-50.

Christensen, L. R., 1975, 'Concepts and Measurement of Agricultural Productivity', *American Journal of Agricultural Economics*, 57, pp: 910-15.

Christensen, L. R., and D. W. Jorgenson, 1973, 'Measuring the Performance of the Private Sector of the US Economy, 1929-1969', in Moss, M. (ed.), *Measuring Economic and Social Performance*, NBER, New York.

Christiano, L. J., 1981, 'A Survey of Measures of Capacity Utilization', *IMF Staff Papers*, 28, pp: 144-98.

Coelli, T., 1995, 'Recent Developments in Frontier Modelling and Efficiency Measurement', *Australian Journal of Agricultural Economics*, 39, pp: 219-45.

Coelli, T., and P. Rao, (forthcoming), *Efficiency and Productivity Measurement*, Centre for Efficiency and Productivity Measurement, University of New England.

Comanor, W. S., and H. Leibenstein, 1969, 'Allocative Efficiency, X-efficiency and the Measurement of Welfare Losses', *Economica*, 36, pp: 304-309.

Corbo, V., and S. Fischer, 1995, 'Structural Adjustment, Stabilization and Policy Reform: Domestic and International Finance', in Behrman, J. and T. N. Srinivasan (eds), *Handbook of Development Economics*, Vol. 3b, Elsevier Science, North Holland, The Netherlands.

Corden, W. M., 1974, *Trade Policy and Economic Welfare*, Clarendon Press, Oxford.

Cowling, K., and M. Waterson, 1976, 'Price-Cost Margins and Market Structure', *Economica*, 43, pp: 267-74.

Craig, C. E., and R. C. Harris, 1973, 'Total Productivity Measurement at the Firm Level', *Solan Management Review*, 14, pp: 13-29.

Curry, B., and K. D. George, 1983, 'Industrial Concentration: A Survey', *Journal of Industrial Economics*, 31, pp: 203-55.

Davidson, R., and J. G. MacKinnon, 1981, *Estimation and Inference in Econometrics*, Oxford University Press, Oxford.

Denison, E., 1961, 'Measurement of Labour Input: Some Questions of Definition and Adequacy of Data', Output, Input and Productivity Measurement, Studies in Income and Wealth, NBER, Volume no. 25.

Denison, E. F., 1962, 'The Sources of Economic Growth in the United States and the Alternatives Before US', Committee for Economic Development, New York, (mimeo).

Denison, E., and W. Chung, 1976, 'How Japan's Economy Grew so Fast', Brooking Institution, Washington D.C. (mimeo).

Denny, M., and M. Fuss, 1981, 'Inter-temporal and Interspatial Comparisons of Cost Efficiency and Productivity', (unpublished manuscript), University of Toronto, Canada

Denny, M., Fuss, M., and L. Waverman, 1981, 'The Measurement and Interpretation of Total Factor Productivity in Regulated Industries, with Application to Canadian Telecommunications', in Cowing, T. G., and R. E. Stevenson (eds), *Productivity Measurement in Regulated Industries*, Academic press, New York, London.

Diewert, W. E., 1975, 'Ideal Log Change Index Numbers and Consistency in Aggregation', Department of Economics Discussion Paper, University of British Columbia, Vancouver, Canada.

Diewert, W. E., 1976, 'Exact and Superlative Index Numbers', *Journal of Econometrics*, 4, pp: 115-45.

Diewert, W. E., 1981, 'The Economic Theory of Index Numbers: A Survey', in Deaton, A. (ed.), *Essays in the Theory and Measurement of Consumer Behaviour* in Honour of Sir Richard Stone, Cambridge University Press, London.

Diewert, W. E., 1992, 'The Measurement of Productivity', *Bulletin of Economic Research*, 44, pp: 163-98.

Diokno, B., 1974, 'Capital Utilization in Government 'Favoured' Export-Oriented Firms', *Philippine Economic Journal*, 13, pp: 149-88.

Dixit, A. K., 1981, 'The Role of Investment in Entry Deterrence', *Economic Journal*, 90, pp: 95-106.

Dixon, B. L., and L. J. Martin, 1982, 'Forecasting U. S. Pork Production Using Random Coefficient Model', *American Journal of Agricultural Economics*, 64, pp: 530-38.

Dodaro, S., 1991, 'Comparative Advantage, Trade and Growth: Export-led Growth Revisited', *World Development*, 19, pp: 1153-66.

Dollar, D., and K. Sokoloff, 1992, 'Patterns of Productivity Growth in South Korean Manufacturing Industries 1963-1979', *Journal of Development Economics*, 33, pp: 309-27.

Domar, E. D., 1961, 'On the Measurement of Technological Change', *Economic Journal*, 71, pp: 709-29.

Eaton, B. C., and R. G. Lypsey, 'Capital Commitment, and Entry Equilibrium', *Bell Journal of Economics*, 12, pp: 593-604.

Esposito, F. F., and L. Esposito, 1974, 'Excess Capacity and Market Share', *Review of Economics and Statistics*, 56, pp: 188-94.

Export Promotion Bureau, 1995, Annual Report 1995, Ministry of Commerce, Government of Bangladesh.

Färe, R., 1984, 'On the Existence of Plant Capacity', *International Economic Review*, 25, pp: 209-213.

Färe, R. *et al* 1994, 'Productivity Growth, Technical Progress and Efficiency Change in Industrialized Countries', *American Economic Review*, 84, pp: 66-83.

Färe, R., Grosskopf, S., and C. A. K. Lovell, 1994, *Production Frontiers*, Cambridge University Press.

Färe, R., Grosskopf, S., and E. C. Kokkelenberg, 1989, 'Measuring Plant Capacity, Utilization and Technical Change: A Nonparametric Approach', *International Economic Review*, 30, pp: 655-66.

Fabricant, S., 1959, 'Basic Facts on Productivity Change', Occasional paper 63, National Bureau of Economic Research, New York.

Fan, S., 1991, 'Effects of Technological Change and Institutional Reform on Production Growth in Chinese Agriculture', *American Journal of Agricultural Economics*, 73, pp: 266-75.

Farrell, M. J., 1957, 'Measurement of Productive Efficiency', *Journal of the Royal Statistical Society*, Part 3, Serial A (General), pp: 253-81.

Feder, G., 1982, 'Exports and Economic Growth', *Journal of Development Economics*, 12, pp: 59-73.

Felipe, J., 1994, 'Total Factor Productivity: A Selective Survey of Methodologies', Department of Regional science, University of Pennsylvania, (mimeo).

Fiege, E. L., and P. A. V. B. Swamy, 1974, 'A Random Coefficient Model of Demand for Liquid Assets', *Journal of Money Credit Banking*, 6, pp: 241-52.

Findlay, R., 1985, 'Primary Export, Manufacturing and Development', in Mat Lundhal (ed.), *The Primary Sector in Economic Development*, London: Croom Helm.

Forest, L. R. Jr., 1979, 'Capacity Utilization: Concepts and Measurement', in Board of Governors of the Federal Reserve Systems, (ed.), *Measures of Capacity Utilization: Problems and Task*, Staff studies, Volume No. 105

Førsund, F., and L. Hjalmarsson, 1979, 'Generalised Farrell Measures of Efficiency: An Application to Milk Processing in Swedish Dairy Plants', *Economic Journal*, 89, pp: 294-315.

Foss, M. F., 1963, 'The Utilisation of Capital Equipment', *Survey of Current Business*, 43, pp: 8-16.

Froehlich, B. R., 1973, 'Some Estimators for a Random Coefficient Regression Model', *Journal of the American Statistical Association*, 68, pp: 329-35.

Fuss, M. A., 1994, 'Productivity Growth in Canadian Telecommunications', *Canadian Journal of Economics*, 27, pp: 371-92.

Garnaut, R., 1991 Economic Reform and Internationalisation: China's Experience in the International Context, paper presented at the 19th Pacific Trade and Development Conference, Beijing, 27-30 May.

Garnaut, R., Grilli, E., and J. Riedel, 1995, *Sustaining Export-Oriented Development: Ideas from East Asia*, Cambridge University Press, U. K., New York.

Garnicott, K., 1984, 'The Developments of Industrial in Australia', *Economic Record*, 60, 231-35.

Geroski, P. A., 1988, 'In Pursuit of Monopoly Power: Recent Quantitative Work in Industrial Economics', *Journal of Applied Econometrics*, 3, pp: 107-24.

Godfrey, L. G., 1988, *Misspecification Tests in Econometrics*, Cambridge University Press, Cambridge.

Gold, B., 1981, 'Improving Industrial Productivity and Technological Capabilities: Needs, Problems and Suggested Policies', in Ali, Dogramaci, (ed.), *Productivity Analysis: A Range of Perspectives*, Martinus Nijhoff publishing, Boston.

Goldar, B., and V. S. Renganathan, 1991, 'Capacity Utilization in Indian Industries', *Indian Economic Journal*, 39, pp: 82-92.

Goldberger, A., 1967, *Econometric Theory*, Wiely, New York.

Goldfled, S. M., and R., E. Quandt, 1988, 'Budget Constraints, Bail-Outs, and the Firm Under Central Planning', *Journal of Comparative Economics*, 12, pp: 502-20.

Goldfled, S. M., and R., E. Quandt, 1990, 'Output Targets, the Soft Budget Constraint and the Firm Under Central Planning', *Journal of Economic Behaviour and Organization*, 14, pp: 205-22.

Goldschmid, H., Mann, M., and J. F. Weston, 1974, *Industrial Concentration: The New Learning*, Little Brown, Boston.

Gollop, F. M., and D. W. Jorgenson, 1979, U. S. *Economic Growth: 1948-1973*, University of Chicago, (mimeo).

Government of Bangladesh, 1981, 1974, 'Population Census', Bangladesh Bureau of Statistics, Statistics Division, Bangladesh Secretariat, Dhaka.

Government of Bangladesh, 1982, 'New Industrial Policy', Ministry of Industries, Dhaka.

Government of Bangladesh, 1985, 'Chemical Industries in Bangladesh', (TIP-MU-DI), October, pp: 77-81.

Government of Bangladesh, 1987, 'Revised Industrial Policy', Ministry of Industries, Dhaka.

Government of Bangladesh, 1988, 'Import Policy Order 1988-89', Ministry of Commerce, Dhaka.

Government of Bangladesh, 1990, *The Fourth Five Year Plan* 1990-95, Ministry of Planning, Dhaka.

Government of Bangladesh, 1993, 'Import Policy Order 1993-95', Ministry of Commerce, Dhaka.

Government of Bangladesh, 1995, 'Bangladesh Handbook 1995', External publicity wing, Ministry of Information, Dhaka.

Greene, W. H., 1990, 'A Gamma-Distributed Stochastic Frontier Model', *Journal of Econometrics*, 46, pp: 141-63.

Greene, W. H., 1993a, 'The Econometric Approach to Efficiency Analysis', in Fried, O. Harold, Lovell, C. A. K., and S. S. Schmidt, (eds), *The Measurement of Productive Efficiency*, Oxford University Press, New York.

Greene, W. H., 1993b, *Econometric Analysis*, Second edition, Macmillan, London.

Greenway, D. and O. Morrissey, 1992, 'Structural Adjustment and Liberalisation in Developing Countries: What Lessons Have We Learned?', *Kyklos*, 46, pp: 241-61.

Griffin, J., 1971, *Capacity Measurement in Petroleum Refining: A Process Analysis Approach to the Joint Product Case*, Heath, USA.

Griffiths, W. E., 1972, 'Estimation of Actual Response Coefficients in the Hildreth-Houck Random Coefficient Model', *Journal of American Statistical Association*, 67, pp: 633-35

Griliches, Z., 1960, 'Measuring Inputs in Agriculture: A Critical Survey', *Journal of Farm Economics*, 42, pp: 1411-27.

Griliches, Z., and V. Ringstad, 1971, *Economies of Scale and the form of the Production Function*, North-Holland, Amsterdam.

Grosskopf, S., 1986, 'The Role of the References Technology in Measuring Productive Efficiency', *Economic Journal*, 96, pp: 499-513.

Grosskopf, S., 1993, 'Efficiency and Productivity' in Fried, H. O., Lovell, C. A. K. and Schmidt, S. S. (eds) *The Measurement of Productive Efficiency: Techniques and Applications*, Oxford University Press.

Grossman, G., and E. Helpman, 1990, 'Trade, Innovation, and Growth', *American Economic Review*, (Papers and Proceedings), 80, pp: 86-91.

Grossman, G., and E. Helpman, 1991, *Innovation and Growth in the Global Economy*, MIT Press, Cambdrige, MA.

Habibullah, M., 1974, 'Some Aspects of Industrial Efficiency and Profitability in Bangladesh', Bureau of Economic Research, University of Dhaka.

Handoussa, H., M. Nishimizu, and J. M. Page, 1986, 'Productivity Change in Egyptian Public Sector Industries After 'The Opening', 1973-179', *Journal of Developemnt Economics*, 20, pp: 53-73.

Harris, R., and J. Taylor, 1985, 'The Measurement of Capacity Utilization', *Applied Economics*, 17, pp: 849-66.

Harris, R., and J. Taylor, 1987, 'Trend-Through-Peaks Methods of Estimating Capacity Utilization', in Bosworth, D. and D. F. Heathfield (eds) *Working below Capacity*, Macmillan Press Limited, London.

Harvard Institute of Development (HIID)/ Employment and Small Scale Enterprise Policy Planning (ESEPP), 1990a, 'Productivity and Economic Development in Bangladesh', Working Paper No. 15, Planning Commission, Dhaka.

HIID/ESEPP, 1990b, 'An Assessment of the Impact of Industrial Policies in Bangladesh', Working Paper No. 16, Planning Commission, Dhaka.

HIID/ESEPP, 1990c, 'An Identification of Dynamic Industrial Subsectors', Working Paper No. 20, Planning Commission, Dhaka.

Harvey, A. C., 1978, 'The Estimation of Time-Varying Parameters from the Panel Data', *Annales de l'insee*, 30-31, pp: 203-26.

Harville, D. A., 1977, 'Maximum Likelihood Approaches to Variance Component Estimation and to Related Problems', *Journal of the American Statistical Association*, 72, pp: 320-338.

Havrylyshyn, O., 1990, 'Trade Policy and Productivity Gains in Developing Countries: A Survey of the Literature', World Bank Research Observer, 5, pp: 1-24.

Heathfield, D. F., 1972, 'The Measurement of Capital Usage Using Electricity Consumption Data', *Journal of Royal Statistical Society* (series A), 135, pp: 208-20.

Helleiner, G. K., 1992, 'Trade, Trade Policy and Economic Development', *Bangladesh Development Studies*, 20, pp: 55-69.

Hemming, R., and A. M. Monsoor, 1988, 'Privatization and Public Enterprises', IMF Occassional Paper No. 56, Washington, D. C.

Herderschee, J., 1994, *Incentives for Exports*, Avebury, Aldershot, Hong Kong, Singapore and Sydney.

Hickman, B. G., 1964, 'On New Method of Capacity Estimation', *Journal of the American Statistical Association*, 59, pp: 529-49.

Hildreth, C., and J. P. Houck, 1968, 'Some Estimators for a Model With Random Coefficients', *Journal of American Statistical Association*, 63, pp: 584-95.

Hill, H., and K. P. Kalirajan, 1993, 'Small Enterprise and Firm-level Technical Efficiency in the Indonesian Garment Industry', *Applied Economics*, 25, pp: 1137-44.

Hogan, W. P., 1967, 'Capacity Creation and Utilization in Pakistan Manufacturing Industry', Economic Development Report no. 84, Harvard University, Cambridge, Mass.

Hoque, A., 1991, 'An Application and Test for a Random Coefficient Model in Bangladesh Agriculture', *Journal of Applied Econometrics*, 6, pp: 77-90.

Hoque, A., 1992, 'Consumption, Cointegration and Varying Coefficients: The Australian Evidence', *Applied Economics*, 24, pp: 775-80.

Hossain, M., 1984, 'Productivity and Profitability in Bangladesh Rural Industries', *Bangladesh Development Studies*, 12, pp: 127-61.

Hulten, C. R., 1973, 'Divisia Index Numbers', *Econometrica*, 41, pp: 1017-1025.

Humphrey, C. E., 1990, *Privatization in Bangladesh: Economic Transition in a Poor Economy*, Westview press, Boulder, San Francisco, & Oxford.

Hutcheson, T. L., 1986, 'Effective Rates of Protection: An Input-Output Analysis', Trade and Industrial Policy Reform Program, Doc.TIP-MU-H.3, Dhaka (mimeo).

Hutcheson, T. L., and J. J. Stern, 1986, Methodology of Assistance Policy Analysis, HIID Development Discussion Paper no. 226, HIID, Harvard University, Cambridge.

ILO-ARTEP, (ed.), 1986, *Bangladesh: Selected Issues in Employment and Development*, New Delhi.

International Labour Organisation (ILO), 1991, Improving Efficiency and Productivity of Small and Medium Scale Enterprises, Regional office, Dhaka, (mimeo).

Islam, N., 1970, 'The Manufactured Exports of Pakistan: Factor Intensity and Related Economic Characteristics', in Robinson, E. A. G. and M. Kidron (eds), *Economic Development in South Asia*, Macmillan, London.

Islam, N., 1981, *Foreign Trade and Economic Controls in Development: The Case of United Pakistan*, New Haven, U.S.A.

Islam, R., 1977, 'Some Constraints on the Choice of Technology', *Bangladesh Development Studies*, 5, pp: 255-84.

Islam, R., 1978, 'Reasons for Idle Capital: The Case of Bangladesh Manufacturing', *Bangladesh Development Studies*, 6, pp: 27-54.

Islam, A. M. *et al* 1993, The Export Garment Industry in Bangladesh: A Potential Catalyst for Breakthrough? Dhaka university, (mimeo).

Islam, A., and M. Chowdhury, 1996, 'Diaster Awaits Garments Sector', *Financial Express*, March 26, P: 5.

Jefferson, G., 1990, 'Chian's Iron and Steel Industry: Sources of Enterprise Efficiency and the Impact of Reform', *Journal of Development Economics*, 33 pp: 329-55.

Jefferson, G., Rawski, T., and Y. Zeng, 1992, 'Growth, Efficiency and Convergence in China's State and Collective Industry', *Economic Development and Cultural Change*, 40, pp: 239-66.

Johansen, L., 1968, 'Production Function and the Concept of Capacity', Recherches recentes sur la Function de Production, Collection *Economic Mathematique et Econometrie*, 2.

Johnston, J., 1960, *Statistical Cost Functions*, McGraw-Hill, New York.

Jorgenson, D. W. and M. Nishimizu, 1978, 'U. S. and Japanese Economic Growth, 1952-1974: An International Comparison', *Economic Journal*, 88, pp: 707-26.

Jorgenson, D. W., and Z. Griliches, 1967, 'The Explanation of Productivity Change', *Review of Economics and Statistics*, 34, pp: 249-84.

Judge, G. G., and T. Takayama, 1966, 'Inequality Restrictions in Regression Analysis', *Journal of the American Statistical Association*, 61, pp: 166-81.

Judge, G. G., *et al* , 1985, *The Theory and Practice of Econometrics*, John Wiley & Sons, New York, Toronto, and Singapore.

Jung, W. S., and P. Marshall, 1985, 'Exports, Growth and Causality in Developing Countries', *Journal of Development Economics*, 18, pp: 1-12.

Kaldor, N., 1966, *Causes of the Slow Rate of Economic Growth of the United Kingdom*, Cambridge University Press, Cambridge, U.K.

Kalirajan, K. P., 1990, 'On estimation of a Regression Model With Fixed and Random Coefficients', *Journal of Applied Statistics*, 17, pp: 237-44.

Kalirajan, K. P., and R. A. Salim, 1997, 'Economic Reforms and Capacity Realization in Bangladesh: An Empirical Analysis', *Journal of Industrial Economics* Vol. XLV, pp:387-403.

Kalirajan, K. P., and M. B. Obwona, 1994, 'Frontier Production Function: The Stochastic Coefficient Approach', *Oxford Bulletin of Economics and Statistics*, 56, pp: 87-96.

Kalirajan, K. P., and M. B. Obwona, 1995, 'Estimating Individual Response Coefficients in Varying Coefficients Regression Models', *Journal of Applied Statistics*, 22, pp: 477-84.

Kalirajan, K. P., and R. T. Shand, 1994a, *Economics in Disequilibrium: An Approach from the Frontier*, Macmillan India limited, New Delhi.

Kalirajan, K. P., and R. T. Shand, 1994b, 'Estimating Technical Efficiency With Non-Neutral Shift of the Frontier' *Journal of Applied Statistics*, 21, pp: 285-94.

Kalirajan, K. P., M. B. Obwona, and S. Zhao, 1996, 'A Decomposition of Total Factor Productivity Growth: The Case of Chinese Agricultural Growth Before and After Reform' *American Journal of Agricultural Economics*, 78, pp: 331-38.

Katrak, H., 1980, 'Industrial Structure, Foreign Trade and Price-cost Margins in Indian Manufacturing Industries', *Journal of Development Economics*, 17, pp: 62-79.

Kemal, A. R., and T. Alauddin, 1974, 'Capacity Utilization in Manufacturing Industries of Pakistan', *Pakistan Development Review*, 7, pp: 231-43.

Kendrick, J. W., 1961, *Productivity Trends in United States*, NBER, New York, Princeton: Princeton University Press.

Khalizadeh-Shiraji, J., 1974, 'Market Structure and Price-Cost Margins in the United Kingdom Manufacturing Industries', *Review of Economics and Statistics*, 56, pp: 67-76.

Khan, A. R., and M. Hossain, 1989, *The Strategy of Development of Bangladesh*, Macmillan and OECD Development Center, London and Paris.

Khan, M., and N. Chowdhury, 'Trade, Industrialisation and Employment' in Islam, R., and M. Muqtada (eds), *Bangladesh: Selected Issues in Employment and Development*, International Labour Organisation (ILO), Asian Employment Programme (ARTEP), New Delhi.

Kibria, M. G., and C. A. Tisdell, 1985, 'Inflexibility of Industrial Labour in a Third World Country: The Case of Jute Spinning in Bangladesh', *Bangladesh Development Studies*, 13, pp: 57-86.

Kibria, M. G., and C. A. Tisdell, 1986, 'Life-time Patterns of Capacity Utilization by Manufacturing Firms in an LDC: A Study of Jute Spinning in Bangladesh', *Indian Economic Review*, 21, pp: 1-19.

Kim, Y. C., and J. K. Kwon 1971, 'A Study on the Level, Trend and Structure of Capital Utilization in Manufacturing in Korea, 1962-1970', Northern Illinois University, Dekalb, (mimeo).

Kim, Y. C., and J. K. Kwon, 1977, 'The Utilization of Capital and the Growth of Output in a Developing Economy: The Case of South Korean Manufacturing', *Journal of Development Economics*, 4, pp: 265-78.

Kim, J., and L. Lau, 1994, 'The Sources of Economic Growth of the East Asian Newly Industrialized Countries', *Journal of the Japanese and the International Economies*, 8, pp: 235-271.

Kirkpatrick, C. H., and N. Lee, and E. I. Nixon, 1985, *Industrial Structure and Policy in Less Developed Countries*, ELBS/ George Allen & Unwin.

Klein, L. R., 1960, 'Some Theoretical Issues in the Measurement of Capacity', *Econometrica*, 28, pp: 272-86.

Klein, L. R., 1962, *Introduction to Econometrics*, Prentice-Hall International, London.

Klein, L. R., and R. S. Preston, 1967, 'Some New Results in the Measurement of Capacity Utilization', *American Economic Review*, 57, pp: 34-58.

Klein, L. R., and R. Summers, 1966, 'The Wharton Index of Capacity Utilization', Working Paper, Wharton school of Finance and Commerce, Philadelphia.

Klein, L. R., and Virginia Long, 1973, 'Capacity Utilization: Concept, Measurement, and Recent Estimates', *Brookings Papers on Economic Activity*, 3, pp: 743-56.

Klotz, B., Madoo, R., and R. Hanson, 1981, 'A Study of High Low Labour Productivity Establishments in Manufacturing', in Kendrick, J. W. and B. N. Vaccara (eds), *New Developments in Productivity Measurement and Analysis*, Chicago: University of Chicago Press.

Kniesner, T. J., and K. M. Smith, 1989, Estimating Labour Supply With Random Coefficient Regression-Econometric Theory and Applications to Labour Supply Disequilibrium and Model Specification, Working Paper no. 181, Faculty of Economics and Departments of Economics, Research School of Pacific and Asian Studies (RSPAS) and Research School of Social Sciences (RSSS), The Australian National University, pp: 1-34.

Koch, J. V., 1980, *Theory of Industrial Organisation*, Prentice-Hall International, U.S.A.

Koenkar, R., 1981, 'A Note on Studentizing a Test for Heteroscedasticity', *Journal of Econometrics*, 17, pp: 107-12.

Koenkar, R., and G. Bassett, 1982, 'Robust Tests for Heteroscedasticity Based on Regression Quantiles', *Econometrica*, 50, pp: 43-61.

Kopp, R. J., and V. K. Smith, 1980, 'Frontier Production Function Estimates for Stem Electric Generation: A Comparative Analysis', *Southern Economic Journal*, 47, pp: 1049-1059.

Kornai, J., 1979, 'Resource-Constrained versus Demand Constrained Systems', *Econometrica*, 47, pp: 802-20.

Kornai, J., 1980, *Economics of Shortage*, Volume no. B, North Holland publishing company, Amsterdam, New York and Oxford.

Kornai, J., 1986, 'The Soft Budget Constraint', *Kyklos*, 39, pp: 3-30

Kornai, J., and J. W. Weibull, 1983, 'Paternalism, Buyers' and Sellers' Market', *Mathematical Social Sciences*, 6, pp: 153-69.

Krishna, K. L., and G. S. Sahota, 1991, 'Technical Efficiency in Bangladesh Manufacturing Industries', *Bangladesh Development Studies*, 19, pp: 89-106.

Krueger, A. O., 1978, *Foreign Trade Regimes and Economic Development: Liberalization Attempts and Consequences*, Cambridge Mass: Ballinger, Lexington, MA.

Krueger, A. O., 1980, 'Trade Policy as an Input to Development', Papers and Proceedings, *American Economic Review*; 70, pp: 288-92.

Krueger, A. O., 1982, 'Comparative Advantage and Development Policy Twenty Years Later', Working Paper, no. 65, Industrial Institute for Economic and Social Research, Stockholm.

Krueger, A. O., and B. Tuncer, 1982, 'Growth of Factor Productivity in Turkish Manufacturing Industries', *Journal of Development Economics*, 11, pp: 307-25.

Krugman, P., 1987, 'The Narrow Moving Band, the Dutch Disease, and the Competitive Consequences of Mrs. Thatcher', *Journal of Development Economics*, 27, pp: 41-55.

Krugman, P., 1994, 'The Myth of Asia's Miracle', *Foreign Affairs*, 73, pp: 62-78.

Kwon, J., 1986, 'Capital Utilization, Economies of Scale and Technical Change in the Growth of Total Factor Productivity: An Explanation of South Korean Manufacturing Growth', *Journal of Development Economics*, 24, pp: 75-89.

Lary, H. B. 1968, *Imports of Manufactures from Less Developed Countries*, Columbia University Press, New York.

Lave, L. B., 1964, 'Technological Change in U. S. Agriculture: The Aggregation Problem', *Journal of Farm Economics*, 46, pp: 200-17.

Lecraw, D., 1978, 'Determinants of Capacity Utilization by Firms in Less Developed Countries', *Journal of Development Economics*, 5, pp: 139-53.

Lee, J. W., 1992, Government Intervention and Productivity Growth in Korean Manufacturing Industries, International Monetary Fund, (mimeo).

Lee, L. F., and W. E. Griffiths, 1979, The Prior Likelihood and Best Linear Unbiased Prediction in Stochastic Coefficient Linear Models, University of New England Working Papers in Econometrics and Applied Statistics No. 1, Armidale, Australia.

Leibenstein, H., 1966, 'Allocative Efficiency vs X-efficiency', *American Economic Review*, Vol. 56, pp: 392-15.

Lieberman, M. B., 1987, 'Excess Capacity as a Barrier to Entry: An Empirical Appraisal', *Journal of Industrial Economics*, 35, pp: 607-27.

Lieberman, M. B., 1989, 'Capacity Utilization: Theoretical Models and Empirical Tests', *European Journal of Operation Research*, 40, pp: 155-68.

Lim, D., 1981, 'Malaysia: Country Study' in Bautista, R., *et al* (eds), *Capital Utilization in Manufacturing*, Oxford University Press.

Lin, J. Y., 1992, 'Rural Reforms and Agricultural Growth in China', *American Economic Review*, 82, pp: 34-51.

Link, A. N., 1987, *Technological Change and Productivity Growth*, Harwood Academic Publishers, London, Paris, New York.

Little, I., Scitovosky, T., and M. Scott, 1970, *Industry and Trade in Some Developing Countries- A Comparative Study*, Oxford University Press, London.

Lovell, K. C. A., 1993 'Production Frontiers and Production Efficiency', in Lovell, K. C. A. *et al* (eds), *The Measurement of Productive Efficiency: Techniques and Applications*, Oxford University Press, New York.

Lucas, R. E. Jr., 1988, 'On the Mechanics of Economic Development', *Journal of Monetary Economics*, 22, pp: 3-42.

Lucas, R. E. Jr., 1990, 'Why Doesn't Capital Flow from Rich to Poor Countries', *American Economic Review*, 80, pp: 139-91.

Lucas, R. E. Jr., 1993, 'Making a Miracle', *Econometrica*, 61, pp: 251-72.

Lucas, R. E., 1981, *Studies in Business Cycle Theory*, Cambridge, MA, MIT Press,

Luger, M. I., and W. Evans, 1988, 'Geographic Differences in Production Technology', Regional Science and Urban Economics, 18, pp: 481-503.

Maddala, G. S., 1971, 'The Use of Variance Models in Pooling Cross-Section and Time Series Data', *Econometrica*, 39, pp: 341-58.

Maddala, G. S., 1977, *Econometrics*, McGraw Hill, New York.

Malenbaum, H., 1969, 'Capacity Balance in the Chemical Industry', in L. R. Klein (ed.) Essays in Industrial Economics, Volume no. 2, University of Pennsylvania, Economic Research Unit.

Mallon, R. D., and J. J. Stern, 1991, 'The Political Economy of Trade and Industrial Policy Reform in Bangladesh', in Perkins, D., and M. Roemer, (eds.), *Reforming Economic Systems in Developing Countries*, HIID, Harvard University, Cambridge, Mass.

Marris, R., 1964, *The Economics of Capital Utilization: A Report on Multiple shifts Work*, Cambridge, Cambridge University Press.

McCain, R. A., 1975, 'Competition, Information, Redundancy: X-efficiency and the Cybernetics of the Firm', *Kyklos*, 28, pp: 286-308.

McIntire, J. L., 1980, 'Problems with the Measurement of Productivity', in United States Congress Joint Economic Committee, (ed.), *Productivity: The Foundation of Growth*, Special Study on Economic Change; 10, Government Publication, Washington, D. C.

McMahon, P. C. and D. J. Smyth, 1974, 'Quarterly Estimates of Capacity Utilization in Ireland', *Economic and Social Review*, 6, pp: 81-105.

Meeusen, W., and J. van den Broeck, 1977a, 'Efficiency Estimation from Cobb-Douglas Production Functions with Composed Error', *International Economic Review* 18, pp: 435-444.

Meeusen, W., and van den Broek, J., 1977b, 'Technical Efficiency and Dimensions of the Firm: Some Results on the Use of Frontier Production Functions', *Empirical Economics*, 2, pp: 109-22.

Mehta, S. S., 1980, *Productivity, Production Function and Technical Change*, Concept Publishing Company, New Delhi.

Merhav, M., 1970, 'Excess Capacity-Measurement, Causes and Uses: A Case Study of Industry in Israel', *Industrialization and Productivity Bulletin*, 15, New York: UNIDO.

Michaely, M., 1977, 'Exports and Economic Growth: An Empirical Investigation', *Journal of Development Economics*, 4, pp: 49-54.

Michaely, M., 1979, 'Exports and Economic Growth: A Reply', *Journal of Development Economics*, 6, pp: 141-43.

Millan, P., 1975, 'The Intensive Use of Capital in Industrial Plants: Multiple Shifts as an Economic Option', Ph. D. Dissertation, Harvard University, Cambridge, Mass.

Mondal, A. H., and S. Ahmad, 1984, 'Factor Proportions and Factor Productivity Changes in Jute and Cotton Textiles Manufacturing Industries in Bangladesh', *Bangladesh Development Studies*, 3, pp: 37-63.

Morawetz, D., 1974, 'Employment Implications of Industrialization in Developing Countries: A Survey', *Economic Journal*, 84, pp: 491-500.

Morawetz, D., 1981, 'Israel: Country Study' in Bautista, R., *et al* (eds), *Capital Utilization in Manufacturing*, Oxford University Press.

Morrison, C., 1986, 'Productivity Measurement with Non-static Expectations and Varying Capacity Utilization', *Journal of Econometrics*, 33, pp: 51-74.

Morrison, C., and W. E. Diewert, 1990, 'New Techniques in the Measurement of Multifactor Productivity', *Journal of Productivity Analysis*, 1, pp: 267-86.

Morrison, C. J., 1985, 'Primal and Dual Capacity Utilization: An Application to Productivity Measurement in the U. S. Automobile Industry', *Journal of Business and Economic Statistics*, 3, pp: 312-24.

Morrison, C. J., 1988, 'Capacity Utilization and Productivity Measurement: An Application to the U. S. Automobile Industry', in Dogramaci, Ali and R. Färe (eds) *Application of Modern Production Theory: Efficiency and Productivity*, Kluwer Nijhof, Netherland

Mueller, J., 1974, 'On Sources of Measured Technical Efficiency: The Impact of Information', *Amerian Journal of Agricultural Economics*, 56, pp: 730-38.

Nadiri, M. I., 1970, 'Some Approaches to the Theory and Measurement of Total Factor Productivity: A Survey', *Journal of Economic Literature*, 8, pp: 1137-77.

Nadiri, M. I., 1972, 'International Studies of Factor Inputs and Total Factor Productivity: A Brief Survey', *Review of Income and Wealth*, 18, pp: 129-54.

Nelson, R. A., 1989a, 'On the Measurement of Capacity Utilization', *Journal of Industrial Economics*, 37, pp: 273-87.

Nelson, R. A., 1989b, 'The Effects of Regulation on Capacity Utilization: Evidence from the Electric Power Industry', *Quarterly Review of Economics and Business*, 29, pp: 37-48.

Nelson, R. R., 1981, 'Research on Productivity Growth and Productivity Differences: Dead Ends and New Departures', *Journal of Economic Literature*, 19, pp: 1029-64.

Nicholls, D. F., and A. R. Pagan, 1985, 'Varying Coefficient Regression', in Hannan, E. J., P. R. Krishnaiah and M. M. Rao (eds), *Handbook of Statistics*, Volume no. 5, Elsevier Science, Amsterdam.

Nishimizu, M., and C. R. Hulten, 1977, 'The Sources of Japanese Economic Growth: 1955-1971', *Review of Economics and Statistics*, 60, pp: 351-61.

Nishimizu, M., and J. M. Page Jr., 1982, 'Total Factor Productivity Growth, Technological Progress, and Technical Efficiency Changes: Dimension of Productivity Change in Yugoslavia, 1965-78', *Economic Journal*, 92, pp: 920-36.

Nishimizu, M., and John Page Jr., 1991, 'Trade Policy, Market Orientation and Productivity Change in Industry', in J. de Melo and A. Sapir, (eds), *Trade*

Theory and Economic Reform: Essays in Honour of Bela Balassa, Cambridge, MA: Basil Blackwell.

Nishimizu, M., and S. Robinson, 1984, 'Trade Policies and Productivity Change in Semi-Industrialized Countries', *Journal of Development Economics*, 16, pp: 177-206.

Nishimizu, M., and S. Robinson, 1986, 'Productivity Growth in Manufacturing', in Chinery, H., *et al*, (eds), *Industrialization and Growth: A Comparative Studies*, Oxford University Press.

Norsworthy, J. R., and S. L. Jang, 1992, *Empirical Measurement and Analysis of Productivity and Technological Change*, North-Holland, Amsterdam.

O'Reilly, L., and B. Nolan, 1979, 'The Measurement of Capacity Utilization in Irish Manufacturing Industry', *Economic and Social Review*, 11, pp: 47-65.

OECD, 1986, 'Main Economic Indicators', Paris, (mimeo).

Ohta, M., 1975, 'A Note on Duality Between Production and Cost Functions: Rate of Returns to Scale and Rate of Technical Progress', *Economic Studies Quarterly*, 25, pp: 63-65.

Oster, S., 1982, 'Intraindustry Structure and the Case of Strategic Change', *Review of Economics and Statistics*, 64, pp: 376-83.

Oulton, N., and M. O'Mahony, 1994, *Productivity and Growth: A Study of British Industry, 1954-1986*, Cambridge University Press.

Pack, H., 1988, 'Industrialization and Trade' in H. B. Chenery and T. N. Srinivasan (eds.) *Handbook of Development Econmics*, Vol. 1, Amsterdam: North Holland.

Pagan, A. R., 1980, 'Some Identification and Estimation Results for Regression Models With Stochastically Varying Coefficients', *Journal of Econometrics*, 13, pp: 341-63.

Papageorgiou, D., Choksi, A. M., and M. Michaely, 1990, *Liberalizing Foreign Trade: The Experience of Developing Countries*, Oxford, Basil Blackwell.

Parry, T. G., 1978, 'Structure and Performance in Australian Manufacturing with Special Reference to Foreign Owned Enterprises', in Kasper, W., and T. G. Parry (eds), *Growth, Trade and Structural Change in an Open Australian Economy*, Centre for Applied Economic Research, University of New South Wales, Sydney.

Pasha, H. A., and T. Qureshi, 1984, 'Capacity Utilization in Selected Industries of Pakistan', *Pakistan Journal of Applied Economics*, 3, pp: 29-56.

Paul, S., 1974a, 'Industrial Performance and Government Controls' in Sandesara, J. C. (ed.), *The Indian Economy: Performance and Prospects*, University of Bombay, Bombay, India.

Paul, S., 1974b, 'Growth and Capacity Utilization of Industrial Capacity', *Economic and Political Weekly*, 7, pp: 2025-32.

Perelman, S., 1995, 'R&D, Technological Progress and Efficiency Change in Industrial Activities', *Review of Income and Wealth*, 41, pp: 349-65.

Perkins, F. C., 1996, 'Productivity Performance and Priorities for the Reform of China's State-Owned Enterprises', *Journal of Development Studies*, 32, pp: 414-44.

Phillips, A., 1970, 'Measuring Industrial Capacity and Capacity Utilization in Less Developed Countries', *Industrialization and Productivity Bulletin* No. 15, UNIDO, Vienna.

Pilat, D., 1995, 'Comparative Productivity of Korean Manufacturing, 1967-1987', *Journal of Development Economics*, 46, pp: 123-44.

Pitt, M. M., and L. Lee, 1981, 'The Measurement and Sources of Technical Efficiency in the Indonesian Weaving Industry', *Journal of Development Economics*, 9, pp: 43-64.

Porter, M. E., 1979, 'The Structure within Industries and Companies' Performance', *Review of Economics and Statistics*, 61, pp: 214-27.

Rahman, A., 1983, *Capacity Utilization in the Large-Scale Manufacturing Industry in Bangladesh*, Institute of Business administration, University of Dhaka.

Rahman, S. H., 1994, 'Trade and Industrialization in Bangladesh: An Assessment', in Helleiner, G. K. (ed.), *Trade and Industrialization in Turbulent Times*, Routledge, London, New York.

Raj, B., and A. Ullah, 1981, *Econometrics: A Varying Coefficients Approach*, London, Croom-Helm.

Ramsey, J. B., 1969, 'Tests for Specification Errors in Classical Linear Least Squares Regression Analysis', *Journal of Royal Statistical Society*, Series B, 31, pp: 350-71.

Rao, C. R., 1965, *Linear Statistical Inference and its Applications*, Wiely & Sons, New York, U. S. A.

Rao, C. R., 1970, 'Estimation of Heteroscedastic Variances in Linear Models', *Journal of the American Statistical Association*, 65, pp: 161-72.

Reza, S., 1993, 'Privatisation of Public Enterprises: The Bangladesh Scenario', *Journal of Economic Cooperation Among Islamic Countries*, 14, pp: 43-60.

Reza, S., and R. Mahmood, 1995, The Economic Impact of Globalisation on Employment and Labour Market in Bangladesh, Bangladesh Institute of Development Studies, Dhaka, (mimeo).

Richter, M. K., 1966, 'Invariance Axioms and Economic Indexes', *Econometrica*, 34, pp: 739-55.

Riedal, J. A., 1984, 'Trade as an Engine of Growth Revisited', *Economic Journal*, 94, pp: 56-73.

Rob, A., 1989, Value of Bangladesh's Policies to Promote Exports, unpublished report to the World Bank.

Rodrik, D., 1992, 'Closing the Technology Gap: Does Trade Liberalization Really Healp', in G. K. Helleiner (ed.) *Trade Policy, Industrialization and Development: New Perspectives*, Oxford: Calendon Press.

Rodrik, D., 1995, 'Trade and Industrial Policy Reform' in J. Behrman and T. N. Srinivasan (eds) *Handbook of Development Economics*, Vol. 3, Amsterdam: North Holland.

Romer, P. M., 1986, 'Increasing Returns and Long Run Growth', *Journal of Political Economy*, 94, pp: 1002-37.

Romer, P. M., 1987, 'Crazy Explanations for the Productivity Slowdown', *NBER Macroeconomic Annual*, Cambridge: MIT Press.

Rosenberg, B., 1972, 'Estimation of Stationary Stochastic Regression Parameters Reexamined', *Journal of the American Statistical Association*, 67, pp: 650-54.

Rosenberg, B., 1973, 'The Analysis of a Cross Section of Time Series by Stochastically Convergent Parameter Regression', *Annals of Economic and Social Measurement*, 2, pp: 399-428.

Rushdi, A. A., 1982, 'Factor Substitubility in the Manufacturing Industries of Bangladesh: An International Comparison', *Bangladesh Economic Review*, 1, pp: 32-46

Ruttan, V. W., 1957, 'Agricultural and Nonagricultural Growth in Output Per Unit of Input', *Journal of Farm Economics*, 39, pp: 1566-1575.

Sahota, G. S. *et al.*, 1991, 'South Asian Development Model and Productivity in Bangladesh', *Bangladesh Development Studies*, 19, pp: 51-88.

Sahota, G. S., 1990, 'An Assessment of the Impact of Industrial Policies in Bangladesh', Development Discussion Paper no. 333, Harvard Institute for International Development, Harvard University.

Sahota, G. S., and M. Huq, 1991, 'Effective Rate of Assistance in Bangladesh', *Bangladesh Development Studies*, 19, pp: 1-50.

Salim, R. A., and K. P. Kalirajan, 1995, 'Impact of Economic Reforms on Capacity Realization and Productivity Growth of Bangladesh Food Manufacturing Industries', Paper Presented at *International Conference on Efficiency and Productivity*, October 22-24, New England, Armidale, New South Wales, Australia.

Salma, U., 1992, Agricultural Price Policy in Bangladesh: General Equilibrium Effects on Growth and Income Distribution, Ph. D. Dissertation, Economics Division, The Australian national University, Canberra.

Sastry, D. U., 1986, 'Capacity Utilization in Cotton Mill Industry in India', *Indian Economic Review*, 14, pp: 1-28.

Sawhney, P. K., and B. L. Sawhney, 1973, 'Capacity Utilization, Concentration and Price-cost Margins: Results of Indian industries', *Journal of Industrial Economics*, 21, pp: 145-53.

Scherer, F. M., 1986, *Industrial Market Structure and Economic Performance*, second edition, Chicago: Rand McNally.

Schmalensee, R., 1972, Variance Estimation in a Random Coefficient Regression Model, Department of Economics, University of California, San Diego, (mimeo).

Schmalensee, R., 1989, 'Inter-industry Studies of Structure and Performance', in Schmalensee, R., and R. D. Willing (eds), *Handbook of Industrial Organization*, II, North-Holland, Amsterdam, London.

Schmidt, P., 1985, 'Frontier Production Functions', *Econometric Reviews*, 4, pp: 289-328.

Schmidt, P., and R. Sickles, 1984, 'Production Frontier and Panel Data', *Journal of Business and Economic Statistics*, 2, pp: 367-74.

Schultz, T. W., 1975, 'The Value of the Ability to Deal with Disequilibria', *Journal of Economic Literature*, 13, pp: 827-46.

Schumpeter, J., 1942, *Capitalism, Socialism and Democracy*, Harper and Row, New York.

Schwallie, D. P., 1982, 'Unconstrained Maximum Likelihood Estimation of Contemporaneous Covariances', *Economic Letters*, 9, pp: 359-64.

Schydlowsky, M. D., 1973, 'On Determining the Causality of Underutilization of Capacity: Working Note', Department of Economics, Boston University, (mimeo).

Schydlowsky, M. D., 1976, 'Capital Utilization, Growth, Employment, and Balance of Payments and Price Stabilization', Discussion Paper Series, No. 22, Department of Economics, Boston University.

Scott, M. F. G., 1993, 'Explaining Economic Growth', *American Economic Review*, (Papers and Proceedings) 83, pp: 421-25.

Segerson, K., and D. Squires, 1993, 'Capacity Utilization Under Regulatory Constraints', *Review of Economics and Statistics*, 75, pp: 76-85.

Segerson, K., and D. Squires, 1990, 'On the Measurement of Economic Capacity Utilization for Multi-product Industries', *Journal of Econometrics*, 44, pp: 347-61.

Sen, B., 1991, 'Privatisation in Bangladesh: Process, Dynamics and Implications', in Kanesaligam, V., (ed.), *Privatization: Trends, and Experiences in South Asia*, Macmillan India Ltd., New Delhi.

Sexton, T. R., S. Sleeper, and R. E. Taggart III, 1991, Data Envelopment Analysis for Nonhomogeneous Units: Pupil Transportation Budgeting in North Carolina, Working Paper, The W. Averill Harriman School for management and policy, The State University of New York, Stony Brook, New York.

Sobhan, R., 1990, 'The Development of the Private Sector in Bangladesh: A Review of the Evaluation and Outcome of State Policy', BIDS Research Report No. 124, Dhaka.

Sobhan, R., 1991, *Debt Default to the Development Finance Institutions: The Crisis of State Sponsored Entrepreneurship in Bangladesh*, University Press Limited, Dhaka.

Sobhan, R., and M. Ahmad, 1980, *Public Enterprise in a Intermediate Regime: A Study in the Political Economy of Bangladesh*, Bangladesh Institute of Development Studies, Dhaka.

Solow, R. M., 1957, 'Technical Change and the Aggregate Production Function', *Review of Economics and Statistics*, 39, pp: 312-20.

Sood, K., 1989, *Trade and Economic Development: India, Pakistan and Bangladesh*, Sage Publications, New Delhi and Newbury park, London.

Spence, A. M., 1977, 'Entry, Capacity, Investment and Oligopolistic Pricing', *Bell Journal of Economics*, 8, pp: 534-44.

Srinivasan, P. V., 1991, 'Relative Importance of Supply and Demand Factors: The Case of Capacity Utilization in Indian Industries', Paper presented at the 28th annual conference of the Indian Econometric Society, West Bengal, Oct. 29-31.

Srinivasan, P. V., 1992, 'Determinants of Capacity Utilization in Indian Industries', *Journal of Quantitative Economics*, 8, pp: 139-56.

Srivastava, V. *et al*, 1981, 'Estimation of Linear Regression Model With Random Coefficients Ensuring Almost Non-negativity of Variance Estimations', *Biometric Journal*, 23, pp: 3-8.

Steel, William F., 1972, 'Import Substitution and Excess Capacity in Ghana', *Oxford Economic Papers*, 24, pp: 212-40

Stern, J. J., Mallon, R. D., and T. L. Hutcheson, 1988, 'Foreign Exchange Regimes and Industrial Growth in Bangladesh', *World Development*, 16, pp: 1419-1439.

Stigler, G. J., 1976, 'The Existence of X-efficiency', *American Economic Review*, 66, pp: 213-16.

Sudit, E. F., and N. Finger, 1981, 'Methodological Issues in Aggregate Productivity Analysis', in Ali, Dogramaci (ed.), *Aggregate and Industry Level Productivity Analysis*, Martinus Nijhoff Publishing.

Swamy, P. A. V. B., 1970, 'Efficient Inference in Random Coefficient Regression Models', *Econometrica*, 38, pp: 311-23.

Swamy, P. A. V. B., 1971, *Statistical Inference in Random Coefficient Regression Models*, New York, Springer-Verlag.

Swamy, P. A. V. B., and A. Havenner, 1981, 'A Random Coefficient Approach to Seasonal Adjustment of Economic Time Series', *Journal of Econometrics*, 15, pp: 177-209.

Swamy, P. A. V. B., and J. S. Mehta, 1975, 'Bayesian and Non-Bayesian Analysis of Switching Regressions and Random Coefficient Regression Models', *Journal of American Statistical Association*, 70, pp: 593-602.

Swamy, P. A. V. B., and G. S. Talvas, 1994, 'Connections Between GARCH and Stochastic Coefficients (SC) Models', *Economic Letters*, 46, pp: 7-10.

Swamy, P. A. V. B., and G. S. Talvas, 1995, 'Random Coefficient Models: Theory and Applications', *Journal of Economic Survey*, 9, pp: 166-96.

Swamy, P. A. V. B., and P. Tinsley, 1980, 'Linear Prediction and Estimation Methods for Regression Models With Stationary Stochastic Coefficients', *Journal of Econometrics*, 12, pp: 103-42.

Swan, T. W., 1957, 'Economic Growth and Capital Accumulation', *Economic Record*, Vol. 32, pp: 334-61.

Theil, H., and van de Panne, 1960, 'Quadratic Programming as an Extension of Classical Quadratic Maximization', *Management Science*, 7, pp: 1-20.

Thoumi, F. E., 1981, 'Colombia: Country Study' in Bautista, R., *et al* (eds), *Capital Utilization in Manufacturing*, Oxford University Press.

Timmer, C. P., 1971, 'Using a Probabilistic Frontier Production Function to Measure Technical Efficiency', *Journal of Political Economy*, 79, pp: 776-94.

Tirole, J., 1992, *Industrial Organisation*, 2nd edition, Macmillan.

Tybout, J. R., 1990, 'Making Noisy Data Sing: Estimating Production Technologies in Developing Countries', *Journal of Econometrics*, 53, pp: 25-44.

Tybout, J. R., 1992, 'Linking Trade and Productivity: New Research Directions', *World Bank Economic Review*, 6, pp: 189-211.

Tybout, J. R., de Melo, and V. Corbo , 1991, 'The Effects of Trade Reforms on Scale and Technical Efficiency: New Evidence from Chile', *Journal of International Economics*, 31, pp: 231-50.

Tybout, J. R., and D. M. Westbrook, 1995, 'Trade Liberalization and the Dimensions of Efficiency Change in Mexican Manufacturing Industries', *Journal of International Economics*, 39, pp: 53-78.

Tyler, W. G., 1979, 'Technical Efficiency in Production in a Developing Country: An Empirical Examination of the Brazilian Plastics and Steel Industries', *Oxford Economic Papers*, 31, pp: 477-95.

United Nations, 1968, 'A System of National Accounts and Supporting Tables, Studies in Methods, series F No. 2 Rev.3, Department of Economics and Social Affairs, Statistical office of the United Nations, United Nations, New York.

Urata, S., and K. Yokota, 1994, 'Trade Liberalization and Productivity Growth in Thailand', *Developing Economies*, 32, pp: 447-58.

Vanlommel, E. *et al*, 1977, 'Industrial Concentration in Belgium: Empirical Comparison of Alternative Seller Concentration Measures', *Journal of Industrial Economics*, 26, pp: 1-20.

Wang, W., 1996, 'Foreign Direct Investment, Spillovers and Catching Up:- The Case of Taiwan', Ph. D. Dissertation, Submitted to the Australian national University, Canberra.

Wenders, J. T., 1971, 'Excess Capacity as Barrier to Entry', *Journal of Industrial Economics*, 20, pp: 14-19.

White, L. J., 1974, *Industrial Concentration and Economic Power in Pakistan*, Princeton University Press, Princeton, NJ.

Williamson, J., 1994, *The Political Economy of Policy Reform*, Institute of International Economics, Washington, D. C.

Winston, G. C., 1971, 'Capital Utilization in Economic Development', *Economic Journal*, 81, pp: 36-60.

Winston, G. C., 1974, 'The Theory of Capital Utilization and Idleness', *Journal of Economic Literature*, 12, pp: 1301-20.

Winston, G. C., and T. O. McCoy, 1974, 'Investment and the Optimal Idleness of Capital', *Review of Economic studies*, 41, pp: 110-25.

World Bank, 1991, 'Bangladesh: Managing Public Resources for Higher Growth', Dhaka, (mimeo).

World Bank, 1992a, 'The Manufacturing Sector in Bangladesh: Selected Issues', (3 volumes), Industry and Finance Division, South Asia Country Department I (memio) Dhaka.

World Bank, 1992b, 'Bangladesh: Report on the Textile Industries Restructuring Study -Phase II', Washington D. C., (mimeo).

World Bank, 1993a, 'The World Table 4 and 5', Washington, D. C.

World Bank, 1993b, Bangladesh: Implementing Structural Reform, Report no. 11569-BD, Washington, D. C.

World Bank, 1994, 'Bangladesh: from Stabilization to Growth, Report No. 12724-BD', Washington, D. C.

World Bank, 1995, *Bureaucrats in Business: The Economics and Politics of Government Ownership*, Oxford University Press.

World Peace Academy of Bangladesh, 1985, 'Technology Transfer and Development: A Study on Bangladesh', Sponsored by Planning Commission, Government of Bangladesh, (mimeo).

Yotopoulos, P. A. and J. B. Nugent, 1976, *Economics of Development*, Harper and Row, New York.

Young, A., 1994, 'Lessons from the East Asian NICs: A Contrarian View', *European Economic Review*, 38, pp: 964-973.

Zellner, A., 1969, 'On the Aggregation Problem: A New Approach to Troublesome Problem', in Fox, K. A., *et al* (eds), *Economic Models, Estimation and Risk Programming: Essays in Honour of Gerald Tintner*, New York: Springer-Verlag.

Zellner, A., 1970, 'Estimation of Regression Relationships Containing Unobservable Variables', *International Economic Review*, 11, pp: 441-54.

Index